THE CITY

OTHER ECONOMIST BOOKS

Guide to Analysing Companies
Guide to Business Modelling
Guide to Business Planning
Guide to Economic Indicators
Guide to the European Union
Guide to Financial Markets
Guide to Management Ideas
Numbers Guide
Style Guide

Dictionary of Business
Dictionary of Economics
International Dictionary of Finance

Brands and Branding
Business Ethics
Business Strategy
China's Stockmarket
Emerging Markets
Globalisation
Successful Innovation
Successful Mergers
Wall Street

Essential Director
Essential Economics
Essential Finance
Essential Internet
Essential Investment
Essential Negotiation

Pocket Asia
Pocket Europe in Figures
Pocket World in Figures

THE CITY

A Guide to London's Global Financial Centre

Richard Roberts

THE ECONOMIST IN ASSOCIATION WITH
PROFILE BOOKS LTD

Published by Profile Books Ltd
58A Hatton Garden, London EC1N 8LX

Typeset in EcoType by MacGuru Ltd
info@macguru.org.uk

Printed in Great Britain by
Creative Print and Design (Wales), Ebbw Vale

A CIP catalogue record for this book is available
from the British Library

ISBN 1 86197 632 1

Contents

For Christopher and Sue

Acknowledgements

I am most grateful to International Financial Services and the Corporation of London, and their helpful staffs, for their invaluable reports on City activities and on London as a financial centre. My thanks to Mark Theisen for researching and putting together Appendix 2 and for other research assistance. To David Kynaston, Barnabas Reynolds, Christopher Robson and Jonathan Ruffer for their comments and insights on this project and over the years. To those who commented on specific sections of the manuscript and for the improvements they suggested. To Martin Liu and Stephen Brough for backing the proposal and to meticulous copy-editor Penny Williams. And last but not least to my wife Sarah for all her affectionate support.

1 About the City

The term "the City" refers to both a place and an industry. The place is London's oldest district, the "Square Mile", settled since Roman times and once bounded by medieval city walls with St Paul's Cathedral at its heart. For centuries this residential and business neighbourhood was host to myriad merchants and bankers conducting international trade and finance. In the 19th century, as the residential population dwindled, the City became synonymous with commercial and financial activities. Today the term is widely used as shorthand for London's wholesale international financial-services industry. It is in this economic sense – referring to activities conducted both inside and outside the Square Mile – that it is used in this book. The Square Mile is used to refer to the City in a geographical sense.

In recent years the activities of the City have spread some way outside the Square Mile in much the same way as financial firms have spread beyond Wall Street in New York. Since the 1990s a number of leading financial firms have set up operations in Canary Wharf, a collection of modern skyscrapers built on the site of London's former docks, about three miles east of the Square Mile. London's West End, a mile or two west of the Square Mile, has become home to other financial services firms, such as hedge funds, private equity funds and private wealth-management businesses. Today, 67% of London's wholesale financial-services industry jobs are in the Square Mile, 14% in Canary Wharf and 19% in the West End.

Two types of financial services activities are conducted in financial centres: retail and wholesale. Retail financial services are found in urban high streets, mostly serving domestic customers and meeting the needs of individuals and small businesses for current and savings accounts, loans and mortgages. Wholesale activities comprise a range of services that meet the requirements of corporations, governments, public agencies and the financial-services industry itself. The provision of these wholesale financial services (sometimes called "City-type" activities) is the City's speciality.

London is one of the world's three global financial centres; the other two are New York and Tokyo. The City's workforce of an estimated 311,000 is similar in size to Wall Street's and probably considerably

Table 1.1 **Wholesale financial services in the EU, 2003**

	€bn
UK (mostly London)	68.3
Germany (mostly Frankfurt)	19.7
France (mostly Paris)	14.3
Italy	10.1
Netherlands	4.0
Rest of EU	10.2
Total	126.6

Source: Corporation of London, *The City's Importance to the EU Economy 2004*, 2004

larger than Tokyo's. London surpasses both of them in the volume of international business it transacts: more international banking, foreign-exchange dealing, trading in international equities, and international bond issuance and trading are conducted in the City than in any other centre. In New York and Tokyo, a substantial proportion of wholesale financial services activity serves domestic clients, reflecting the scale of the American and Japanese economies. The three global centres have strong connections with one another and ties to other important international and regional financial centres, such as Hong Kong, Singapore, Frankfurt, Paris, Zurich, Los Angeles and Chicago.

London is the largest financial centre in the European time zone and is substantially bigger than either Frankfurt or Paris (see Table 1.1). The value of the UK's (mostly London's) output of international wholesale financial services exceeds that of the rest of the EU combined.

The City matrix

The City, like all financial centres, is made up of a matrix of complementary elements – financial and commercial services sectors, financial markets and financial institutions – and financial-services industry firms (see Appendix 2).

Financial and commercial services sectors

These consist of:

- investment banking and securities (the sell-side)
- investors and asset management (the buy-side)

- banking
- insurance
- professional and support services (such as legal, accounting, human resources, information technology, public relations)
- shipping and commodities.

These sectors are discussed in Chapters 4–9. Each has its own trade association (some have several) representing its members' interests to government, the media and other parties.

Financial markets
There are two types of financial market:

- formally constituted exchanges with membership, rules and (traditionally) a physical marketplace; and
- over-the-counter (OTC) markets.

The main formally constituted City-based exchanges are as follows.

Securities and derivatives
- London Stock Exchange (LSE): trades shares of large companies and government bonds
- Alternative Investment Market (AIM): trades shares of small companies
- Euronext–London International Financial Futures Exchange (LIFFE): trades financial derivatives
- OM London Exchange: trades financial derivatives

Insurance
- Lloyd's of London

Commodities, shipping and gold
- London Metal Exchange (LME): trades mineral commodities and derivatives
- London Commodity Exchange (LCE): trades agricultural commodities and derivatives
- International Petroleum Exchange (IPE): trades energy derivatives
- Baltic Exchange: trades shipping, cargoes, air freight and air cargoes
- Gold

The major OTC markets in London are:

- the foreign-exchange market
- the Eurobond market
- the money market
- the interbank market
- the OTC derivatives market.

In OTC financial markets, trading takes place by negotiation between the parties to a deal. As there is no physical marketplace, transactions are executed by telephone or computer.

The London Clearing House (LCH), one of the world's leading clearing houses, plays a crucial role in the operation of several City markets. It acts as the central counterparty to contracts issued by exchange members enabling the centralised settlement of obligations. This increases the efficiency and underpins the integrity of the markets it serves – the IPE, LIFFE and the LME – and a variety of OTC products such as swaps and repos. The operation of London's financial markets is covered in Chapter 3.

Institutions

The Bank of England. Founded in 1694, the Bank of England is the UK's central bank. Before 1946 it was privately owned, but it acted as the government's bank from the outset. It is responsible for the operation of UK monetary policy and the maintenance of financial stability, having been given operational independence to do so by the government in 1997. It has to meet a government-defined inflation target and to take account of government economic objectives in its conduct of monetary policy. Its principal instrument for the fulfilment of its duties is the setting of UK interest rates. The Bank holds the government's bank accounts and issues the country's bank notes. Its account holders include banks (including central banks), other financial institutions and some large corporations. The Bank of England is the subject of Chapter 10.

Financial Services Authority. Located at Canary Wharf, the Financial Services Authority (FSA) is the City's regulatory authority. It has four main aims:

- Maintenance of confidence in the UK's financial system through the supervision of market infrastructure and market surveillance.

- The promotion of public understanding of the financial system.
- Securing an appropriate degree of protection for consumers.
- Helping to reduce financial crime.

The FSA was created in 1997 as the sole regulatory body for the financial-services industry. It incorporated an array of existing regulatory bodies and was vested with the regulatory responsibilities hitherto exercised by the Bank of England and several government departments. The FSA became operational in 2001. It is covered in Chapter 11.

International Financial Services, London. IFSL represents the City's wholesale financial-services industry. It is funded by the Bank of England, the Corporation of London and more than 100 other members drawn from every facet of financial services activity. Its purpose is the worldwide promotion of the financial services provided by its members' UK operations. It works for the liberalisation of trade in international financial services. IFSL staff produce authoritative research reports and statistics on the UK's financial-services industry.

Corporation of London. As the Square Mile's local government authority, the Corporation of London provides such municipal services as policing, education, refuse collection, housing and social services. It also plays a leading role in the promotion of London as a financial centre through its Economic Development Office. It publishes two quarterly reports, City Economy Digest and City Research Focus, giving data about City activity and relevant research, together with other reports researched and written by consultants and universities.

City employment and activities

At the beginning of 2004, 311,000 people were employed in wholesale financial services in London (see Table 1.2 overleaf). The largest sector is securities – buying and selling equities and bonds – which employs 77,500 people (25% of the total). International banking – borrowing and lending at the wholesale level – provides 56,500 jobs (18%). Insurance and asset management each employ 39,000 people (12.5%). There are fewer people working in corporate finance, foreign exchange and derivatives than in other areas, but the low head count is not a yardstick of their significance. Lastly, some 70,500 people provide specialist professional support services to meet the legal, accounting and other

Table 1.2 **Employment in wholesale financial services and related activities in London, January 2004**

	Number of people	% share
Securities	77,500	25.0
of which:		
domestic equities	31,000	10.0
international equities	15,500	5.0
bonds	31,000	10.0
International banking	56,500	18.2
Insurance	39,000	12.5
Asset management	39,000	12.5
Corporate finance	13,500	4.3
Foreign exchange	8,000	2.6
Derivatives	7,000	2.3
Professional services	70,500	22.7
Total	311,000	100.0

Source: Corporation of London, *The City's Importance to the EU Economy 2004*, 2004

requirements of banks, investment banks, asset managers and other financial and non-financial firms and public bodies.

A further 20,000 people work in the City in the commodities markets and marine services, and a similar number in British banks' head offices.

Since the 1960s, when London re-emerged as a leading international financial centre, employment in wholesale financial services has grown by an average of 1.6% a year. The City head count rose from around 200,000 in 1971 to a peak of 340,000 in 2000 (see Figure 1.1).

There were rapid rates of expansion from 1978 to 1987 and from 1994 to 2000. There were also three significant downturns. In the mid-1970s, 40,000 jobs were lost (19% of the total) as a consequence of the market slump and recession that followed the quadrupling of the oil price in 1973. In the late 1980s and early 1990s, the City shed 60,000 jobs (22% of the total) following the crash of October 1987 and the recession of the early 1990s. When the dotcom bubble burst in 2000, an across-the-board retreat of overvalued share prices and a global economic slow-down resulted in job losses in 2001 and 2002 of around 35,000 (10% of the total) – a somewhat smaller setback than previous downturns. Hiring resumed in 2003 as business began to recover.

Employment in wholesale financial services and related activities in London
1971–2004

1.1

Sources: Corporation of London, *Growth Prospects of City Industries*, 2003; *The City's Importance to the EU Economy 2004*, 2004

Front office, back office, middle office

Firms in the financial-services industry have long drawn a distinction between so-called front-office and back-office activities. Three criteria are used for classification:

- The degree to which an activity involves interaction with parties outside the firm, especially clients.
- Whether the activity is revenue-generating or a business cost.
- The degree to which an activity is routine.

Front-office activities involve interaction with clients or counterparties (outside and inside) the firm, are revenue-generating and are generally non-routine. Examples include the origination of new business, selling, trading, analysis, client account handling, product development, corporate communications and central management.

Back-office activities generally involve little interaction with people outside the firm, are funded by internal financial transfers and are often routine and clerical. The processing of transactions and the compiling and supplying of data to the front office are the principal forms of financial services back-office work, including internal audit, cheque and security transactions processing, call centres, claims processing and payment, clearing-house operations, and internal management support.

These days people also talk about the middle office, whose functions include information technology (IT) management and development, risk management, regulatory compliance, human resources, legal and tax issues, and accounting and reporting. These are non-routine functions, but they are not revenue-generating and their focus is mostly internal rather than external. Nonetheless, they are so important to the bottom line of the business that they usually accompany the front office.

Traditionally, City firms located their back-office activities near to the front office to process transactions and service the revenue generators. But since the 1970s, computing and telecommunications have allowed a physical separation of these activities. As a result, some firms moved their back-office activities out of the Square Mile to places such as south coast seaside towns and the Bristol area where operating costs are lower.

The availability of huge new office buildings with cheap rents at Canary Wharf and elsewhere allowed firms to reunite front- and back-office activities. This was partly prompted by notable instances – most famously the collapse of Barings in 1995 – where controls over dealing rooms and transaction processing had proved ineffective or had been ignored. Another stimulus is the increasing importance of IT for both front-office and back-office operations, generating internal economies of scale in its provision.

City pay

The level of City remuneration is famously high across the board relative to other occupations. Between 1970 and 2002, the average salary of a male worker in the City rose from £2,256 to £61,838, compared with national average white-collar salaries of £1,856 and £31,741 respectively.

Similarly, the earnings of women in the City rose from an annual average of £1,138 at the start of the 1970s to £36,306 in 2002, compared with national averages of £915 and £21,070 respectively. Although at the end of the 1990s the average earnings of men in the City were 80% higher than those of women, a gender discrepancy far larger than in the nation as a whole, the gender gap had closed a little over the three decades.

Overall, the City's labour force is composed of 55% men and 45% women, compared with the national average of 51% and 49%. In the banking and securities sectors, the proportions are 59% men and 41% women, although in other activities females are more numerous, particularly in legal services where the ratio is reversed: 58% women and 42%

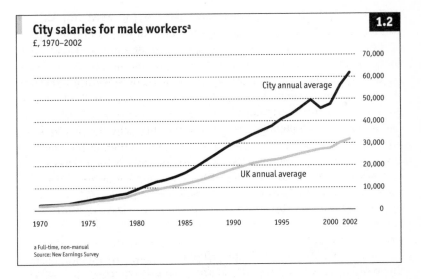

City salaries for male workers[a]
£, 1970–2002

`1.2`

City annual average

UK annual average

70,000
60,000
50,000
40,000
30,000
20,000
10,000
0

1970   1975   1980   1985   1990   1995   2000 2002

a Full-time, non-manual
Source: New Earnings Survey

men. Nationally, almost half of females in the workforce are employed part-time, but in the City 92% of women work full-time. Among men, 96% work full-time, the same as the national average. During the downturn in the early 2000s, the proportion of men in the City's workforce rose slightly as the number of male part-time workers increased and that of female full-time workers decreased.

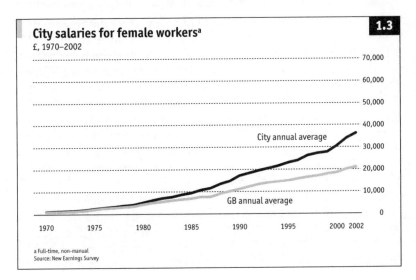

City salaries for female workers[a]
£, 1970–2002

`1.3`

City annual average

GB annual average

70,000
60,000
50,000
40,000
30,000
20,000
10,000
0

1970   1975   1980   1985   1990   1995   2000 2002

a Full-time, non-manual
Source: New Earnings Survey

Workers in the City are better paid than those in other sectors, and over the years the pay premium has increased. In the 1970s the average income in the City was around 20% higher than national average white-collar earnings. The City's earnings premium grew rapidly in the 1980s, rising for men from 25% in 1980 to 60% in 1988. These were the years of "Big Bang", the deregulation of the securities industry, which resulted in a fundamental restructuring of the way many City firms did business and an influx of foreign banks and securities houses into London. Both processes had the effect of bidding up City salaries – the so-called "yuppie boom". In the wake of the October 1987 stockmarket crash, many City firms shed staff and the salary premium stabilised. But salaries took off again in the mid-1990s; according to government data, by the beginning of the 2000s the average City salary (full-time adult employees of both sexes) was £45,419, more than double the national average of £21,842.

The fivefold increase in the premium of City salaries compared with the national average since 1970, from 20% to more than 100%, is explained partly by the changing composition of City jobs and partly by the productivity of City workers. An ever greater concentration of highly skilled front-office jobs and the relocation of back-office staff to less costly places is one part of the story. The other is the dynamism of the international financial services sector, whose productivity growth has exceeded that of the UK economy as a whole by 2–3% a year.

The remuneration packages of many City workers comprise a salary plus a discretionary bonus, which for key executives in a good year may exceed their basic pay. In theory, the bonus system provides City firms with a flexible cost base that allows them to weather the ups and downs of variable revenues without having to undermine their effectiveness by laying off staff. It also means that revenue generators are rewarded in proportion to performance, either individually if this is possible, as in the case of traders, or by team or division.

The bonus season at the end of the calendar year has been a feature of City life since the mid-1980s. Although modest bonuses had existed in the City for years, it was competition for staff by American banks, where big bonuses were already a feature, at the time of Big Bang that really launched them in London. Substantial bonuses were paid in the boom years 1986 and 1987, but payouts were much smaller in the late 1980s and early 1990s following the October 1987 stockmarket crash. Big bonuses returned in 1993, the year in which more than 100 partners at the London offices of Goldman Sachs received year-end bonuses of more than $1m each. In 1996, the next bumper year, City bonuses totalled £750m and the following year they hit £1 billion for the first time.

The unprecedented largesse of the 1996 and 1997 bonus rounds made a few conscience-stricken souls uneasy about the size of their remuneration packages. In January 1998 a debate was held at the Mansion House on the motion "This house believes that City salaries are totally fair and justified". The motion was defeated, but there is no record of anyone returning their bonus.

The big bonus payouts of 1996 and 1997 prompted speculation as to whether a fundamental shift was taking place in the financial-services industry. A plausible proposition was that with the internationalisation of investment, the big European and American investment banks had started to compete with each other on a global basis. This had created a single elite labour market, and London pay was catching up with Wall Street pay levels and American remuneration practices.

The financial crisis in East Asia, the Russian default and the near-collapse of Long-Term Capital Management cast a pall over the financial services sector in 1998 and bonus payouts fell to £600m. But a takeover boom and the dotcom bubble led to bonus payments in 1999 and 2000 totalling respectively £1 billion and £1.5 billion, the latter a new record. The downturn in City activity and job losses in 2001 and 2002 were accompanied by sharp cuts in bonuses and their restriction to key staff. But 2003 saw the return of more generous and more widespread bonus payouts.

Driving forces

Underlying the expansion of City employment from the 1960s was a set of fundamental forces driving the expansion of international financial services. It is a well-known feature of long-term economic development that the stock of financial assets – deposits, loans, shares, bonds, mortgages and so on – grows faster than the rate of increase of overall output. In other words, as a society becomes more prosperous and economically more sophisticated, the ratio of financial assets to national product rises. The management of financial assets is the activity performed by the financial services sector; thus as an economy grows, typically the financial services sector increases faster than national output.

This relationship between economic development and the growth of the financial services sector also applies to the international economy and international financial services; as the international economy grows, the international financial-services industry expands even more rapidly. In recent decades world output has grown at an average of 3-4% a year, with the output of international financial services expanding at an annual rate of around 7%, according to a pioneering report on the City's growth prospects by Lombard Street Research for the Corporation of London. The latter is a much faster rate of growth than that achieved by the UK economy and is the principal factor underlying the growth and prosperity of the City since the 1960s. As the leading location of the international financial-services industry, London has been the main beneficiary of the long boom in demand for international financial services.

There have been four key dynamics:

- The rapid expansion of international trade.
- The growth of international financial flows.
- The internationalisation of investment.
- The increasing conduct of international financial transactions "offshore".

Since 1945 the world economy has grown more or less continuously. This expansion was fostered by the dismantling of restrictions on trade and financial flows under the generally benign regime of the post-war set of international economic institutions, notably the International Monetary Fund, the World Bank, the World Trade Organisation (formerly the General Agreement on Tariffs and Trade, or GATT) and the Bank for International Settlements. Global economic growth stimulated the expansion of international trade, which increased at a faster rate than world output. The buoyancy of world trade provided a direct boost to several City activities – trade finance, foreign-exchange trading, ship and aircraft broking and international insurance – and an indirect stimulus to others.

Initially, banks were responsible for most overseas lending. But from the 1960s an enormous international capital market – the Eurobond market (see Chapter 3) – grew up as an offshore alternative source of funds for borrowers. The bulk of international financial flows was between developed countries, but emerging countries also began to borrow from Western banks and in the international capital market to fund economic development, not to mention the purchase of armaments and other unproductive activities. As the leading international banking centre and the principal Eurobond market location, London benefited greatly from these developments.

The internationalisation of investment has been fostered by the abolition of bureaucratic barriers to free financial flows and by advances in communications. In the 1950s and 1960s, many countries operated exchange controls to support the value of their currencies under the system of fixed exchange rates agreed at the Bretton Woods Conference in 1944. Following the collapse of the Bretton Woods system in the early 1970s, the leading industrial countries gradually scrapped exchange controls, thereby allowing their citizens to invest their money wherever they wished.

Advances in communications stimulated both the increase in international capital flows and the internationalisation of investment by broadening perceptions of opportunities and reducing the risks. Improvements in telecommunications dramatically improved the availability of information and the speed of dissemination, and cut the cost. Developments in aviation technology reduced the time and cost of air travel, making it easier for asset managers and private investors to visit financial centres in other countries. Extended horizons and a quest for better performance led to the international diversification of assets by pension funds and other investors.

In the 1980s, the City emerged as the principal provider of international asset-management services to institutional investors. It also expanded international bond dealing and pioneered international equities trading, which soon dwarfed transactions in domestic equities. Cross-border mergers and acquisitions work developed, as did other international corporate finance advisory work in areas such as privatisation.

Since the 1960s there has been a rapid expansion in the conduct of international financial transactions "offshore", which in the context of the international financial system means the transfer of financings of all sorts from high-tax rigidly regulated centres to relatively low-tax and lightly regulated centres. The latter are often not the domestic location of savers and investors or lenders and borrowers.

Offshore transactions are subject to the regulatory and legal framework selected by the contracting parties, not that of their domicile. This enables borrowers to find cheaper funds or more flexible types of finance than are available in their domestic market, and for lenders to achieve better rates of return. An offshore transaction is denominated in a currency other than that of the financial centre in which it is conducted (which is subject to that centre's domestic constraints). Initially, most offshore transactions were in US dollars held on deposit at European banks (Eurodollars), but now most convertible currencies can be used.

Three main kinds of financial activity are conducted offshore: banking; bond issuance, underwriting and trading; and swaps and derivatives. The offshore markets have eclipsed their onshore counterparts by providing a greater range of products and more dynamic product innovation, as well as lower costs. Not surprisingly, the volume of business conducted offshore has mushroomed. In theory, offshore financial facilities can be located anywhere and everywhere. But in reality, the principal centre for the conduct of offshore financial activities and the main beneficiary of the overall expansion in offshore financial services since the 1960s has been London, the leading location of the Euromarkets.

Financial services clustering

For centuries banking and trading involved face-to-face transactions with clients and counterparties, for instance on the floor of a stock exchange. Hosting such activities was the origin of financial centres. Modern communications technology means that a physical presence is no longer necessary for the conduct of much wholesale financial business, such as most forms of securities trading, banking or investment. Yet financial firms continue to cluster in financial centres. Why?

A report commissioned by the Corporation of London, *Financial Services Clustering and its Significance for London*, published in 2003, pinpoints four "critical benefits" for financial firms from location in the Square Mile/Canary Wharf financial services cluster:

- ◪ The London "brand". A Square Mile/Canary Wharf address confers credibility and status upon firms. For example, a City address turns a law firm into a City law firm. Likewise, if an investment bank wants to be taken seriously as an international player, it has to have an operation in London.
- ◪ Proximity to customers, skilled labour and regulatory bodies. This is important for winning business, recruitment of specialist staff and contacts, both formal and informal, with regulators and professional bodies.
- ◪ Access to knowledge. Closeness to competitors, support services and customers facilitates knowledge acquisition and accumulation. Proximity also fosters social interaction, which remains an "important vector" for knowledge transfer. So is proximity between colleagues within firms, one of the factors

that leads firms to consolidate highly skilled front-office activities in a single building to internalise the intra-firm exchange of expertise.

■ The wider attractions of London. As a major world city, London has lifestyle attractions few other cities can match. Its cosmopolitan nature, arts, shops and restaurants make it a vibrant city, a place where people want to work and live.

The report also identified four "major clustering engines" that promote the growth and sustainability of the Square Mile/Canary Wharf financial services cluster:

■ The labour market. This is one of London's greatest assets. The supply of skilled labour, both from domestic and international pools, sustains the growth of the Square Mile/Canary Wharf cluster. The size of the financial services skills pool means that people are attracted into the cluster because of the prestige of developing a career in the City, and the size of the labour market encourages mobility between firms and sectors.

■ Personal relationships. Personal contacts between buyers and sellers of wholesale financial services, suppliers of support services, professional bodies, government and financial regulators are "vital processes" that sustain London as a financial centre. Face-to-face contact – business and social, formal and informal – remains a "fundamental requirement" for building trust, acquiring knowledge and the execution of complex transactions that require the input of many parties. Subscription markets (see Chapter 3) work better when participants know each other through face-to-face contact. So do activities that require close liaison between professional advisers and clients, such as mergers and acquisitions and the development of bespoke financial solutions.

■ Promotion of innovation through close contacts between financial services firms, clients and suppliers of support services. The encouragement of innovation and access to new products and markets are of great benefit to firms in a strong financial services cluster.

■ Creative competition between providers. Competition between financial services providers is an important spur to efficiency and innovation. The quest for market share provides an impetus for product innovation and differentiation, the development of new markets and more efficient ways of delivering services and products to clients.

Empirical research has found that financial services firms that locate in strong clusters grow faster than average, and this superior performance is attributed to the benefits of clustering. The report recommends that the authorities should pursue policies that assist the Square Mile/Canary Wharf cluster to remain as compact as possible. There is currently no evidence that core firms or functions are de-clustering, but the Square Mile/Canary Wharf needs to be nurtured if it is to continue to deliver substantial benefits to London, the UK and the European Union.

Financial centre economies of scale, scope and agglomeration
Firms that operate from larger financial services clusters generally enjoy significant competitive advantages compared with firms based in smaller centres. This is because of the operation of external economies of scale, economies of scope and economies of agglomeration. But these benefits may possibly be diminished by contrary diseconomies of scale.

Firms benefit from economies of scale when there is a positive correlation between the size of the firm and the efficiency of its operations. External economies of scale accrue to firms when a positive relationship exists between efficiency and the size of the industry (financial centre) in which they operate. Larger financial centres provide a more advantageous operating environment than smaller centres for several reasons:

- The larger the pool of skilled labour, the easier it is for firms to function, grow and diversify.
- The greater the range of associated financial activities, the more opportunity there is for creative interaction, integration and innovation. These are known as external economies of scope.
- The quality of financial markets – that is, their liquidity and efficiency – is strongly correlated with the scale of operations. These are highly desirable features, meaning better prices, lower dealing costs and diminished likelihood of market failure. There may be a positive reinforcement effect, with liquidity attracting further liquidity.
- Innovation is stimulated by the number of rival financial firms, the quantity and quality of skilled labour, and the variety of

financial activities. New business opportunities arise from both customers and other financial firms.

◪ Competition among firms promotes keener pricing for transactions, higher-quality work and product innovation. Higher standards help firms operating from larger financial centres to win business away from firms accustomed to a less vigorous competitive environment.

◪ Activities that require co-ordinated activity on the part of a number of independent firms can be undertaken more readily and effectively with a larger population of firms and specialist personnel; for example, subscription markets, such as loan syndication or the primary issuance of securities.

◪ Firms operating from larger and more prestigious financial centres enjoy a reputational and credibility advantage compared with those operating from smaller centres. Location is an important part of a financial firm's brand.

Financial firms operating in large financial centres also enjoy economies of agglomeration, which are reductions in transaction costs that result from a concentration of specialist support services and other business services. The ready availability of commercial lawyers, accountants, specialist printers, IT experts, financial public-relations consultants and many other support services enhances a firm's efficiency and competitiveness. The bigger the centre, the more extensive, varied and keenly priced is the range of complementary specialist support services.

Once firms are established in a financial centre, there are powerful reasons for them to remain there. Sunk costs – necessary but irrecoverable expenditures, such as start-up costs – are an important factor. So too is the work of building relationships with clients, other financial firms, the regulatory authorities and staff. Such relationships make it difficult and costly to relocate and lead to location inertia.

External economies of scale and economies of scope are powerful forces in the global financial-services industry, bestowing a big competitive advantage upon well-established, leading financial centres such as London. Indeed, in theory, the logical outcome of their operation is that most wholesale international financial activity should concentrate in a single global centre. But centralisation can also generate diseconomies of scale, such as crowding and congestion, high costs of accommodation and labour, and perhaps increased information costs because of distance from clients. Moreover, in the real world, political factors, regulatory barriers and incentives, and time-zone differences distort the operation of the centralising economic forces. So a role remains for regional and local financial centres.

The City: strengths and weaknesses

Based on surveys of City firms and practitioners, the top 20 factors that make London an attractive location for international financial services firms are as follows:

- ◪ Critical mass. The large number of firms and the wide range of activities undertaken generate external economies of scale and scope.
- ◪ Labour market size. The depth and breadth of the skills pool.
- ◪ Labour flexibility. The ability to hire and fire to adjust the ratio of costs to revenue.
- ◪ Professional and support services. High-quality support services generate economies of agglomeration.
- ◪ Physical infrastructure. The availability of abundant, state-of-the-art office accommodation, particularly at Canary Wharf.
- ◪ Financial infrastructure. High-quality payments and settlements systems.
- ◪ Clustering. The spatial concentration of participants which facilitates face-to-face contact.
- ◪ Openness. A tradition of welcoming foreign firms and allowing relatively easy access to markets.
- ◪ Trading and investment culture. A long-standing familiarity and affinity with financial markets.
- ◪ Financial innovation. Stimulated by the trading culture, the wealth of expertise and competitive environment.
- ◪ Regulation. A fair and rigorous regulatory framework applied proportionately.
- ◪ Tax. A relatively low-tax environment for companies and individuals.
- ◪ International transport links. Five international airports serving 100m passengers a year and Eurostar rail connections to Paris and Brussels.
- ◪ Information flow. London has a flourishing business and financial press and information culture. It is also regularly rated top European city for telecommunications in the annual Cushman &

Wakefield European Cities Monitor survey of business executives.

- ■ English language. The language of international finance. The common tongue was one of the reasons in the 1960s most American banks decided to establish their Euromarket operations in London rather than elsewhere.
- ■ Rule of law. The enforceability of contracts and arbitration procedures. English law is much used in commercial contracts, with disputes resolved in UK courts or through London-based arbitration and mediation.
- ■ Financial education and training. The presence of leading academic centres for the study and teaching of finance, as well as specialist financial training companies.
- ■ Time zone. A central position between the Asian and American time zones.
- ■ Metropolitan life. The appeal of living in a vibrant, cosmopolitan city.
- ■ Stability. Both political and economic.

Nevertheless, a number of complaints are regularly cited by respondents in polls:

- ■ Transport. The poor quality and reliability of the London Underground and links to airports and the cost of transport delays.
- ■ Cost. The high cost of office and residential accommodation and staff, as well as the overall expensiveness of living and working in London.
- ■ Government complacency. The lack of policy co-ordination and support for City interests.
- ■ Tax. The erosion of the UK's relatively low-tax regime.
- ■ Labour market regulation. The erosion of UK labour flexibility.
- ■ Regulation. The gradual erosion of London's business-friendly environment.

Importance of the City to the London, UK and EU economies

The City's workforce of 311,000 comprises a little over 1% of the UK's labour force. However, because of the vitality and efficiency of London's international financial-services industry, it makes a disproportionately important contribution to the UK's prosperity in terms of output, tax and overseas earnings. Estimates of the City's output range as high as £47 billion, 4% of UK GDP. In 2000 City firms and workers contributed nearly £10 billion in tax to the public purse, around 4% of total tax revenues. It has been estimated that on average each employee at a foreign bank generates £75,000 in tax revenue to the British government, a total contribution of £2.25 billion. Furthermore, the City's overseas earnings help offset the long-standing deficit in trade in goods: manufactures, foodstuffs and raw materials. Between 1992 and 2003, the financial sector's net exports rose more than threefold from £5 billion to over £16 billion. Indeed, Gordon Brown, the chancellor of the exchequer, deems the City's contribution to be so significant that one of his famous "five tests" of the UK's readiness to join the euro when Labour took power in 1997 was that entry should not damage the City.

The City is of even greater significance to the economy of London, its host city. City workers constitute around 8% of London's workforce and generate 14% of its GDP. They are among the highest paid London workers, receiving total incomes of £13–15 billion. Their demand for goods and services sustains many of London's leading restaurants, designer shops and luxury goods outlets, as well as underpinning thousands of more modest enterprises. The New York municipality estimates that each job on Wall Street supports two additional jobs in the city. If this ratio is applied to London, City jobs and pay packets support almost a quarter of London jobs.

The City accounts for 54% of total wholesale financial services activity in the EU. A calculation of the benefits this brings to the EU economy has been attempted by the Centre for Economic and Business Research, a City-based consultancy, on behalf of the Corporation of London. The method used is to compare the actual situation in 2003 with a hypothetical model of the EU economy (on the basis of some "heroic assumptions" and bold estimates), in which wholesale financial services are spread evenly across the countries of the EU proportionate to the size of their GDP. This is called the fragmented market hypothesis.

The fragmented market hypothesis model estimates that the even dispersion of wholesale financial services around the EU would lead to a fall in the scale of the City's output from €68.3 billion to €16.3 billion, a reduction of three-quarters. Around two-thirds of City employment, 207,000 jobs, would disappear. Loss of the economies of scale, scope and agglomeration that arise from the existence of the Square Mile/Canary Wharf cluster would result in increases in the prices of many services and products, leading customers to seek services outside the EU. The study suggests that only €14.4 billion of the €52 billion of business lost by the City would go elsewhere in the EU. Of the remainder, €21.3 billion would migrate to financial centres outside the EU, principally New York or Switzerland, and €16.3 billion of business would simply disappear, made uneconomic by the higher costs without the efficiencies of the large market in London. The macroeconomic outcome would be that the EU's GDP would be €31 billion lower (0.33%) with a net loss of 199,000 jobs across the region. The UK would bear the brunt of adjustment, with its GDP falling by €36 billion (2.1%), but Luxembourg, the Netherlands, Germany, France and Belgium would suffer too.

Back to the future

Will the City continue to grow and prosper? It ought to, because the underlying reasons for its growth in recent decades still exist. Demand for international financial services continues to expand rapidly, driven by global economic growth, the liberalisation of cross-border trade and capital flows, and the growth of international financial markets. These forces may even gather momentum in coming decades as more and more countries, including the potential giants China, India, Russia and Brazil, adopt convertible currencies and become integrated into the international financial system.

The City's leading position, reinforced by the powerful effect of economies of scale, scope and agglomeration, should ensure that a substantial portion of the growth of international financial services business is handled in London. There will certainly be competition from other centres, perhaps most challengingly in the long run from smaller centres with low taxes and less cumbersome regulatory regimes designed to attract international financial business. Hong Kong and Dubai are possible candidates. So are established tax havens such as the Bahamas and the Cayman Islands, although in such cases most of the high-value-added work, as well as the staff conducting it, remain in the major financial centres, including London.

The continuing dynamic expansion of demand for international financial services, coupled with the City's entrenched advantages as the world's foremost international financial centre, has led forecasters to estimate that the real output of the London wholesale financial services sector will grow by at least 6% a year over the next 10–20 years, repeating the performance of the last three decades. This is a much more rapid rate of expansion than the historic trend rate of UK economic growth, meaning that the City will loom even larger as a factor in the UK economy as well as in society and politics.

The difference between the 6% a year projected rate of growth of real output and a much lower rate of employment growth, 1.7% per annum over the last 30 years, implies the continuation of substantial increases in real output per head and hence in personal incomes. This would be consistent with factors promoting greater productivity in the wholesale financial-services industry, particularly investment in IT. Another factor helping productivity along is the increasing size of deals – equity issues, bond and currency trades, mergers and acquisitions – in global financial markets. The outcome will be that the gulf between remuneration levels in the international financial-services industry and other forms of employment will grow even wider. Nice work – if you can get it.

2 From the Royal Exchange to Canary Wharf

The origins of the City as an international financial centre go back five centuries and its development is entwined with Britain's evolution as a leading trading nation and naval power. In the second half of the 16th century, during the reign of Queen Elizabeth I, English seafarers began to voyage to Asia and the Americas and there was an expansion of mercantile contact with the commercial centres of northern Europe and the Mediterranean.

The growth of trade and shipping prompted the provision of a centralised marketplace for the conduct of mercantile and financial transactions. Such bourses existed in some European cities, notably Antwerp, where they stimulated trade through providing the amenities of centralisation, competition, price transparency, ancillary services, market information and sometimes a degree of regulation. In 1571, on the initiative of Sir Thomas Gresham, a leading merchant, the Royal Exchange was established in London's Cornhill to furnish these services. The opening ceremony was performed by Queen Elizabeth herself, setting the seal at the outset upon the symbiotic relationship between what was to become known as the City and the state.

At the time, the leading financial and mercantile centre in Europe and indeed the world was Antwerp. One reason for this was its geographic location on the River Scheldt, which is so large that even though Antwerp was some 60km from the North Sea, it became a convenient port for trading ships. The other was that it was Antwerp's cosmopolitan merchants who perfected the negotiability of the foreign bill of exchange, the principal instrument for the finance of international trade until the late 20th century. A bill of exchange is an IOU by which the "drawer" (a purchaser of goods) makes an unconditional undertaking to pay the "drawee" a sum of money at a given date, typically three months ahead. Like a post-dated cheque, it can be assigned by the drawee for payment to any named party or simply to the bearer. To enhance negotiability, the bills were endorsed by prominent merchants, who charged a commission for their guarantee. As merchants became more involved in finance, such activities became known as merchant banking.

Antwerp's golden age came to an abrupt and violent end in 1585 when the city was sacked by Spanish troops. Its merchants and bankers fled, taking with them their financial expertise. Many relocated in Amsterdam, which for the following two centuries became the world's leading financial centre. But some made it to London, enhancing its financial and mercantile acumen.

It was over the oceans, not across the Channel, that merchants in London sought profitable opportunities:

- In Asia, where trade in spices and exotic textiles was dominated by the East India Company, arguably the world's first multinational corporation formed in 1600 with a monopoly conferred by Royal Charter.
- In the Caribbean, where colonies were established in Jamaica, the centre of the sugar trade, in 1655, and other islands.
- In South America, where initially commerce was conducted illegally with the Spanish and Portuguese colonies.
- Along the eastern seaboard of North America, where British settlers harvested cod and timber and later grew crops such as cotton and hemp.

Another monopoly trading company, the Hudson Bay Company, was given a charter in 1670 to develop trade in the remote north; and in 1711 the South Sea Company was granted exclusive rights to trade with Spanish America, chiefly in slaves from Africa. However, the slave trade proved disappointingly unprofitable and the company's management decided to deploy its resources by buying up a large part of the British national debt. These financial manoeuvres led to the development of a speculative boom in the company's shares – the South Sea Bubble of 1720 – the first British securities bubble. Fraud and deception on the part of some of the company's directors and the bribery of officials and members of Parliament were contributory factors, as was the public's greed and credulity. When prices collapsed, thousands of speculators were ruined and three government ministers were implicated in corruption.

By 1700 London was the world's busiest port and with a population of 600,000 the world's largest city. The expansion of maritime and mercantile activity led to the development of markets in ship chartering, marine insurance and commodities. For many years transactions took place in coffee houses, which served as meeting places for different activities. For instance, Lloyd's coffee house, which opened in 1688, became the centre for marine underwriting. In time, those who met regularly to transact business became dissatisfied with their accommodation in the coffee houses and formed themselves into membership organisations with their own premises (custom built to their requirements), rules of conduct, listings of transactions and restrictions on entry.

London's position, convenient for shipping from the Baltic, the Mediterranean and the Atlantic, helped it establish itself as a thriving port. Amsterdam was in an equally advantageous geographic position, yet its trade languished while London's soared. The principal reason was the three wars waged by the British navy in the years 1652–74, which took a heavy toll of Dutch shipping. Naval superiority was also the key to the rapid expansion of British colonial territories in the 18th century, some seized from other European powers, notably France, Spain and Holland, while others, such as Australia and the Cape of Good Hope, were new settlements. The growth of empire contributed to the expansion of London's entrepôt activities because under the prevailing mercantilist regulations, all trade with British colonies had to be carried in British ships and to go through a British port before transshipment. Thus London became the prime market for most internationally traded commodities.

All that trade needed financing. Since the demise of Antwerp, Amsterdam was the leading market for international bills of exchange and retained its pre-eminence as an international money market despite being overtaken by London as a port. Nevertheless, London developed its own bill of exchange facilities as some merchants increasingly specialised in trade financing, becoming known as merchant banks. One of the leading houses undertaking this activity was Baring Brothers, established in 1762 by émigrés from Bremen in Germany.

War and government finance, 1694–1815

War is an expensive and potentially financially ruinous undertaking, particularly for countries with ramshackle public finances such as Britain in the 1670s. Indeed, the Anglo-Dutch wars imposed such a strain on the public finances that in 1672 the government defaulted on its debts, the last time a British government has done so. The Anglo-Dutch wars came to an end with the succession to the British throne of William III, a Dutchman, in 1688. But William was also at war, fighting Louis XIV of France, so Britain immediately found itself committed to that struggle, putting new pressure on the public finances.

The formation of the Bank of England in 1694 was the solution to the government's financial difficulties. In return for a substantial loan, the Bank was appointed the government's banker and received a monopoly of "joint stock" (shareholder) banking in England and Wales; all other banks had to operate as private partnerships with a maximum of six partners. The Bank not only made loans to the government itself but also organised the issue of government bonds and bills to raise funds from the public. Loans to the government took the form of Bank of England notes (convertible into gold on demand at the Bank), which soon dominated London's note circulation. But it was not a public institution, it was a privately owned company formed by a group of wealthy merchants, and in the 18th and 19th centuries it endeavoured to maximise shareholder value as well as serving the state.

Between 1739 and 1815, Britain was waging war or preparing to do so for two out of every three years. The result was an increase in public debt, in the form of outstanding long-term bonds, from £44m to £820m at the time of the battle of Waterloo in 1815. In these years, government bond issues were purchased by loan contractors in a competitive auction. The contractors put together syndicates of merchants who undertook to subscribe for a part of the total, which they then sold to smaller investors. Notable among the loan contractors were the firms of Barings and N.M. Rothschild (founded in 1798). But not all were so successful, and despite the sharing of risk by underwriting, many went bust.

The large scale of issuance of government bonds in the 18th century and particularly in the years of the French wars, 1793–1815, led to the growth of a secondary market where such bonds were traded. After more than a century of trading in coffee houses, in 1801 the leading brokers and jobbers (marketmakers) formed a membership organisation, the Stock Exchange, with a list of securities that could be traded, fixed settlement days and a rule book. The following year it moved to its present site in Old Broad Street.

Banking in London traces its origins to silversmiths who safeguarded gold and silver coins brought to London by country landowners attending the royal court at Westminster. Safeguarding turned into deposit taking, which provided the basis for lending, often to country landowners against the security of a mortgage on their estates.

These London "private banks" also developed correspondent relationships with provincial "country banks", both types being partnerships. The latter became widespread in the 18th century to serve the financial needs of farmers, merchants and industry by purchasing their bills of exchange (at a discount to face value), paying with their own banknotes. The bills were to be either held to maturity or sent to a correspondent in London for sale in the London bill market (discount market). Specialist bill brokers emerged around 1800, matching buyers and sellers of bills and receiving a commission for the service. By the 1830s some bill brokers had developed into "discount houses", firms specialising in investment in a portfolio of bills and financing their activities with short-term borrowings from London banks. Thus emerged the London money market.

The French occupation of Amsterdam in 1795 and blockade of Hamburg from 1803 devastated the trade and financial activities of these major international centres and led to the migration of merchants to London. The founder of Schroders, for instance, was a member of a Hamburg merchant dynasty who set up in London in 1804 in the middle of the French wars; the London firm subsequently became the leader in the family's international network. By closing down the competition for a generation, the wars boosted London's position as the world's primary trading and financial centre.

The City supreme, 1815–1914

By the end of the French wars in 1815, many elements of the City matrix were already present, in rudimentary form at least: a government bond market; a money market trading domestic bills; a government bank that was developing the functions of a central bank; and some elements of a national banking system. There were also various institutions connected with maritime and trading activities, notably Lloyd's of London, the marine insurance market, shipbroking at the Baltic coffee house and the Mincing Lane commodity markets, as well as a handful of joint-stock insurance companies. During the following century the scale and scope of all these activities and the internationalisation of London as a financial centre grew.

Between 1815 and the Boer war of 1899–1902, Britain was an antagonist in only one major war, the Crimean war of 1854–56, so there was less need for government borrowing for military purposes. The *Pax Britannica* was one reason why British government bonds (or gilts) became a smaller and smaller proportion of stockmarket securities, falling from 70% in 1853 to 9% in 1913 (see Table 2.1 overleaf); the other was the growth of borrowing by other borrowers.

In the 1830s and again in the 1840s there was a boom and bust in domestic railway stocks, technology bubbles comparable with the 1990s

Table 2.1 **London Stock Exchange securities, 1853–1913 (£m, nominal value)**

	1853	%	1873	%	1893	%	1913	%
Domestic								
British government (gilts)	854	70	859	38	810	12	1,013	9
Municipal	–	–	–	–	91	1	277	2
Railways	194	16	374	16	855	13	1,217	11
Commercial & industrial companies	22	2	20	1	93	1	439	4
Other companies (domestic & foreign)	44	4	178	8	454	7	1,640	15
Total domestic	1,114	92	1,431	63	2,303	34	4,586	41
Overseas								
Foreign governments	70	6	404	18	2,385	36	3,134	28
Dominion & colonial governments	–	–	83	4	309	5	612	5
Foreign railways (private companies)	31	3	354	16	1,564	24	2,931	26
Total overseas	101	9	841	38	4,258	65	6,677	59
Grand total	1,215		2,270		6,561		11,262	

Note: Percentage totals may not add to 100 because of rounding.
Source: Morgan, E.V. and Thomas, W.A., *The Stock Exchange: Its History and Functions*, Elek, 1962

dotcom bubble that burst in 2000. As the boom took off, UK railway securities (mostly bonds) emerged as a second major stockmarket sector, yielding a premium for investors over gilts. Before the early 1860s, the only way a company could get limited liability was through a private act of parliament, an expensive procedure that only large undertakings such as railways could afford. New company legislation introduced registration, which greatly facilitated company formation and joint-stock (shareholder) ownership. Nevertheless, it was not until the late 1880s that companies began to float on the Stock Exchange in substantial numbers. Many of these were utilities, infrastructure, dock, gas, electricity, tramway and mining companies, all with heavy capital requirements.

Manufacturers made little use of the capital-raising facilities available on the London capital market; in 1913 UK commercial and industrial securities constituted only 4% of the total (see Table 2.1). The capital requirements of the industrial revolution were met from other sources: private and family fortunes, short-term borrowing from banks and provincial stock exchanges. It was partly a matter of demand, as companies were able to raise sufficient funds from traditional sources and preferred to remain private and finance expansion from retained profits. But it also reflected the Stock Exchange's orientation to meet the demand for funds of large and increasingly overseas borrowers.

International capital market

The first foreign sovereign bond issue in the London capital market was in 1795 by Austria to finance its war effort against France (Austria ended up defaulting). The next milestone in the development of this segment of the market was the massive loan organised by Barings on behalf of France to enable it to make reparations payments in 1818. This opened the market to foreign sovereign borrowers, and in the 1820s there was a boom in foreign loans, especially to newly independent republics in Latin America. Many of them soon defaulted on interest payments and the episode culminated in a massive crash in 1825, the first of four Latin American debt crises at roughly half-century intervals. The outcome was that for a generation the London capital market was closed to most foreign borrowers: in 1853 foreign loans constituted only 9% of the total (see Table 2.1).

Lending to foreign governments resumed in the 1850s and accelerated in the 1860s. By the early 1870s bond issues were being made by borrowers of distinctly dubious creditworthiness, including a number of Latin American countries. Again the speculative euphoria was followed by a market crash (including a second Latin American debt crisis), and a parliamentary inquiry in 1875 revealed unscrupulous practices on the part of some of the City firms that acted as intermediaries for the borrowers. After a hiatus, foreign lending resumed in the 1880s but was interrupted by the Barings crisis of 1890. The problem was that Barings' funds had become temporarily locked up in unmarketable Argentinian bonds and it was unable to meet its immediate liabilities. Its failure threatened to bring down other City firms and precipitate a crash. This was avoided by decisive leadership on the part of the Bank of England, which organised a guarantee fund that enabled Barings to pay its creditors. The episode was a milestone in the evolution of the Bank's assumption of the central bank responsibility of lender of last resort (see Chapter 10).

Globalisation and the City, 1860s–1914

In the half-century from the mid-1860s to the first world war, the global economy expanded rapidly as a growing number of countries participated in international trade and industrialised. Two technologies played crucial roles: steam power and the electric telegraph. From the 1850s steam began to replace sail in powering the world's shipping fleet, cutting journey times and enhancing reliability. The construction of railways in North America, Latin America, Australia, South Africa and elsewhere opened up vast productive hinterlands as well as new markets. The effect was a sustained fall in world commodity prices between 1873 and 1896, making goods cheaper and consumers more prosperous. Much of the massive investment required was raised through the London capital market, and the bulk of the £6.6 billion of securities outstanding in respect of overseas borrowers in 1913 was for railway building by private companies and governments.

The electric telegraph led to huge reductions in communications time, promoting the integration of the major financial markets. London and Paris were connected by telegraph in the early 1850s. The laying of a transatlantic telegraph in 1866 cut communications time between London and North America from weeks by ship to minutes by cable. By the 1880s telegraph communication was possible with the whole of the economically developed world, revolutionising international commerce. Again the City played a crucial role, financing much of the cable-laying and being a major client. Moreover, it was a pair of City firms, Reuters and the Exchange Telegraph Company (Extel), that pioneered the provision of telegraphic news and data services.

Much of the rapidly expanding international trade was denominated in sterling and financed in the City. The 1880s to the first world war was the era of the gold standard, a system of fixed exchange rates in which each participating currency was worth a specified weight of gold. Bank of England banknotes were exchangeable for gold on demand and the Bank fulfilled the role of guardian of the system.

From the middle of the 19th century the London money market was increasingly dominated by "foreign bills", bills of exchange arising from the finance of international trade. The market grew substantially and had no equivalent in any other financial centre. Overseas banks, first from the British Empire, then continental Europe and subsequently elsewhere, established branches in the City to invest deposits in the liquid but interest-bearing securities of the London money market, enhancing the market's depth and liquidity.

In the City the merchant banks emerged as the undisputed kings of the jungle. There were two thoroughly international sides to their business: the endorsement of bills of exchange arising from international trade, enhancing their negotiability in the London money market; and the sponsorship and organisation of large securities issues by foreign governments, overseas railway companies and other international borrowers in the London capital market. Before the 1920s merchant banks rarely acted for British borrowers, focusing on their international clientele. The successful merchant bankers became very rich. Some bought country houses and married into the aristocracy, sometimes moving on from the City. Members of the leading merchant banking families dominated the Court of Directors of the Bank of England.

The Bank's monopoly of joint-stock banking ended in the provinces in 1826 and in London in 1833. This resulted in the formation of well-capitalised shareholder-owned banks (which became known as clearing banks) and the development of extensive branch networks, supplanting or absorbing the country banks. Pursuit of scale led to mergers between the clearing banks, and by the 1920s the British banking system was dominated by seven giant clearing banks, each with a corporate headquarters in the City. The clearing banks were not allowed to issue their own banknotes, and as the country banks disappeared so did their notes. Gradually, Bank of England notes became the sole banknotes in circulation, although it was not until 1928 that the process was completed.

War, depression and controls, 1914–58

On the outbreak of the first world war the Stock Exchange closed for five months and the money market was thrown into turmoil, because one-third of the bills of exchange (money-market short-term instruments) in circulation were due to be redeemed by German, Austrian or Russian firms from which payments would not be forthcoming. Many merchant banks and discount houses faced ruin, and their collapse threatened other City houses and the national banking system. However, prompt government action led by the Bank of England prevented a wave of bankruptcies. With the money market dominated by Treasury bills and a ban on the issue of foreign securities, the war years 1914–18 were bleak for many City firms.

The City's problems provided an opening for New York to emerge as a major international financial centre. With encouragement from the Federal Reserve Bank of New York, a discount market based on dollar bills of exchange developed on Wall Street. It captured the financing of US commodity imports and much Latin American and Asian trade that had hitherto used the London money market. With the London capital market reserved for British government borrowing to raise war finance, the international capital market moved to Wall Street and the relocation proved permanent. Even the British government turned to the US capital market for war loans, giving a further boost to Wall Street, as well as selling off dollar assets held by British nationals to pay for munitions.

The end of the war brought a quick relaxation of wartime economic and financial controls. This led to a frenetic, short-lived boom in 1919–20 which was followed by a severe recession in 1920–21. During the boom, a City takeover frenzy led to the acquisition of companies at massively inflated prices, saddling the bidders with weak balance sheets when the value of the assets so expensively purchased collapsed. Money-market activity revived in the boom, although on an inflation-adjusted basis the volume of business was only half of its pre-war level. But activity fell sharply in the downturn. The brightest sector of the City in the early 1920s was foreign-exchange dealing, which boomed as never before in the currency turmoil that followed the end of the war. The major clearing banks dominated the activity.

Although by no means the principal cause, the departure of sterling from the gold standard in 1919 contributed to the post-war currency instability. It was government policy to return to the gold standard when conditions permitted. This led to big cuts in public expenditure to balance the budget, exacerbating the severity of the 1920–21 recession. Proponents of the austerity measures, notably the governor of the Bank of England, Montagu Norman, argued that sterling's return to the gold standard would stimulate trade, boosting the manufacturing sector, and restore the City to its pre-war pre-eminence as an international financial centre. In 1925 sterling returned to the gold standard at the pre-war parity of £1:$4.86 – a matter of principle for the Bank of England, honouring the trust of external holders of sterling. However, a well-known and controversial economist, John Maynard Keynes, a fellow of King's College, Cambridge, argued that the parity was 10% too high, creating an exchange-rate problem for UK exporters, who had already been hit by the penetration of their Latin American and Asian export markets during the war by US and Japanese competitors. This led to accusations that the interests of industry and the unemployed had been sacrificed to the City.

Following the return to the gold standard, controls on securities issues for overseas borrowers were rescinded and there was a minor revival of such issues. Nevertheless, Wall Street and the dollar remained pre-eminent in the international capital market. The volume of international trade bills in the money market also picked up, although on an inflation-adjusted basis business was lower than in 1913. Moreover, the clearing banks muscled into the business in the 1920s, to the fury of the merchant banks. Relative to the pre-war "golden age", the 1920s were difficult years for most City firms, but they were a lot better than the 1930s and 1940s.

The 1931 crisis and the slump

In 1928, soaring stock prices on Wall Street and rising interest rates persuaded American banks to begin to repatriate short-term loans to European banks to take advantage of domestic opportunities. The Wall Street crash of October 1929 accelerated the withdrawal of funds, which were needed to meet losses at home. But the banking systems of central Europe had become dependent on these funds and their removal caused a crisis. It began in Austria in May 1931 and soon spread to Germany, which in July 1931 imposed a moratorium on all external debt payments. In September it was the UK's turn to feel the pressure, leading to the departure of sterling from the gold standard (the value of the pound dropped from $4.86 to $3.50) and the formation of a coalition national government to confront the crisis. These events discredited the economic policy associated with the Bank and the City, as well as giving rise to a conspiracy theory on the political left that the Bank had engineered the downfall of the Labour administration.

The 1931 financial crisis ushered in the international economic slump that reached its nadir in 1932–33, with millions unemployed in the industrial economies. The developing countries suffered too, triggering widespread defaults on loans by countries in eastern Europe and Latin America (the third Latin American debt crisis). The slump blighted many City activities. The two-thirds drop in the value of world exports between 1929 and 1934 had a devastating impact on the City's trade finance, shipping, marine insurance and commodity market sectors. Securities issues for overseas borrowers crashed from £150m in 1929 to £21m in 1935.

The money market was hit by a dearth of foreign trade bills when the Treasury adopted a policy of cheap money (low interest rates), which was intended to revive economic activity and ran from 1932 to 1951. Low interest rates made the business of the discount houses uneconomic and several failed. To avoid extinction (with encouragement from the authorities), firms and clearing banks made defensive arrangements, eliminating price competition and ensuring modest profits, which lasted until 1971.

The German suspension of external payments in July 1931 caused problems similar to those at the outbreak of the first world war for many merchant banks with substantial trade finance credits outstanding to German firms. They survived during the 1930s and 1940s thanks to facilities made available by the Bank of England and the clearing banks, but as shadows of their former selves. Overall, the 1930s were little short of disastrous for the City's international activities: the UK's invisible exports from financial services, insurance and shipping fell from an annual average of £200m in 1926–30 to £110m in 1931–33 and £51m in 1934–38.

For a generation, from the 1930s to the 1960s, the City turned its focus away from the international market towards the domestic market. Protected by trade tariffs, UK manufacturing firms staged a recovery from the slump in the 1930s, a decade that saw the large-scale development of new sectors such as motor manufacturing, electrical products and the chemicals industry. The merchant banks cultivated relationships with UK firms, offering corporate advisory services and access to the capital market, displacing the stockbrokers and company promoters that hitherto had provided these services. It was to serve the City's new-found interest in the domestic market that the *Financial News* (acquired by the *Financial Times* in 1945) launched a new stockmarket index in 1935. Composed of the 30 leading shares, it became the FT Ordinary Share Index, which until the 1980s was the most widely used benchmark for share prices.

The second world war and the post-war years

The outbreak of the second world war in 1939 was accompanied by the introduction of comprehensive controls on activity in the financial markets in order to satisfy the government's war finance needs. The Stock Exchange closed briefly and then business became dominated by government debt: by 1946 gilts constituted 56% of quoted securities, a proportion last seen in the 1860s. Share prices tumbled with the coming of war, but staged a recovery from 1941 and were back to pre-war levels by 1945. The commodity markets closed at the beginning of hostilities and stayed shut until the early 1950s. The City was badly bombed during the Blitz in 1941, one-third of the Square Mile being razed by German bombs. Survival, both physical and financial, was the order of the day.

The first major measure of the post-war Labour government elected in 1945 was the nationalisation of the Bank of England, a symbolic act of revenge for 1931. In following years the fuel, power, steel and transport

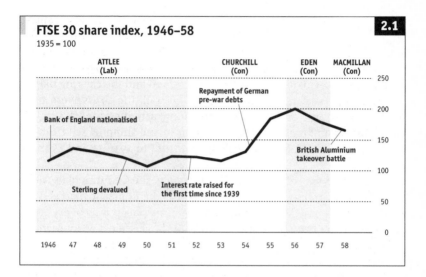

FTSE 30 share index, 1946–58
1935 = 100

industries were also nationalised, leading to the disappearance of several large sectors of securities from the Stock Exchange (as well as fears in the City that the banks would be next). The government retained the full array of wartime controls, making it difficult for the financial markets and financial firms to operate without official consent, as was intended.

In the post-war era, Wall Street was unrivalled as the world's leading international financial centre. The dollar became the reference point for the new Bretton Woods system of fixed exchange rates and the world's principal reserve currency. The business of the City's merchant banks and stockmarket firms revived in the 1950s along with the stockmarket (see Figure 2.1) but remained focused on the UK's domestic economy. The return of a Conservative government in 1951 led to the scrapping of many of the wartime controls and the reopening of the commodity markets, although exchange controls were retained to shore up sterling in the new fixed exchange-rate system. In 1954, a turning point in the revival of the City's fortunes, the bullion market reopened and German credits frozen in 1931 were repaid (with interest). But the prevailing atmosphere in the City for most of the 1950s was cautious and clubby, and innovation was looked on with suspicion.

A tale of two cities, 1958–79

A challenge to the established order of things in the City was

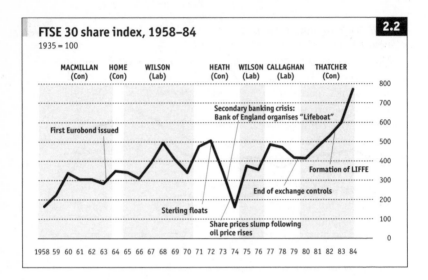

FTSE 30 share index, 1958–84   **2.2**

1935 = 100

MACMILLAN	HOME	WILSON		HEATH	WILSON CALLAGHAN	THATCHER
(Con)	(Con)	(Lab)		(Con)	(Lab) (Lab)	(Con)

Secondary banking crisis:
Bank of England organises "Lifeboat"

First Eurobond issued

Formation of LIFFE

End of exchange controls

Sterling floats

Share prices slump following
oil price rises

800
700
600
500
400
300
200
100
0

1958 59 60 61 62 63 64 65 66 67 68 69 70 71 72 73 74 75 76 77 78 79 80 81 82 83 84

mounted by S.G. Warburg, a merchant bank founded by two German Jewish banker refugees in the 1930s. In the winter of 1958–59 S.G. Warburg organised a hostile takeover bid for British Aluminium, a virtually unprecedented move that united almost the whole of the rest of the City against it. But the battle was won in the marketplace, where S.G. Warburg's aggressive accumulation of shares made it victorious. The "aluminium war" put the City on the front pages and turned merchant bankers into celebrities. Change was under way in the Square Mile.

Before the late 1950s corporate mergers and acquisitions had been handled by accountants, but in the 1960s the resurgent merchant banks made the business their own. They also moved into pension-fund management, taking business from life insurance companies and getting new mandates as their corporate clients began their own self-administered schemes. There was even a revival of their trade finance and other banking activities and the development of hire purchase and leasing.

During 1958–68 the bull market on the London Stock Exchange revived the fortunes of brokers and jobbers (marketmakers). In both the early and late 1960s there were takeover booms and headline-grabbing corporate contests, such as ICI's unsuccessful bid for Courtaulds in 1961 and GEC's bids for AEI (Associated Electrical Industries) in 1967 and English Electric in 1968, which resulted in the creation of a British engineering giant. The restructuring of British industry was promoted by the

1964–70 Labour administration, keeping the corporate finance departments of the major merchant banks very busy.

The UK's post-war domestic financial system featured strict demarcation between different types of financial institution: merchant banks, clearing banks, discount houses, building societies, stockbrokers, jobbers and others. There was not only little competition between sectors, but also little price competition within sectors, since they operated as cartels with restrictive practices that set rates and commissions. These arrangements were legacies of the survival measures of the 1930s and wartime. The Conservative administration that came into power in 1970 was sympathetic to arguments that the controls were inhibiting the UK's economic performance and in 1971 adopted a new policy for the banking sector, "Competition and Credit Control". This package of reforms eliminated the banking cartel and allowed competition among bankers in lending. The immediate and unanticipated effect was a credit boom that fuelled a property boom and price inflation.

Rise of the Euromarkets

The drama of takeover bids and the revival of the City's domestic business overshadowed the rise of a new international market: the Eurodollar market. A Eurodollar is a dollar held on deposit in a bank outside the United States (see Chapter 3). The rise of a market in offshore dollars in Europe in the late 1950s was the outcome of a mixture of economic and political factors. The most important was the recurrent American balance-of-payments deficits, resulting in a large pool of externally held dollars. These were augmented by dollars placed offshore by American corporations and investors, where they earned higher rates of interest than available domestically because of a regulatory ceiling on the rate that American banks could pay. Another source was the dollar balances of communist countries that were wary of placing them on deposit in New York lest they be taken hostage by the American government in a cold war crisis.

The Euromarkets span the maturity spectrum, and each market has a different pattern of development:

- Short-term – the Eurocurrency market.
- Medium-term – syndicated loans and Euronotes.
- Long-term – the Eurobond market.

The first to develop was the Eurocurrency market, for short-term deposits and loans, mostly between banks. It expanded rapidly in the late 1950s and 1960s. In 1963 the overall market was estimated at $12 billion; by 1970 it was $65 billion, an annual compound rate of growth of 31%. The establishment of the Eurocurrency market in London was encouraged by the Bank of England, and it was British commercial banks that nurtured the new market. But it was major American commercial banks that really developed the market in London, soon being joined by European and Japanese banks. In 1960 77 foreign banks had a presence in London; by 1970 the number had more than doubled to 163. Except in the early days, the merchant banks played only a minor part in the development of the Eurocurrency market, their balance sheets being too small for them to be significant receivers of dollar deposits relative to the scale of the market.

The Eurobond market developed to meet the requirements of governments and corporations for long-term finance. It was created and developed by European banks as a means of competing with the American investment banks that dominated the international capital market in New York and thus got the lion's share of the fees and commissions, while the European banks that handled most of the distribution to European investors received only meagre sales commissions. The Eurobond market was launched in July 1963 in London with a $15m issue on behalf of Autostrade, the Italian national highways authority. S.G. Warburg was the lead manager of the issue, with prominent German, Belgian and Dutch banks as co-managers.

Within weeks of the opening of the Eurobond market, the president of the United States, John F. Kennedy, announced the introduction of a tax on foreign borrowing in the American capital market to curb the outflow of dollars that was contributing to the country's gaping balance-of-payments deficit. This was a stroke of fortune for the fledgling market and the City, ensuring that a substantial volume of international capital market activity shifted from New York to London. Seeing the writing on the wall, the leading Wall Street international bond firms, including Morgan Stanley, First Boston, Smith Barney and Lehman Brothers, established offices in Europe in the years 1964–67. Between 1963 and 1972 the volume of Eurobond new issues rose from $148m to $5.5 billion. Some City merchant banks and British commercial banks were significant players in the market's first decade, but in the 1970s they were sidelined by the leading Wall Street investment and commercial banks and the major European universal banks that built up a major presence in London to undertake this business.

The continuing problem of the American balance-of-payments deficit lay behind the announcement by Richard Nixon in August 1971 of the suspension of the convertibility of externally held dollars for gold, the linchpin of the Bretton Woods system. Although the system was patched up by the Smithsonian Agreement of December 1975, this in turn collapsed in March 1973 and the world moved to floating exchange rates. Floating rates gave a big boost to foreign-exchange trading and led to the creation of a market in Chicago in 1972 specialising in trading currency futures, the first financial derivatives. The devaluation of the dollar hit the earnings of the oil-producing countries (oil is denominated in dollars), leading to moves by OPEC to restore the real value of revenues through price rises. The outbreak of the Yom Kippur war in October 1973 led to a tightening of oil prices and the application of sanctions against western countries that openly supported Israel.

The quadrupling of the oil price in 1973 triggered a global recession in 1974–75. This caused the UK stockmarket to plummet: the FT Ordinary Share Index fell from 543 at its peak in May 1972 to 146 in early January 1975 (see Figure 2.2 on page 36). Naturally, this was very bad news for investors and for the business of the domestic securities industry and the merchant banks. It also triggered a crash in property values. This led to problems at the so-called secondary or fringe banks, a new type of City firm that specialised in short-term borrowing on the money market and long-term lending to property companies. Their business model depended on them being able to regularly re-borrow at reasonable rates, but with the collapse of property values they found that funds were either unavailable or ruinously expensive. One of them collapsed and others were on the brink when the Bank of England intervened and organised a "lifeboat" of City banks that provided funds to prevent more failures and supervised an orderly winding up of the sector.

The recession led to rising unemployment and a mounting budget deficit in the UK. This, together with rampant inflation, caused foreign holders to lose confidence in sterling, which crashed. The government appealed to the IMF, which in 1976 provided a loan to help the UK over its difficulties. In order to repay its borrowing, in 1977 the government sold off a tranche of its holding of British Petroleum (BP) shares in a public offering that raised £564m, at the time the world's largest equity offering and a forerunner of the privatisations of the 1980s.

But the oil-price hike had a silver lining for the Euromarkets. Over the years 1972–80, international commercial banks, mostly in London and New York, received $154 billion in short-term petrodollar deposits.

These funds were lent to countries with balance-of-payments deficits caused by the oil-price shock. The bulk of this "petrodollar recycling" was arranged in London. It mostly took the form of large floating-rate loans with medium-term maturity (3–10 years). These loans to sovereign (government) borrowers and international institutions, or multinational corporations, were often so huge that they were made by syndicates of banks, the risk exposure being too great for even the biggest international banks to shoulder alone. The British clearing banks and major American and European banks were active as arrangers and participants in syndicated loans.

From the abolition of exchange controls to Canary Wharf, 1979–2004

From the end of the 1970s to the middle of the 2000s the domestic City and the international City of London came together as a global financial powerhouse. The transformation that took place in this quarter century was extraordinary and involved the following sweeping structural changes:

- Deregulation and the reconfiguration of markets and market participants.
- Institutional reorientation and innovation.
- Increased scale of markets and size of market participants.
- Convergence of domestic and international markets and activities.
- Increase in foreign ownership.
- Enhanced significance of institutional investors.
- Rebuilding and spatial expansion.

These were the long-term trends behind the headlines that reported day-to-day market highs and lows, changes in ownership of City firms, financial scandals and calamities, reforms of regulatory and institutional structures, and individual and corporate achievements.

Abolition of exchange controls, 1979

The beginning of the process of transformation can be pinpointed exactly: Tuesday 23rd October 1979. That day there were two political developments of profound significance for the City: first, a surprise announcement by the recently elected Conservative government led by Margaret Thatcher of the immediate removal of sterling exchange controls, transforming opportunities for investors and setting in motion fundamental changes in the UK securities industry; second, a ministerial decision to back the reference by the Office of Fair Trading (OFT), a UK antitrust body, of the rule book of the London Stock Exchange to the Restrictive Practices Court. This was because of its long-standing requirement that members charge minimum commissions for securities transactions, eliminating price competition. These two decisions – unconnected and fortuitously coincidental, but self-reinforcing – set the City on the road to fundamental change.

Exchange controls – restrictions on capital movements by investors and companies – had been introduced 40 years earlier at the beginning of the second world war to direct financial resources to the war effort. They were retained after the war to protect sterling against devaluation under the Bretton Woods system of fixed exchange rates by preventing capital outflows. With the collapse of the Bretton Woods system and the floating of sterling in 1972, that reason for their existence disappeared. Yet the controls were retained because politicians and officials were terrified of the foreign-exchange market, which had repeatedly humiliated British governments.

In the late 1970s there was a rapid increase in the output of North Sea oil, turning sterling into a petrocurrency. When the Iranian revolution led to a second OPEC oil-price shock in summer 1979, the pound soared. The lifting of exchange controls was an attempt, vain as it transpired, to curb the rise in the exchange rate to help British exporters. But abolition was also consistent with the Thatcher government's avowed devotion to the free market and its determination to roll back the post-war corporatist arrangements. Remarkably, this fundamental financial decision was taken in such haste and secrecy that there was virtually no consultation with City firms or institutions and no careful consideration of its consequences for the City.

At liberty to invest anywhere in the world for the first time in a couple of generations, British institutional investors went on an overseas shopping spree, especially for dollar securities. In 1978 (under exchange controls), net investment in equities by British institutional investors comprised domestic shares worth £1.9 billion and foreign shares worth £459 million; in 1982 (after abolition), the figures were domestic shares worth £2.4 billion and foreign shares worth £2.9 billion.

Although it was predictable that some of the purchases of foreign securities would be handled by foreign brokerage firms, especially the London offices of American brokerage houses, the revelation that British stockbrokers handled only 5% of the overseas investments made by the 20 leading British pension funds in the couple of years immediately following abolition shocked the authorities. This was partly because of the predominantly domestic orientation of British brokers following 40 years of restrictions on foreign investment. But the crucial factor was the Stock Exchange rule on minimum commissions, which made it almost impossible for them to win business against foreign houses that were unhindered by constraints on price competition.

The Stock Exchange's rule on minimum commissions was already under fire for other reasons, which had led to the OFT's challenge. First, the abolition of minimum commissions at the New York Stock Exchange in May 1975 had set an example of this form of deregulation. Second, such restrictive practices were anathema to the new government's market-oriented ideology. Third, institutional investors were up in arms about the level of commission rates in London and were increasingly finding ways of avoiding paying them. The hindrance minimum commissions were to the international competitiveness of the UK's securities industry was yet another reason for reform.

Big Bang, 1983–86

The outcome was a deal in July 1983, largely brokered by the Bank of England, by which the government halted the OFT's legal challenge in exchange for reform undertakings on the part of the London Stock Exchange. The package of reforms that was eventually implemented affected a lot more than commission rates and transformed the City securities market along Wall Street lines, radically changing the centuries-old market structure:

- Minimum commissions were scrapped, permitting competitive pricing in securities brokerage.
- The rule that securities firms could conduct either brokerage or marketmaking (but not both) was abolished (in the jargon, dual capacity replaced single capacity).
- Restrictions on the ownership of Stock Exchange firms were relaxed, allowing them to be purchased by banks for the first time.
- Greater competition was introduced in the government bond (gilts) market.

This transformation of the UK securities industry soon came to be known as "Big Bang".

The abolition of restrictions on the ownership of Stock Exchange firms led to a restructuring of the securities industry, one of the bastions of the traditional City along with the merchant banks. In the three years up to October 1986, when the new trading and institutional arrangements became fully operational, all but two of the leading British securities firms were acquired by new owners. In total, 77 of the 225 Stock Exchange firms were sold, turning more than 500 of their former partners into millionaires: 16 were bought by British merchant banks; 27 by British commercial banks; 14 by American banks; and 20 by other foreign, mostly European, banks.

The deregulation of the ownership of Stock Exchange firms presented City merchant banks with an opportunity to develop into investment banks on the "integrated" Wall Street model. The pre-Big Bang business model of the leading merchant banks was a mixture of specialist banking (traditional trade finance and other activities), corporate finance (mergers and acquisitions and capital raising) and asset management. The pattern of business of the leading Wall Street investment banks was a combination of corporate advisory and capital-raising, and secondary-market securities trading and brokerage, the latter providing distribution capability for securities issues organised by the firm. Securities trading was conducted both as an agent for clients and on the firm's own account (proprietary trading). The integrated American investment banking model was riskier and required more capital than the traditional British pattern of business, but it could be highly profitable, especially in a bull market.

Big Bang opened the UK domestic securities and corporate advisory markets to the major American investment banks, which had hitherto confined their activities to the Euromarkets. From the mid-1980s they began to build up their presence in London and to compete aggressively for domestic business. In September 1985, for instance, City stockbrokers were awestruck when Goldman Sachs purchased an entire portfolio of securities being offloaded by Robert Maxwell, a publishing tycoon, as a single "block trade" for $300m. Between 1986 and 1989 Salomon Brothers increased its London staff from 150 to 900, Merrill Lynch from 760 to 1,600, Morgan Stanley from 600 to 950 and Goldman Sachs from 520 to 750. However, the real interest of the Wall Street firms was not the UK market, it was the process of European economic integration, which it was believed would generate an investment-banking bonanza.

Anticipation of the American challenge led most of the leading British merchant banks – Barings, Hambros, Hill Samuel, Kleinwort Benson, Morgan Grenfell and S.G. Warburg – to adopt the American integrated model, developing securities activities in addition to their traditional corporate advisory work. So did the three British clearing banks with investment banking ambitions: Barclays, Midland and National Westminster (NatWest). The opposite strategy of sticking to their established pattern of business was pursued by Robert Fleming & Co, Lazard Brothers and Schroders, among the merchant banks, and Cazenove, one of the remaining pair of independent stockbrokers. N.M. Rothschild hedged its bets by forging an alliance with Smith Brothers, the other independent British securities house, which was renamed Smith New Court.

Clearing banks

The British clearing (commercial) banks were much bigger than the merchant banks in capital, assets and manpower, especially the "big four": Barclays, Lloyds, Midland and NatWest. Competing only against each other in most parts of the domestic banking market, they were also very profitable. These profits provided management with the means to build the business, but the highly concentrated retail banking market offered little scope for domestic expansion. So growth meant either expansion abroad or diversification into some related or new activity. The profits also provided the means for NatWest to build itself a spanking new City headquarters, the NatWest Tower in Bishopsgate, which at the time of its opening in 1981 was the tallest building in the UK.

In the 1960s and 1970s Barclays and National Westminster established a significant, though not particularly profitable, presence in the United States while Lloyds had a substantial footprint in Latin America through its acquisition in 1971 of Bank of London and Latin America (BOLSA), which became Lloyds Bank International. Eager to catch up, in summer 1980 Midland agreed to buy the San Francisco-based Crocker Bank, which had been active in lending to Latin American borrowers in the 1970s. The onset of the less-developed country debt crisis in summer 1982 was disastrous for Crocker and its new owner, Midland (see Chapter 13). Midland eventually succeeded in extricating itself from Crocker, which was sold to Wells Fargo Bank in 1986. Overall, the disastrous foray into North America cost Midland at least £1 billion and its reputation never recovered. In June 1992 it was acquired by the Hongkong and Shanghai Banking Corporation (HSBC), which moved its headquarters from Hong Kong to London at around the same time.

Lloyds Bank also found its balance sheet riddled with non-performing Latin American loans because of the traditional focus of its subsidiary Lloyds Bank International on that region, although its problems were nothing like as acute as Midland's. Nevertheless, the experience was chastening and was one of the factors that prompted the management to seek to define the bank's fundamental objectives. The exercise was undertaken in 1983, the outcome being a shift from multiple objectives to a single goal: a doubling of shareholder value every three years. This was to be achieved through focusing solely on the most profitable aspect of the bank's operations, its UK retail banking business. It proved a spectacularly successful strategy, and Lloyds was soon one of the most profitable banks in the world and one of the most admired.

As Lloyds set about divesting non-core activities, Barclays and NatWest decided to take advantage of the Big Bang restructuring to supplement their retail banking businesses with investment banking. With their enormous resources they were able to assemble substantial investment-banking operations by acquiring some leading stockbroking and securities marketmaking firms and by hiring. At Barclays, the outcome was Barclays de Zoete Wedd (BZW), and NatWest developed securities activities at County Bank, its investment-banking arm. Midland too, though more modestly as befitted its straitened circumstances, added a securities brokerage capacity to Samuel Montagu, its merchant-banking subsidiary. Backed by their parents' big balance sheets, BZW, County and Samuel Montagu appeared to be well positioned to meet the growing challenge from American investment banks.

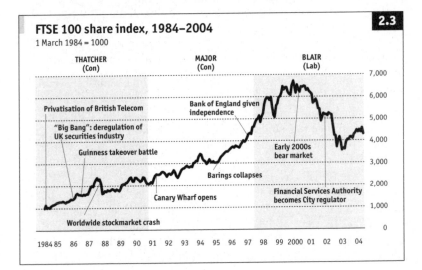

FTSE 100 share index, 1984–2004
1 March 1984 = 1000

2.3

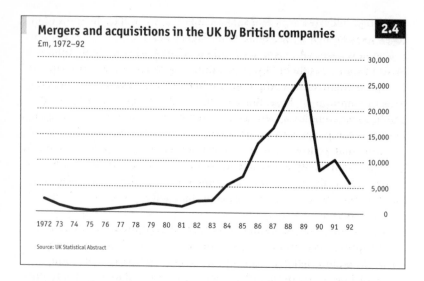

Mergers and acquisitions in the UK by British companies
£m, 1972–92

2.4

30,000

25,000

20,000

15,000

10,000

5,000

0

1972 73 74 75 76 77 78 79 80 81 82 83 84 85 86 87 88 89 90 91 92

Source: UK Statistical Abstract

1980s bull market

The Big Bang restructuring of the City took place against the background of a bull market on the stock exchange that ran from November 1979 to summer 1987 (see Figure 2.3). Rising share prices and soaring turnover for both equities and gilts encouraged banks to believe that it was a good idea to buy stockbroking and marketmaking firms and to pay fancy prices. The growing sophistication of trading and asset management required a better benchmark than the FT Ordinary Share Index that had been introduced in 1935. Accordingly, in February 1984 a more comprehensive and up-to-the-minute index – the FTSE 100 Share Index – was introduced.

In the mid-1980s there was an upsurge in primary market securities issuance on the London Stock Exchange. In 1980 the total amount raised through the issuance of securities was £1.6 billion. In 1982 it increased to £3 billion, in 1984 to £9 billion, in 1986 to £23 billion and in 1987 to £26.6 billion. These totals include initial public offerings by new companies, additional securities issues by existing companies and privatisation sales by the British government, which in some years surpassed corporate fundraising. Some of this capital was used to fund a UK corporate mergers and acquisitions boom, which began in 1982 and generated substantial fees for the merchant banks' corporate finance departments and other advisers. In 1981 British companies spent £1.1 billion on acquiring other British companies. Spending doubled in 1982 to £2.2 billion, reached £7 billion in 1985 and £13.5 billion in 1986, and at the peak of the boom in 1989 it was £27.2 billion (see Figure 2.4).

The new takeover wave was kicked off in April–June 1983 by a successful £600m hostile bid by BTR, a thrusting conglomerate, for Thomas Tilling, an engineering company. The bid had a number of features that became common in these showdowns: a "dawn raid" to accumulate a significant shareholding before the announcement of the bid; an aggressive press campaign; and a hard sell to institutional investors. Like many of those that followed, it was masterminded by a merchant bank, Morgan Grenfell, which emerged as the City's principal organiser of hostile bids, using muscular, and sometimes illegal, tactics. Other merchant banks, notably S.G. Warburg, became known for the skill of their bid-battle defence work.

Three contested bid battles received massive media attention. The first, in spring 1985, was the contest between the Al Fayed brothers and "Tiny" Rowland, head of Lonrho, a trading company, for control of House of Fraser, the owner of Harrods. This final chapter in a complex struggle for control of the famous department store that had been going on for years was won by the Al Fayed brothers. The second, in winter 1985, was the fight between United Biscuits and Hanson Trust for control of Imperial Tobacco, a tobacco and consumer goods conglomerate. Hanson won, prompting Sir Hector Laing, head of United Biscuits, to protest loudly about the loss of an opportunity to forge a major new UK-based international food company and to condemn the short-term outlook of City asset managers. The episode placed the issue of City short-termism on the public and political agenda and established Laing as a leading critic.

The third episode, in a class of its own, was the acrimonious struggle between Argyll Group, a British retail multiple, and Guinness, a leading British drinks industry company, over Distillers, the largest independent Scotch whiskymaker (see Chapter 13). The contest, played out between December 1985 and April 1986, featured the most extensive use ever made of financial public relations to sway shareholders and belittle the other side. Guinness and its advisers won the battle by resorting to illegal tactics that later led to a major scandal and a high-profile series of trials. Similar conduct on Wall Street also led to scandal and arrests, most notably of Ivan Boesky, an arbitrageur involved in a notorious Wall Street insider trading scandal. Such episodes inspired the film *Wall Street*, which was released in 1987.

Privatisation, 1979-87

Margaret Thatcher came into office in 1979 determined to reverse three decades of poor economic performance by the UK. The large public sector was deemed to be a prime culprit, and the privatisation of public assets became a key dimension of government policy. Initially, attention was focused on the sale of public-sector housing stock to occupiers, and the privatisation programme of the first Thatcher administration of 1979-83 was modest compared with what came later.

Privatisation was intended to achieve a variety of objectives, which were sometimes difficult to reconcile with each other. The transfer of industries to the private sector was meant to instil market disciplines and thus increase the efficiency of the economy. The sales were a source of funds for the government, allowing lower taxes than might otherwise have been the case. Privatisation was a means of enticing individual citizens to become participants in a shareholding democracy. It was a device for weakening the public-sector trade unions. In the public utility monopoly industries, it offered an opportunity for restructuring and the introduction of competition. The sales also generated substantial fees for the City merchant banks that arranged them.

The Conservative Party manifesto for the 1979 election contained a commitment to privatise the aerospace, shipbuilding and freight industries, which were deemed to be subject to normal competitive disciplines that had no place in state ownership. The first public asset to be sold was another tranche of the government's holding of BP shares, following the example set by the previous Labour government. The eight privatisations conducted by the first Thatcher government raised a total of £1,404m (see Table 2.2). The second Thatcher government conducted a dozen privatisation sales between 1983 and 1987 that raised a total of £14.5 billion, ten times the amount in the first phase (see Table 2.3).

The privatisation of British Telecom (BT) in December 1984 was of a different order of magnitude and significance to all previous privatisations. The new private company would have a market capitalisation of £8 billion, half as large again as GEC, then the UK's biggest company. Initially, 51% of the equity – valued at around £4 billion – was to be sold, breaking a series of records. It was four times larger than the biggest gilt issues, the largest initial public offering and the largest equity offering ever made in any stockmarket. The project was met with incredulity in much of the City on the basis that it was too large to be absorbed by investors. Partly for this reason, but also with the deliberate aim of creating a new class of share-owning citizens, the offer was accompanied

Table 2.2 **Privatisations, 1979–83**

Year	Company	%	Proceeds (£m)
1979	BP	5	290
1980	Ferranti	50	54
1981	British Aerospace	51	150
	British Sugar	24	44
	Cable & Wireless	49	224
1982	Amersham International	100	71
	Britoil	51	549
1983	Associated British Ports	49	22
Total			1,404

by an unprecedented press and television campaign to stimulate public interest and participation.

Institutional investors were allocated 47% of the issue, the British public 39% and overseas investors 14%. When the offer closed a couple of weeks later the public tranche was five times oversubscribed, applications having been received from 2.3m prospective individual shareholders for a total of 12,750m shares. Individual applicants were allocated 800 shares each, irrespective of the size of their application.

Table 2.3 **Privatisations, 1983–87**

Year	Company	%	Proceeds (£m)
1983	BP	7	542
	Cable & Wireless	22	262
1984	Associated British Ports	48	48
	BT	50	3,916
	Enterprise Oil	100	392
	Jaguar	100	297
1985	British Aerospace	49	363
	Britoil	49	434
	Cable & Wireless	22	602
1986	British Gas	100	5,434
1987	British Airways	100	900
	Rolls-Royce	100	1,362
Total			14,552

When dealing opened the shares immediately soared to a 100% premium, a gratifying outcome for the hordes of first-time shareholders but laying the government open to criticism for undervaluing public assets.

The successful privatisation of BT was a milestone because it transformed attitudes in the City and the country to privatisation and opened up the prospect of the wholesale return of UK utilities industries to the private sector. It increased the number of individual shareholders several-fold and led to an unprecedented upsurge in public interest in financial and business matters. It filled the government's coffers and pointed the way to a source of further funds. Moreover, it established a new financial services activity in which the City, notably Kleinwort Benson and N.M. Rothschild, led the way and exported around the world.

The next major privatisation was British Gas in December 1986, in the wake of Big Bang. The British Gas initial public offering was even bigger than BT's, raising £5.4 billion, another record. For a second time, a privatisation issue was targeted at individual investors, particularly the company's 16m customers, who were offered discounts. A ubiquitous television, press and poster advertising campaign exhorted the public to "tell Sid" about the share offer, 40% of the issue being reserved for the public, 40% for institutional investors and 20% for overseas buyers. Again, the offer was a success, although this time it was only twice oversubscribed and the opening premium was modest.

Financial Services Act, 1986

The advent of mass share ownership through privatisation made the protection of investors a topical issue in the mid-1980s. So did the Big Bang reforms, particularly the elimination of the functional separation between stockbrokers (who acted as independent agents on behalf of buyers and sellers) and marketmakers, which removed a traditional form of investor protection.

Traditionally, City markets had been self-regulating and most participants were eager for this to continue. They argued that supervision by regulators drawn from their own ranks was most effective, since they knew best who the miscreants were, and that self-regulation allowed markets to remain flexible and adaptable. Observers, particularly from the political left, dismissed self-regulation as hopelessly compromised and advocated statutory regulation with a policing body along the lines of the American Securities and Exchange Commission. It was a question of devising a pattern of regulation that was rigorous in the protection of retail investors but did not hobble the operation and development of the

City's wholesale financial markets.

The Financial Services Act of 1986, which came into operation in 1988, established a hybrid regulatory system that endeavoured to combine the strengths of self-regulation with firmer external control. Overall responsibility for supervision was entrusted to the Securities and Investments Board (SIB) appointed by the government. Self-regulation was retained in the form of five Self-Regulatory Organisations (SROs), which covered most financial services activities (but not insurance): securities; fund management; financial advisers; the futures and options markets; and life assurance and unit trusts. The SROs were responsible for setting rules for their members, but these had to be consistent with the SIB's overall rulebook, a monumental document weighing four and a half pounds.

Nor was this the end of regulatory complexity. The Department of Trade and Industry retained authority in several areas, such as insider dealing and the authorisation of new unit trusts. The Stock Exchange, Lloyd's and other "recognised investment exchanges" retained control over their markets, as did "designated investment exchanges" such as the AIBD (Association of International Bond Dealers, forerunner of the International Securities Market Association – ISMA). Mergers and acquisitions were scrutinised by the Takeover Panel (a self-policing body composed of City financial and business institutions) and might be referred to the statutory Monopolies and Mergers Commission. The Bank of England supervised the banking system. Ultimately, there was the police Fraud Squad, which had the ability to undertake its own investigations.

The outcome of the regulatory reform of the mid-1980s satisfied almost nobody. Advocates of a statutory system complained that it was feeble, ineffective and unfathomable. Many people working in the City, however, protested about the bureaucracy and the expense: the SROs were financed by their members, and the SIB by a levy on the SROs. The estimated cost to the financial-services industry of the new regulatory arrangements was £100m a year.

Euromarket expansion

The Eurobond market continued to expand rapidly in the 1970s and 1980s: in 1970 total primary issuance was $2.7 billion; by 1987 it was $143.7 billion. The end of the American Interest Equalisation Tax in 1974 was followed by a surge in dollar-denominated foreign bond issues in New York. In 1974–78, the value of dollar issues in the American capital market exceeded the amount of dollar Eurobond issues. This led some to predict that the international dollar bond market would return to New York. However, the sharp hike in American interest rates in 1979 to counter inflation wrought havoc in the American bond market and stifled the recovery; the international market remained offshore principally in London. The weakness of the dollar in the 1970s led to a big expansion of other currency sectors, notably Eurodeutschemarks and Euroyen, and in that decade the Eurodollar market evolved into the Eurocurrency market.

Innovation is a characteristic of the Eurobond market, in both product development and distribution methods. In the 1970s, with the parameters of the market broadly defined, it began a series of innovations that substantially broadened its product range and attracted business away from the national capital markets. There were three major innovations, as well as a multitude of lesser improvements to established products:

- In 1970, the floating-rate note (FRN), a medium-term security with an interest rate tied to a benchmark (usually the London interbank offered rate – LIBOR).
- Beginning in 1975–77, the introduction of fixed-price and fixed-bid issue techniques that provided greater price security for investors.
- In the late 1970s and early 1980s, the development of the swap market, allowing an exchange of liabilities, such as currency or interest rates (fixed to floating and vice versa).

The FRN segment of the Eurobond market was an alternative source of funding to the syndicated loan. By the late 1970s, FRNs accounted for 20–30% of the Eurobond market. They appealed to borrowers because of the relatively low cost at which they could raise vast amounts and to investors because of the ready marketability of a securities instrument. Syndicated lending went distinctly out of fashion for banks with the onset of the less-developed country debt crisis in August 1982. Borrowers turned to the FRN market and issuers hastened to accommodate them. The market boomed, with the volume of outstanding FRNs increasing from $10 billion in 1980 to $150 billion in 1986. The boom featured the proliferation of ever more complex instruments issued by more and more market participants: 50 firms were operating as market-makers in FRNs by 1986. The competition led to tighter and tighter pricing, making investment in FRNs less and less profitable. In late 1986, with massive oversupply and virtually no demand, the market collapsed. Banks and investors sustained severe losses, and this was followed by a savage contraction of the market and job cuts.

Stockmarket crash of 1987

The FRN crash of 1986–87 went unnoticed outside the financial markets, but this was not the case with the stockmarket crash of October 1987, the most sensational financial event since the 1929 Wall Street crash. The 1987 crash originated on Wall Street where it was fundamentally a panic retreat from the stratospheric valuations of American equities. On October 19th, after a jittery couple of weeks but for no specific reason, investors suffered a collective loss of nerve and scrambled to sell at once. That day the Dow Jones Index crashed 508 points, an unprecedented 23% fall in a single day. In London, the FTSE 100 lost 250 points, an 11% drop, and the following day it fell a further 251 points to 1,801, making an aggregate fall over the two days of 23%. The decline continued at a slower pace for a few more weeks and in mid-November the FTSE 100 touched 1,573, a 36% retreat from its peak of 2,443 in mid-July. The sell-off in New York had a contagion effect on London for several reasons: the dumping of UK securities by American investors; the interconnections between global financial markets and the impact on investor sentiment; and because the downturn in prices triggered automatic selling by computer-driven "program trading" portfolio systems on both sides of the Atlantic.

The crash of October 19th–20th 1987 occurred in the middle of the largest UK privatisation to date, the sale of the government's remaining 31.5% stake in BP, and some new fundraising by the company involving shares worth £7.25 billion, another record-breaking equity offering. Details of the offer had appeared on October 15th, a few days before the crash. The issue was underwritten by some 400 financial institutions in London, the United States and Europe. As the market plunged, BP's share price slumped from 350p to 286p, way below the underwriting price of 330p, leaving the underwriters facing potential losses of £1 billion.

The prospect of such losses led to intense lobbying of Nigel Lawson, the chancellor of the exchequer, for the issue to be pulled, especially from across the Atlantic. In London the potential losses were widely diversified, but in the United States and Canada, because of the North American system of underwriting, they were concentrated among the leading investment banks, which pulled every political string they could grasp. But Lawson was unmoved, responding that the purpose of the generally handsomely remunerated underwriting system was to provide insurance against unforeseen developments.

The doldrums, 1987–92

In the closing months of 1987 and during 1988, the FTSE 100 remained around its post-crash low. But in 1989 there was a significant recovery, and in the summer the index touched 2,360, just a little below its 1987 peak. For the following three years share prices drifted sideways. Equity turnover measured by value slumped to £325 billion in 1988, two-fifths below the record panic volume of 1987, and remained around that level for several years. Gilts turnover declined too but by much less than equity turnover. As on other occasions when equity activity falls, fixed-income earnings helped City firms sustain revenues. Securities issues for British companies fell in 1988, but in the early 1990s there was a recovery to pre-crash levels. Mergers and acquisitions expenditure by British companies remained high in 1988 and 1989, largely because of deals in the pipeline, but activity collapsed in the early 1990s (see Figure 2.3 on page 45). A further depressant was that the City became a target for IRA (Irish Republican Army) terrorists. Although most attacks were thwarted, two IRA bombs perpetrated mass murder at St Mary Axe in 1992 and Bishopsgate in 1993.

The feeble financial-market conditions of the late 1980s and early 1990s generated insufficient demand for the capacity that had been created in the bull market. As activity and profits fell, firms took measures to cut costs. This meant job cuts and between 1988 and 1993, 60,000 City jobs disappeared. Many of the foreign banks that had bought City brokerage firms a few years earlier swallowed their pride and shut them down. The most sensational episode was the closure in December 1988 of Morgan Grenfell Securities, which was losing £1m a week. This involved a £45m write-off and the loss of 770 jobs. One employee got his revenge by dialling the weather announcement in Sydney, Australia, and leaving the phone dangling – it was found 24 hours later.

Guinness and other scandals

The excesses of the 1980s boom were exposed in a series of scandals that came to light after the crash. Foremost was the illegal share-price support operation by Guinness and its advisers during the takeover of Distillers, which led to a widely reported trial in 1990 and jail sentences (see Chapter 13). The Blue Arrow scandal that came to court in 1991 was also about an illegal share-support scheme (see Chapter 13). The misdemeanours of Robert Maxwell began well before the 1980s, although it was in the closing years of that decade that he stole at least £400m from the pension funds of his employees to prop up his faltering business empire. The sorry story came out in November 1991 after he was reported missing from his luxury yacht and his body was found in the sea near Tenerife (see Chapter 13).

In July 1991 the Bank of England led concerted action in several countries to close down BCCI (Bank of Credit and Commerce International). Subsequent investigation revealed the biggest bank fraud in history, with estimates of the losses of investors and depositors ranging from £5 billion to £20 billion (see Chapter 13). Although BCCI was registered in Luxembourg, its operational headquarters was in London and the Bank of England was accused by some of supervisory negligence. It was the second time in less than a decade that the Bank had been blamed for a major failure in bank supervision, the previous incident being the collapse of Johnson Matthey Bankers in 1984 (see Chapter 13). This had led to the Banking Act 1987, which tightened prudential regulation of banks. These episodes fostered a perception among some sections of the public and politicians that fraud and wrongdoing were commonplace in the City and that the Bank of England was not up to the job.

The climate of suspicion about the City at the end of the 1980s and in the early 1990s was the context of a public debate about City "short-termism", the alleged tendency of institutional investors to prioritise immediate gains over the long-term interest of companies and the full range of stakeholders. Critics such as Sir Hector Laing maintained that companies were obliged to focus so much on current earnings per share that important long-term investment was being neglected for fear that the share price would be marked down, making the company vulnerable to a hostile takeover bid. The short-term focus of City investment institutions was criticised by a CBI (Confederation of British Industry) report in November 1988, and Lord Young, the trade and industry secretary, added his voice to the chorus of complaints. Alarmed by the outcry, the Institutional Fund Managers Association commissioned a report, *Short-termism on Trial*, by Paul Marsh, a professor at London Business School, which was published in 1989. Marsh was generally sceptical of the claims of the critics and found "a paucity of evidence" to support their assertions. As the 1990s progressed, the short-termism issue became subsumed by the universal acceptance of the pursuit of "shareholder value", to which both management and institutional investors became obliged to subscribe.

Canary Wharf

The downturn in the City in the early 1990s was disastrous for Olympia & York, the developers of the Canary Wharf office complex in London's docklands. Unable to attract tenants for Canary Wharf, where occupancy was only 55%, and buffeted by simultaneous property slumps in London, New York and Toronto, the firm collapsed in May 1992.

Canary Wharf was the brainchild of Michael von Clemm, the London head of investment bank Credit Suisse First Boston, who was frustrated at being unable to find suitable state-of-the-art premises for his rapidly expanding operations. Located in a district of derelict docks, the site had plenty of room to accommodate the vast trading floors that modern investment banks require, unlike the narrow Victorian frontages of the Square Mile. Yet it was only three miles down the road. Development got under way in summer 1985, in the heyday of Big Bang euphoria. Von Clemm put together a consortium to undertake the largest real-estate development in western Europe, comprising 8.5m square feet of office space on a 71-acre site. In July 1987, Paul Reichmann, head of Olympia & York, the world's leading commercial property-development company and builder of New York's World Financial Centre, took control of the project.

The development enjoyed support from the British government, which in 1981 had designated the London docklands a special development zone where projects were eligible for public subsidies. The initial stages of the Canary Wharf scheme received support of £1.3 billion from British taxpayers. It also enjoyed the public support of Margaret Thatcher, the prime minister, who herself initiated construction with a pile-driver in May 1988. The centrepiece of the vast project, One Canada Square, comprising 4.5m square feet of office space, was completed on time in just three years. The first tenants arrived in August 1991.

Canary Wharf's biggest problem was transport: the roads were choked and rail links were non-existent. From 1987 access from the Square Mile was provided by the Docklands Light Railway, initially from Tower Hill and from 1991 from Bank. London City Airport opened nearby in 1987, giving access to Europe. Construction of a new road, the Limehouse Link, began in 1989 – at £4,588 per inch the most expensive road ever built in the UK – but it did not open until May 1993. In the meantime, Olympia & York went into receivership.

Canary Wharf became the property of the 11 banks to which it owed £576m. Sir Peter Levene, formerly head of procurement at the Ministry of Defence, was appointed to run it on behalf of the new owners.

Assisted by the upturn in City activity from 1993, Levene was able to attract prestigious new tenants. In 1995 it was announced that the banks had accepted an offer from a private consortium to buy Canary Wharf for £800m. The consortium was led by none other than Reichmann, who thus reassumed control of the project in which his faith had never wavered. (It was subsequently put up for sale again, and this long-running saga was still unresolved when this book was published.)

More privatisation, 1987–92

The Conservative Party's manifesto for the June 1987 election included commitments to privatise the water and electricity industries, completing the transfer to the private sector of the four major utilities that had begun with telecommunications in 1984 and gas in 1986. As natural monopolies and essential services, water and electricity involved complex issues about industry structure, regulation and the introduction of competition that required lengthy preparation. While this work was being undertaken several more straightforward privatisations were mounted, including British Airports Authority, National Bus Company, Rover Group and British Steel (see Table 2.4).

The water industry was divided into ten regional companies for privatisation in November 1989. Water privatisation aroused more public opposition than any previous sale, with opinion polls suggesting that 70% were hostile. Nevertheless, the shares reserved for public subscription were six times oversubscribed and the sale raised £5.2 billion for the

Table 2.4 **Privatisations, 1987–91**

Year	Company	%	Proceeds (£m)
1987	BP	32	5,750
	British Airports Authority	100	1,280
	National Bus Company	100	300
1988	British Steel	100	2,500
	Rover Group	99	150
1989	Water companies	100	5,240
1990	Electricity distribution companies	100	5,180
1991	BT	25	5,400
	National Power and PowerGen	60	2,160
	Scottish Power and Scottish Hydro	100	2,880
Total			30,840

government. The electricity industry was divided into 12 retail distribution companies and four power generation companies, which were privatised in three phases in December 1990, February 1991 and June 1991. In total the sales generated £10.2 billion.

In the third phase of privatisation from 1987 to 1992, the government raised a total of £30.8 billion. Around half, £15.4 billion, came from the sales of the water and electricity industries, £11.1 billion from divestments of state holdings in BP and BT, and £4.3 billion from the privatisation of airports, bus services, steelmaking and motor manufacture. The total was double the £14.5 billion raised by privatisation in 1983–87 and 22 times the £1.4 billion raised in 1979–83. These substantial revenues transformed the public purse, permitting income-tax cuts, including in 1988 a reduction of the higher rate from 60% to 40%, and even reductions in the national debt in the years 1988–90, a phenomenon last witnessed in the 1920s. This was good news for taxpayers, but it was not so popular in the gilts market.

ERM debacle, 1992

The privatisation programmes involved the City and the government working together for a common purpose. The ERM crisis of September 1992 pitted the financial markets against the government. The Exchange Rate Mechanism (ERM) was a fixed exchange-rate arrangement among European currencies created in 1979. There were 37 ERM rate realignments in the years 1979–87, but then the system settled down and from January 1987 to August 1992 there were no realignments at all. The UK joined the ERM in 1990 as a step towards participation in the creation of the single market and possibly a single currency. The creation of a single currency was agreed in the Maastricht treaty of February 1992. It was assumed that the stability of the ERM and the convergence of inflation rates and other economic indicators among European Union members would continue, paving the way for the introduction of the euro. But the ink on the treaty had scarcely had time to dry before the ERM faced a crisis.

In September 1992 the pound and several other currencies came under attack from hedge funds and other speculators who believed that they were overvalued at their current ERM parities. The British government, led by John Major, determined to defend sterling at all costs. In City dealing rooms, playing the one-way bet against sterling was a once-in-a-lifetime Klondike. Despite the government's spending £15 billion on buying pounds in the market and hiking interest rates to 15% (briefly), the market had its way: sterling was forced out of the ERM and deval-ued and Major's administration suffered a blow to its authority from which it never recovered.

The IMF's analysis of the cause of the ERM crisis of 1992 was that high levels of inflation in some countries and a lack of compensating realignments from 1987 had resulted in the overvaluation of several cur-rencies, including the pound. Another factor was the tension between the reduction in interest rates needed by most ERM members to stimu-late economic activity and the higher rates required by Germany to con-tain the inflationary pressures stemming from German unification. The European Commission, by contrast, placed the blame squarely on inter-national currency speculators, and Jacques Chirac, the French prime minister, fulminated that they were "the AIDS of the world economy".

The most prominent of the pariahs was George Soros, whose hedge fund made a profit of $1 billion in September 1992 by speculating against sterling and forcing it out of the ERM. Soros, based in New York but also active in London, was by no means bashful about wreaking havoc with the British government's exchange-rate policy or of making such profits at the expense of the British taxpayer. As he explained to a journalist, the opportunity only arose because the British government's policy was fundamentally misjudged and untenable: "If it hadn't been untenable, our 'ganging up on it [sterling]' wouldn't have pushed Britain out of the ERM ... we were not the only ones playing, and the process would have unfolded more or less the same way even if I had never been born."

The episode provided a vivid demonstration of the power of the financial markets in the modern world and their ability to discipline governments that step out of line with their expectations.

1990s bull market, 1993–2000

Share prices embarked upon a sustained upward movement in the clos-ing months of 1992, and in summer 1993 the FTSE 100 reached 3,000 for the first time. It hit 4,000 in 1996, 5,000 in 1997, 6,000 in February 1999 and peaked at 6,720 in December 1999 (see Figure 2.3 on page 45). The bull market went hand in hand with the creation of 130,000 additional City jobs and big bonuses (see Chapter 1).

In the 1990s bull market there was a final wave of privatisations by Major's Conservative administration. The privatisation of British Coal in 1994 and British Energy and AEA Technology in 1996 completed the sell-off of the energy sector and raised in total £3.1 billion for the govern-ment. The privatisation of the railways in 1996/97 involved splitting the industry into Railtrack, the owner and operator of the infrastructure, and a clutch of operating companies that provided rail services. Although the sales were successfully completed, Railtrack alone bringing in £2 billion, the operational outcome was less than satisfactory. In 2001, in a desperate attempt to sort out the chaos, Railtrack was effectively renationalised, although in a maladroit manner that outraged shareholders.

The Private Finance Initiative (PFI), launched in 1992, was a kind of successor to the privatisation programme. Instead of selling off government assets, under the PFI the City raises private finance for public-sector infrastructure projects – bridges, schools, hospitals and prisons – that do not yet exist. The government pays for the services provided, but payments are spread over 20 or 30 years. The PFI got off to a slow start, but lift-off was achieved in 1996 and by the time of the election in May 1997 contracts worth £6 billion had been agreed.

Instead of reversing the Conservative government's privatisations, the Labour government accepted the new boundaries of the private and public sectors. It also continued to support the PFI, and by the end of 2003 630 projects had been signed with a capital value of £57 billion. Since 1996, PFI schemes have funded around 15% of UK public-sector capital investment. City banks had an unrivalled head start in PFI work, which had originated in the UK. As they began to market the idea around the world, it looked as if it would become the City's most successful new export since privatisation.

Virtually the first action of the new Labour administration in 1997 was to confer independence on the Bank of England and give it operational responsibility for UK monetary policy (see Chapter 10). At the same time it transferred responsibility for bank supervision to a new unitary super-regulator, the Financial Services Authority (see Chapter 11). It also decreed "five tests" to assess the readiness of the UK to join the euro, one of which was that membership should not have an adverse impact on the City. Neither in 1999, at the launch of the euro, nor in 2003, when the Treasury conducted an assessment, was the UK deemed ready to join (see Chapter 14).

The great City sell-off

The process of European economic and financial market integration, in which the launch of the euro was an important milestone, lay behind the expansion of the presence of the leading American investment banks in London. The build-up began in the 1980s but really got under

BLACKWELL
53-62, South Bridge
Edinburgh
EH1 1YS
Tel: (0131) 622 8222
Fax: (0131) 557 8149
VAT No: GB 532585539

Thank you for shopping at Blackwell

Shop online www.blackwell.co.uk

SALE
475 13 339756   15 Jan 2011 15:39

CASHIER: SH
5029378004361 LARGE CARRIER B   0.10
9780470744512 OFFICIAL GUIDE   19.99

TOTAL   ITEMS   2   20.09

CASH   21.00
CHANGE CASH   0.91-

VAT INCLUDED IN ABOVE TOTAL AMOUNT

RATE   0.00%   0.00 IN   20.09
    Refunds and exchanges on any item
  must be returned in person within 10
  days with your receipt or proof of
  purchase. Exchanges can be for another
  item of equal value, gift vouchers or a
  refund by the original method of payment

way in the early 1990s, when on the back of record profits in 1992 and 1993 Wall Street firms launched a worldwide expansion drive, targeting London in particular as the bridgehead for Europe.

The mounting challenge from American firms and anticipation of a boom in European corporate finance and capital market business arising from European integration led some major European banks to seek to enhance their Anglo-Saxon style investment-banking capabilities. The most straightforward way to do this was to buy a City merchant bank, creating an off-the-shelf capability. Deutsche Bank was the first to do so. In 1989 it bought Morgan Grenfell, whose senior management had become discredited through the firm's involvement in the Guinness scandal and whose balance sheet had been weakened by big losses as a result of the 1987 crash. It was the first merchant bank to pass into foreign ownership.

The burgeoning activity of Wall Street investment banks in London squeezed British merchant banks from two directions. First, competition for talent sent compensation costs soaring. Second, competition for business led to keener pricing and deprived them of mandates they would traditionally have expected to win. The American firms were in a position to bid aggressively for people and business because of the profits generated by their Wall Street operations, which enjoyed higher fee levels than were customary in London and were booming. Continental banks were also able to subsidise their London operations, thanks to the infinite patience of their shareholders. The squeeze on profits led some of the integrated merchant banks to attempt to boost profits from proprietary securities trading, like the American investment banks. One of them was Barings, which went spectacularly bust in February 1995 (see Chapter 13) and was acquired by ING, a Dutch bank, for £1. Another victim of proprietary trading losses as well as a botched merger with Morgan Stanley was S.G. Warburg, which was acquired by Swiss Bank Corporation in spring 1995 for just its net asset value. In other words, the S.G. Warburg brand name, a year earlier the City's foremost franchise, had been rendered virtually valueless. Between 1995 and 2000 almost the whole sector was sold to overseas owners.

Some firms – Barings, Hambros, Morgan Grenfell and S.G. Warburg – ended up with new owners because they got into trouble. Others – Robert Fleming & Co, Kleinwort Benson, MAM, Schroders and Smith New Court – came to the conclusion that they were too small to compete with the global players and sold out to one of the European or

Table 2.5 **Sale of City merchant banks and securities firms, 1989–2000**

Date	Firm	Purchaser	Price (£m)
1989	Morgan Grenfell	Deutsche Bank	950
1995	Barings	ING	–
	Kleinwort Benson	Dresdner Bank	1,000
	Smith New Court	Merrill Lynch	526
	S.G. Warburg	Swiss Bank Corporation	860
1997	BZW (Barclays) (part)	CSFB	100
	Hambros	Société Générale/Investec	738
	Mercury Asset Management	Merrill Lynch	3,100
	NatWest Markets (part)	Bankers Trust/Deutsche Bank	129
2000	Robert Fleming & Co	Chase Manhattan	4,800
	Schroders (part)	Citigroup	1,350

American banks seeking to enter the business or expand its presence. With the sale of Schroders and Flemings in 2000, all that was left of the independent British merchant bank and securities sector was the privately owned firms N.M. Rothschild, Cazenove and Lazard Brothers, and some small niche players.

British commercial banks Barclays and NatWest had the capital to operate in the global marketplace, but to compete effectively with the American investment banks they needed a substantial presence on Wall Street. Still smarting from losses from earlier forays into the United States, their directors balked at the cost and the risk. But if they were not prepared to place a firm footprint in New York they were out of the global game. Accordingly, in 1997 both banks took the strategic decision largely to pull out of investment banking and focus on commercial banking. HSBC was also wary of making a major acquisition on Wall Street, although rumours of such a move were a hardy perennial. Instead, it steadily built up its investment-banking capabilities in London and elsewhere.

As the investment-banking business globalised, British merchant banks found themselves struggling in the face of the huge advantage enjoyed by American firms, whose domestic market constituted half of the world market. Hence the imperative to establish a substantial presence on Wall Street, a challenge flunked by all the British firms. When large European corporate clients began to shed medium-sized advisers in favour of the leading American investment banks, the writing was on the wall for the middle-rank firms. On the sale of Schroders, the *Financial Times* commented (January 19th 2000): "The demise of the UK investment banks is a natural part of the process of international specialisation that results from globalisation."

Others blamed parochial shortcomings rather than global processes. Philip Augar, an investment banker during the 1990s and author of *The Death of Gentlemanly Capitalism* (Penguin Books, 2000), ascribed considerable culpability to amateurish management at the merchant banks. As for the failure of the clearing banks to stay in the game, he blamed irresolute and short-termist senior executives, class-based internal warfare and failure at the political level to defend a national interest – which would surely not have happened in France or Germany.

Yet it could be argued that far from being a national humiliation, the City sell-off was a triumph of economic rationality, and that the sales of stockbroking and marketmaking firms in the 1980s and of merchant banks in the 1990s were shrewd cash-outs at the top of the market cycle in an industry that had been artificially cosseted by barriers to entry and cartel-like practices. Furthermore, it was a sector with highly cyclical and thus poor-quality earnings, in which British banks would always be at a disadvantage relative to those with much larger domestic economies. In short it was better – not just for the owners but also for the national interest – to get out while the going was good rather than suffer a lingering decline and attrition of value, like the motor and shipbuilding industries.

The new millennium

The rise and fall of the dotcom and technology bubble of 1995–2000 was a spectacular financial finale to the 20th century. Although principally a Wall Street phenomenon played out on the NASDAQ market, it also caught on in the City. There was a spate of initial public offerings of home-grown dotcom firms, one of the best known being Lastminute.com, most of which ended in tears for investors. But it was not just start-ups that were aboard the technology bandwagon. So was Marconi, the new name under new management for GEC, once the UK's largest company and one of the most respected. The thrusting new management team decided to transform the stodgy engineering company into a feisty player in the fashionable telecoms industry, and in the process managed to turn a company with a £35 billion market capitalisation into one worth just £1 billion (see Chapter 13).

The bull market came to an end at the beginning of 2000. Between then and early 2003 the FTSE 100 fell by nearly 50% from 6,700 to 3,500 (see Figure 2.3 on page 45), a similar magnitude to the Dow Jones Industrial Average (although the crash of the Nasdaq was much more sensational). The downturn was accompanied by around 35,000 City job losses in 2001 and 2002 (see Chapter 1). But in 2003 share prices in London began a gradual climb back, and by spring 2004 the FTSE 100 was up around 4,500. As the market picked up so did the profitability of City activities and recruitment. Soon it was being forecast that the green shoots of recovery were harbingers of expansion to yet further heights.

3 Financial markets and instruments

The fundamental economic function performed by financial markets is the transfer of funds from households and others with surplus funds (lender-savers) to corporations, governments and other parties that require funds (borrower-spenders). This process is economically important since it channels resources from those that have accumulated funds to those that have a productive use for them.

There are two routes by which transfers of funds are made (see Figure 3.1):

- Direct finance. Direct lending by lender-savers to borrower-spenders, and lending via the financial markets through the direct purchase by lenders-savers of securities issued by borrower-spenders.
- Indirect finance through financial intermediaries. Lender-savers entrust their funds to financial intermediaries that either lend themselves to borrower-spenders (banks) or lend via the financial markets (contractual savings institutions and investment intermediaries).

Direct finance forms a small proportion of lending in modern economies. One reason is the mismatch between the demands of

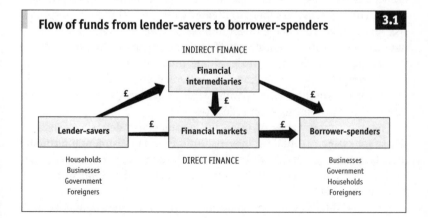

Flow of funds from lender-savers to borrower-spenders 3.1

INDIRECT FINANCE

Financial intermediaries

£ £

£

Lender-savers £ Financial markets £ Borrower-spenders

Households   DIRECT FINANCE   Businesses
Businesses   Government
Government   Households
Foreigners   Foreigners

borrower-spenders, typically for long-term, illiquid and higher-risk borrowing, and the preference of lender-savers for short-term, readily realisable and low-risk lending. Another is the transaction costs incurred by investors, such as: search costs, verification costs, monitoring costs and enforcement costs, which may be prohibitive for small-scale, non-professional investors. Then there are the problems arising from asymmetric information, which is when one party to a transaction has better information than the other party. For example, borrowers have better information about the risks and potential returns of an investment project than lenders, giving rise to problems in the evaluation of proposals and in monitoring and enforcing contracts.

Financial intermediaries

Financial intermediaries provide solutions to many of these problems. However, the employment of the services of an intermediary involves an additional transaction cost for lender-savers. This means that the advantages of intermediated finance must outweigh the additional transaction costs.

Financial intermediaries act as middlemen, transferring funds from lender-savers to borrower-spenders. They do so in two stages: first, by sourcing funds from lender-savers, such as bank deposits, premiums from life insurance policies or the issue of units by a unit trust, incurring their own primary liabilities to them; second, by investing the funds in a variety of primary assets issued by borrower-spenders to raise money, such as loans, mortgages, equities and bonds.

Financial intermediaries are usually better placed than individual lender-savers to assume and spread the risks of ownership of primary assets. Their size enables them to diversify their asset holdings to spread risk and to take advantage of economies of scale in buying and selling assets. They are able to employ staff with the expertise and proximity to the market to enable them to evaluate investment opportunities and risks. Competition among financial intermediaries ensures that both lender-savers and borrower-spenders enjoy keen prices, protecting their interests and promoting economic efficiency.

There are three types of financial intermediary: depository institutions (banks), contractual savings institutions and investment intermediaries (see Table 3.1). Banks differ from the other financial intermediaries in that they lend directly to borrower-spenders, rather than through a financial market.

Financial intermediaries transform the primary assets issued by bor-

Table 3.1 **UK financial intermediaries, primary liabilities and primary assets**

Type	Primary liabilities (sources of funds)	Primary assets (principal uses of funds)
Depository institutions		
Clearing banks	Deposits	Business and retail loans, mortgages, money-market securities, municipal bonds
Building societies	Deposits	Mortgages
Mutual savings societies	Deposits	Mortgages and retail loans
Contractual savings institutions		
Pension funds	Employee/employer contributions	Equities, bonds
Life insurance companies	Policy premiums	Equities, bonds, mortgages
Investment intermediaries		
Unit trusts	Units	Equities, bonds
Investment trusts	Shares	Equities, bonds, unlisted investments
Private equity funds	Partnership investment	Private companies
Hedge funds	Partnership investment	Various

rower-spenders into investments of the sort sought by lender-savers. They issue deposit, premium or unit claims with the characteristics of small size, low-to-medium risk and high liquidity, and use the funds raised to acquire larger, higher-risk and relatively illiquid claims issued by borrower-spenders.

Financial intermediaries bring about three types of financial transformation:

- Size transformation. Small sums from lender-savers are parcelled into large amounts required by borrower-spenders.
- Maturity transformation. The primary liabilities of intermediaries, such as banks, are typically much more short-term than their primary assets, but by pooling deposits they are able to meet the demand of borrower-lenders for long-term funds.
- Risk transformation. Financial intermediaries hold primary assets with higher risk of default than their own primary liabilities. They are able to minimise these risks (and profit from the disparity in yields) through a combination of the diversification,

pooling, screening and monitoring of assets, and the holding of reserves.

Financial intermediaries are also able to reduce the problems arising from asymmetric information by their expertise and research, through requirements for collateral and by placing restrictive covenants on uses to which loans may be put.

Financial markets

Borrower-spenders raise funds for investment either from banks or by issuing financial securities that are purchased directly or indirectly by lender-savers. The initial sale of a financial security to raise funds for borrower-spenders is known as the primary market. All subsequent selling and buying of the securities occurs in the secondary market. Secondary-market transactions generate no additional funds for the issuer, but an active secondary market in a security encourages lender-savers to buy securities issued by a borrower-spender, and the price at which a security trades provides a yardstick of the borrower-spender's performance and the market's sentiment towards it.

Financial markets perform a variety of important functions for participants and for the economy as a whole:

- Price discovery. Determining the price of assets through supply and demand; in a well-functioning market buyers and sellers can be confident that the price at which they trade is fair and reasonable.
- Asset valuation. Market prices provide a detached basis for determining the value of corporations and other assets.
- Fundraising. For borrower-spenders, allowing corporations and governments to raise substantial sums at a reasonable price by accessing a large number of lenders.
- Income and saving. For lender-savers, enabling them to earn a return on their funds and to accumulate assets that may grow in value.
- Arbitrage. Providing price transparency that leads to the reduction of price discrepancies, making for greater economic efficiency.
- Risk management. Futures, options and swaps derivatives contracts permit investors to protect themselves against unfavourable market developments and to hold only those risks that they want to assume.

◪ Watchdog. Helping to ensure prudent financial conduct on the part of the borrower-spenders in whose securities the market deals. If market participants lose confidence in government policy, or in a company's strategy or incumbent management, the price of its securities will be adversely affected, drawing attention to doubts about its conduct.

Features of financial markets

Financial markets are organised in various ways and have a mixture of features.

◪ Exchanges. Membership organisations with buildings, staff, rule books, standard contract units, settlement dates and delivery specifications. The Financial Services Authority (FSA) authorises and supervises seven recognised investment exchanges in the UK:
  - London Stock Exchange, the main securities exchange in the UK.
  - Virt-x, a pan-European exchange owned by a consortium of leading London-based and Swiss investment banks launched in 2001. It was formed to allow trading in the shares of leading European companies on a single exchange.
  - Derivatives exchanges: London International Financial Futures and Options Exchange (LIFFE); International Petroleum Exchange (IPE); London Metal Exchange (LME); OM London; EDX London

◪ Over-the-counter markets. OTC markets have no physical form or formal membership listing, although they do have market associations and participants are regulated by the FSA. Trading takes place by screen or telephone on the basis of principal-to-principal negotiations. All risks are between the two parties to a transaction and the terms of the deal are often confidential. Participants are constantly in touch with each other by trading platform or telephone and are aware of the prices at which other trades are being conducted. The main OTC markets are highly competitive and the prices quoted are generally as keen as on formal exchanges. The foreign-exchange market, the Euromarkets, the money markets, the bullion market and the interbank market are OTC markets. Derivatives are traded both on LIFFE and over the counter.

◪ Batch markets. Purchase and sale orders are accumulated and matched at set times.

- ◪ Continuous markets. Trading between buyers and sellers occurs continuously while the market is open. A continuous market is more convenient than a batch market but requires a sufficient volume of transactions.
- ◪ Auction markets. Order-driven markets where deals are struck directly between two participants.
- ◪ Dealer markets. Quote-driven markets where marketmakers guarantee to provide both buy (bid) and sell (offer) prices while the market is open. The gap between the prices (the bid-offer spread) constitutes the marketmaker's profit. The presence of marketmakers ensures that buyers and sellers are, in theory, always able to deal.
- ◪ Trading:
  - Open outcry trading takes place on a trading floor, trading pit or trading ring. Traders verbally or by hand-signals publicly announce bids and offers and execute trades. A feature of open outcry markets is the presence of local traders, who deal mainly on their own account, usually taking small, temporary positions. Locals often generate a considerable trading volume, enhancing the market's liquidity. Open outcry is still used in many American exchanges but in Europe it has been supplanted by electronic trading (see below). The London Stock Exchange and LIFFE have abandoned open outcry trading in favour of electronic trading. The lower trading costs and the ability to have remote access provided by electronic trading have outweighed claims of inferior liquidity advanced by supporters of open outcry.
  - Electronic trading is conducted from remote trading platforms, comprising information and dealing screens in bank dealing rooms. Bids and offers entered into the remote trading platforms are despatched to a host computer that ranks them according to price (for bids/offers at identical prices according to the time received). Traders see only the best bid and offer prices. The host computer automatically executes orders.
- ◪ Maturity:
  - securities with a short-term maturity of less than a year are traded in the money market;
  - securities with a maturity of more than a year and equities (which have no maturity date at all) are traded in the capital market.

- Means of settlement:
  - spot or cash markets deal on the basis of immediate settlement;
  - forward or futures markets deal on the basis of settlement being made sometime in the future.
- Completion:
  - in spot markets the parties to a transaction (the counterparties) are obliged to exchange immediately;
  - in forward or futures markets the counterparties exchange at a predetermined future date;
  - in options markets the holder buys the right, but not the obligation, to buy or sell an asset within a defined period at a set price.

Desirable attributes

There are a number of attributes that are desirable in financial markets and are generally characteristic of the main markets:

- Liquidity. The ease with which a trade can be executed at a reasonable price. In an illiquid market an investor may have difficulty selling an asset for a reasonable price, if at all. Larger markets generally have greater liquidity than smaller markets. Because of the presence of effective marketmakers, quote-driven markets may have greater liquidity than order-driven markets.
- Transparency. The availability of up-to-date and reliable information about trading and prices. The less transparent a market, the more reluctant traders are to conduct business there. Transparency is the key to price efficiency.
- Price efficiency. Prices in the market reflect all available information.
- Operational efficiency. Competitive transaction costs, that is a mixture of the costs of conducting trades, regulation and taxes.
- Reliability. Mechanisms that ensure that trades are processed correctly.
- Immediacy. Transactions are completed rapidly.
- Redress through law. Appropriate institutions, laws and procedures to enforce contracts and resolve disputes.
- Appropriate regulation and investor protection. An appropriate balance of regulations that protect investors and safeguard the market's reputation but do not stifle trading volumes or market innovation.

Market participants

Households are the main lender-savers, but corporations, governments, central banks and foreign investors may also be significant. Corporations and governments are the principal borrower-spenders, but others include local authorities, government agencies, international organisations (such as the World Bank) and foreign borrowers. Financial intermediaries that act on behalf of lenders and borrowers, or on their own account, include commercial banks, investment banks, insurance companies, asset management firms, pension funds, private equity funds and hedge funds. The make-up of participants varies from market to market and between financial centres.

There are two types of investors: individuals and institutions. In the UK, individual investors now own only 14% of equities. This is a much lower proportion than in the United States (39%) and Spain, Italy and Greece (30%), but higher than in France (8%). Private clients are active traders and generated 65% of trades in 2000, although the small size of the deals meant they constituted only 8% of market turnover. However, small deals incur higher commission rates than institutional trades, so private investors contributed 29% of the London Stock Exchange's total commission income.

The major institutional investors – insurance companies, pension funds, unit trusts and investment trusts – and overseas institutional investors (principally pension funds) own in aggregate 82% of the UK's equity market (see Table 5.1 on page 113). The grip of institutional investors on British companies is firmer than in other major economies. Often 80–90% of the shares of large and medium-sized companies are owned by institutional shareholders, compared with 60–65% in the United States. Institutional owners and the asset managers who work for them are under pressure to deliver short-term investment performance. Many believe that the ownership structure of the UK's public companies places unhealthy pressure on senior management to pursue short-term goals and behave in ways that win the approval of asset managers but may not serve the long-term interests of the companies they manage.

Financial market traders deal either as agents, buying and selling on behalf of clients, or as principals, using the firm's own capital as the basis for their dealings (proprietary trading). As proprietary traders their dealings can be divided into three types:

- Arbitrage. Taking advantage of price or yield discrepancies between different markets, buying at a lower price in one market and selling at a higher price in another. Such opportunities are generally rare and short-lived because of modern communications technology and because the activities of arbitrageurs eliminate them.

- ▪ Hedging. The purchase or sale of financial instruments to minimise or eliminate risk; for example, the risk of loss to investments or deals from currency or interest-rate fluctuations.
- ▪ Speculation. The assumption of risk by buying or selling financial assets in the hope of making a profit from a change in the price of an asset; the opposite of hedging. By buying when prices are perceived to be low and selling when prices are believed to be high, speculators smooth price fluctuations. Though sometimes attacked for supposedly causing market instability, speculators provide liquidity and enhance the efficiency of markets.

London Stock Exchange

The London Stock Exchange (LSE) is the principal exchange for trading UK equities and government and corporate bonds, and the leading exchange for trading international equities. The Alternative Investment Market (AIM), formed in 1995, is the LSE's second-tier market for shares in small and growing companies that do not meet the criteria for a listing on the main market. There is also OFEX, also established in 1995, where companies too small for either the LSE or the AIM may be listed. A listing on OFEX is often used as a springboard to the achievement of a listing on the AIM.

UK equity market

The shares of around 1,550 British companies are quoted on the LSE, with a combined market capitalisation of £1,360 billion at the beginning of 2004. A further 750 companies are quoted on the AIM, with a market capitalisation of £18 billion. Over the decade up to 2003, £171 billion was raised in the primary market for British companies. Initial public offerings, when new companies join the market, raised £73 billion from investors, and further issues and privatisations raised £98 billion.

The size distribution of companies listed on the UK equity market is highly skewed – the 80 largest companies (each with a market capitalisation greater than £2 billion) account for 80% of total market capitalisation. BP, the biggest of all, alone accounted for 8.3% of market capitalisation in 2002. At the other end of the scale, 1,466 companies with a market capitalisation under £50m comprise around 65% of the quoted companies but only 1% of total market capitalisation.

Table 3.2 **London Stock Exchange, market capitalisation by sector, 2002**

	Market value		Turnover	
	£bn	%	£bn	%
Services	615	55	1,005	53
of which:				
– non-financial	297	31	571	26
– financial	318	24	434	27
Consumer goods	227	18	319	20
Mineral extraction	188	13	227	16
Information technology	9	2	35	1
Utilities	46	4	80	4
General industrials	24	3	57	2
Basic industries	35	3	62	3
Other	14	2	32	1
Total	1,158	100	1,815	100

Services sector companies make up more than half of total market capitalisation (see Table 3.2); consumer goods manufacturing and mineral extraction are the other major sectors. General industrial shares comprise only 3% of total market capitalisation.

Member firms of the LSE are broker-dealers, meaning that they can trade either on behalf of a client (broker) or on their own account (dealer). Many of the larger firms are also authorised to act as market-makers, undertaking to buy and sell the shares of a chosen set of firms. There are rules and regulations designed to prevent conflicts of interest between the roles of broker, dealer and marketmaker. Some brokers act only for institutional investors, whereas others focus on retail clients.

Secondary-market turnover in UK equities totalled £1,876 billion in 2003, a fourfold increase over the previous decade. The growth in turnover has been driven by the expansion of both customer and intra-market trading. Much of the increase is attributable to trading on SETS (Stock Exchange Electronic Trading Service), a streamlined and low-cost electronic order-driven system covering the 200 largest and most traded UK equities, introduced in 1997. Trading in FTSE 100 companies comprised 85% of UK equity turnover in 2002, compared with 57% in 1996. Trading in smaller companies is conducted on SEAQ, a real-time screen-based quotation system. Turnover on the AIM in 2003 was £6.6 billion, 0.3% of total turnover in UK equities.

Institutional investors dominate the ownership of UK shares. British institutional investors – insurance companies, pension funds, and unit and investment trusts – owned 50% of UK equities in 2002 (see Table 5.1 on page 113). Overseas investors, mostly pension funds, owned 32%, compared with just 4% in 1981. The increase was principally a result of the internationalisation of American pension fund portfolios. Share ownership by individuals has been in decline since the 1960s; in 2002 only 14% of UK shares were directly owned by private investors.

Around 380 foreign companies listed on overseas stock exchanges are also listed on the LSE. International companies seek additional listings on foreign stock exchanges to gain access to capital. The LSE has a 56% market share of the global trading turnover in foreign listed equities and the second largest number of listings after the New York markets (see Table 12.3 on page 240). In 2003 international equity turnover on the LSE was £1,759 billion, slightly less than the £1,876 billion turnover in UK shares. More than 70% of foreign equity turnover arises from trading in the shares of major European companies, principally from France (16%) and Germany (13%). In 2003, as part of its drive to attract more foreign company listings, the LSE introduced a fast-track procedure for admission to the AIM for companies already quoted on nine overseas exchanges.

UK bond market

The UK bond market is also focused on the LSE. The largest element is British government bonds, which had a market value of £273 billion at the beginning of 2003. UK corporate bonds quoted on the LSE total only £16 billion, reflecting the tendency of British companies to raise debt finance through the Euromarkets and the banking system. There are also bonds issued by local authorities and foreign borrowers, the latter having an outstanding value of around £100 billion. Trading turnover in non-government bonds on the LSE in 2001 was £115 billion.

The issuance of British government bonds, known as gilt-edged securities (gilts), is the responsibility of the Debt Management Office (DMO), an executive agency of the Treasury. Gilts have a maturity of a year or more. Shorter-term government securities (Treasury bills) are traded in the money market. The bulk of British government bonds in issuance are "straight" gilts with a fixed coupon (rate of interest), although about 20% pay interest linked to a benchmark of price inflation (index-linked). Around 1% are "perpetuals" with no redemption date.

Trading in gilts in 2003 was £2,552 billion, substantially more than UK and international equities. There are 16 authorised Gilt-Edged Market-makers (GEMMs) firms, which act as both marketmakers and brokers. They are required to be prepared to make a market in gilts whatever the trading environment and are expected to participate actively in the issuance of new gilts by bidding at gilts auctions. In return they have various market privileges. The gilts market is also supported by specialist stock exchange money brokers. Part of their business is lending gilts and funds to the GEMMs. The FSA is responsible for the regulation of the gilts market.

Clearing and settlement
The clearing of security trades involves the transmission, reconciliation and confirmation of payments orders and security transfer instructions. The presence of a central counterparty assists trading by removing counterparty risk (the risk of non-payment or non-delivery) and increases market liquidity. Settlement involves the transfer of securities and funds between buyers and sellers and is normally executed via a central securities depository. The pattern of central counterparties and central securities depositories for the major European stock exchanges is shown in Figure 3.2.

For domestic equities, settlement on the LSE takes place three working days after a trade. The settlement system for equities and gilts traded on the LSE is CREST, a market membership organisation introduced in 1996. CREST is also the settlement system for money-market instruments, unit trusts and open-ended investment companies (OEICs) (see Chapter 5); it settles 300,000 transactions a day. In 2002 CREST merged with Euroclear, the central securities depository serving the Euronext exchanges, to create a pan-European securities settlement system.

The London Clearing House (LCH) is the UK's principal central counterparty, acting for trades on the LSE, Euronext.LIFFE, the International Petroleum Exchange and the London Metal Exchange, as well as for some of the smaller overseas exchanges and for some OTC transactions. Established in 1888, it is the largest central counterparty in Europe by value cleared and the leading global central counterparty by range of services provided. Its income in 2002 was £69m: futures and options accounted for £38m, swaps for £16m, equities for £8m and repos for £7m (see page 88 for a definition of repo).

In summer 2003 a merger was announced between the LCH and Clearnet, the central counterparty subsidiary of Euronext, the French-led amalgamation of the Amsterdam, Brussels, Lisbon and Paris bourses.

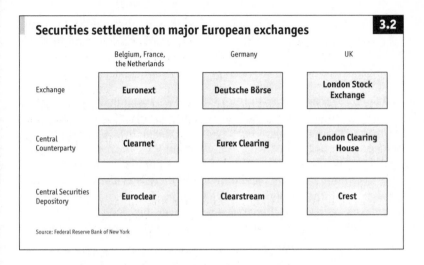

Securities settlement on major European exchanges — 3.2

	Belgium, France, the Netherlands	Germany	UK
Exchange	Euronext	Deutsche Börse	London Stock Exchange
Central Counterparty	Clearnet	Eurex Clearing	London Clearing House
Central Securities Depository	Euroclear	Clearstream	Crest

Source: Federal Reserve Bank of New York

The merger was complicated because of different ownership structures (the LCH is mutually owned by its members and Clearnet is a limited company), the issue of where the cross-border entity would be regulated and the influence of Euronext. A holding company, LCH.Clearnet Group, was formed to own the two operating entities in London and Paris, which would be regulated by their respective authorities. Euronext undertook to limit its influence over LCH.Clearnet by capping its voting rights at 24.9% and reducing its 41.9% economic interest over time. Through the LCH, 45.1% of LCH.Clearnet is owned by users, mostly big banks.

The merger upset the LSE, which questioned the independence of LCH.Clearnet and announced publicly that it was exploring "alternative clearing arrangements". The LSE argued that clearing and settlement were functions that should be executed and owned by an exchange's users, not a rival bourse. It took as its model the mutually owned Depository Trust & Clearing Corporation, the dominant clearing house for American securities trading. LCH.Clearnet's vision, however, is that users should be able to choose which counterparty to use for clearing when trading on one of Europe's exchanges. It argued that competition between central counterparties would reduce costs and lead to greater efficiency, and that the merger was an important step in the consolidation of European central counterparty infrastructure and would help transform the EU's capital markets. Moreover, with its "major global reach", LCH.Clearnet announced that it was set to become the "partner of choice" for central counterparties and international markets around the world. But, as *The Economist* observed circumspectly, "it may take a few years before the vision becomes reality".

Derivatives

Derivatives is a generic term for a range of financial instruments based on dealings in an underlying asset, such as bonds, equities, commodities, currencies and indices representing financial assets. Their primary function is to hedge financial risk, although they may also have been used for speculation. They have become popular with companies, banks, commodity traders and others, and there is evidence that quite a few have not understood – or have been reckless with regard to – the complexity or risks attached to the derivatives they have bought.

Derivatives are traded on exchanges and over the counter. There are three basic types of instrument:

- Futures. Contracts to buy or sell an underlying financial instrument or product on a future date at a prearranged price. They are negotiable instruments that can be traded in futures markets.
- Options. Contracts conferring on the holder a right to buy or sell an underlying financial instrument at an agreed price within a specified time period. The seller of the option has a contractual obligation to honour the contract, but the buyer is not obliged to exercise the option.
- Swaps. Transactions in which two parties undertake to exchange cash flows. They are used to change an existing market exposure on account of a loan, security, currency or interest rate to a different exposure.

OTC derivatives markets are wholesale markets in which contracts tailored to the purchaser's requirements are bought directly from banks by financial institutions and companies. OTC derivatives include forward contracts, options and swaps.

Exchange-traded derivatives are bought and sold on an organised financial exchange in which large numbers of buyers and sellers participate in a competitive, transparent and fully regulated marketplace. Exchange-traded contracts have standardised features – lot size, quality and settlement – which enhance market liquidity. They have a central counterparty clearing house, which effectively eliminates counterparty risk for market participants. Exchange-traded contracts include financial futures and traded options.

Modern derivatives business began with the introduction of a grain futures contract by the Chicago Board of Trade in 1865. They made their first appearance in the City in 1878 when the London Corn Trade Association introduced a futures contract, and thereafter futures contracts became standard features of commodity exchanges. Financial derivatives first appeared in the early 1970s following the breakdown of the Bretton Woods system of fixed exchange rates, which led to much greater volatility in currencies and interest rates. In 1972 the Chicago Mercantile Exchange introduced currency futures and in 1975 the Chicago Board of Trade launched the first interest-rate futures contract. The first financial derivatives exchange in Europe was the London International Financial Futures and Options Exchange (LIFFE), which opened in 1982. It was followed by OM London in 1989, the MATIF (now Euronext) in Paris in 1986 and the DTB (now Eurex) in Frankfurt in 1990.

There are three main financial derivatives exchanges in Europe: Euronext.LIFFE, OM London and Eurex. London is an important location for trading on all three exchanges. Remote trading by London-based dealers constituted 45% of Eurex turnover in 2003.

Exchange-traded derivatives markets

London has three financial derivatives exchanges – LIFFE, the OM London Exchange and EDX – and two commodities derivatives exchanges – the London Metal Exchange (LME) and the International Petroleum Exchange (IPE) (see Table 3.3 overleaf).

LIFFE is much the largest of the London-based derivatives exchanges; in 2001 the value of contracts traded was £96 trillion. In 2001 LIFFE was acquired by Euronext, the pan-European cash and derivatives exchange formed by the merger of the Amsterdam, Brussels and Paris exchanges in 2000. Euronext.LIFFE ranks second to the Chicago Mercantile Exchange as the world's largest derivatives exchange by value. Short-term interest-rate products constitute 75% of contracts: it is the principal exchange for trading euro money-market derivatives with 99% of exchange-traded business. It claims to offer the most comprehensive range of financial futures and options products of any exchange. There are also some commodities contracts.

LIFFE's recent success has been based on the effectiveness of its LIFFE CONNECT electronic trading platform for remote screen-based trading. This has delivered significant trading economies and efficiencies,

Table 3.3 **Trading on London-based derivatives exchanges, 2003**

	Number of contracts (m)
LIFFE	336
LME	72
IPE	33
OM London/EDX	66
Total	507

Source: IFSL, *International Financial Markets in the UK*, May 2004

supporting a wide range of instruments irrespective of their complexity. Other exchanges have adopted LIFFE CONNECT under licence as their trading platform, including the Chicago Board of Trade, NASDAQ and TIFFE in Tokyo.

OM London is part of the OM Group of exchanges, together with Stockholm and Calgary, which operates as a single marketplace. Swedish and Norwegian securities, as well as pulp products, constitute a substantial proportion of trading. A quarter of OM business is conducted in London. OM's leading exchange technology is licensed to 25 other exchanges and clearing houses.

EDX London is a derivatives exchange tailored to the requirements of equity market participants, a joint venture of the LSE and OM launched in July 2003. The LME is the world's biggest non-ferrous metals market, handling 90% of such contracts, and the IPE is the leading market for energy futures and options in Europe (see Chapter 9).

The LCH acts as central counterparty for contracts on LIFFE, the LME and the IPE, clearing 300m contracts a year on their behalf. Since 1999, the LCH has also been developing clearing services for the major OTC products.

Over-the-counter derivatives markets
The UK is the largest market for OTC derivatives trading, accounting for 36% of world turnover (see Table 3.4). The Bank for International Settlements's triennial survey of OTC derivatives trading in April 2001 recorded average daily turnover in London of $275 billion. This was 61% more than in 1998, when the previous survey was done, and 300% more than in 1995. In the 2001 survey, interest-rate contracts constituted 86% of UK OTC derivatives business and currency contracts 14%. The recent

Table 3.4 **OTC derivatives turnover, 2001[a]**

	$bn	%
UK	275	36
United States	135	18
Germany	97	13
France	67	9
Japan	22	3
Switzerland	15	2
Others	153	19
Total	764	100

a Average daily turnover in April 2001.
Source: Bank for International Settlements

growth in the market was mostly driven by interest-rate swaps, which are of increasing importance as trading and pricing benchmarks. Swaps constitute half of UK OTC derivatives market activity. The euro is the principal currency in interest-rate derivatives with a 48% market share. The introduction of the euro in 1999 reduced currency derivatives volume as the currencies it replaced disappeared. Activity in currency derivatives is dominated by the dollar, which forms one side of 81% of transactions.

A new OTC market in credit derivatives developed rapidly in the late 1990s and early 2000s. Credit derivatives permit lenders – banks and bondholders – to spread the risk of loan default to other investors. There was a boom in credit derivatives in Europe following the launch of the euro. With much of the currency and interest-rate risk eliminated by the single currency, banks looked for an instrument to manage the remaining credit risk. At the same time, European institutional investors were looking for higher-yielding investments and credit derivatives met their requirements. The market mushroomed, and the estimated worldwide value of credit derivatives rose from $170 billion in 1997 to $1.5 trillion in 2002; it is forecast to reach $4.8 trillion by the end of 2004. Around half of this booming business is conducted in London. The market is currently one of the City's most highly paid niches, with leading traders reported to earn an average of £1.6m a year.

Activity in OTC derivatives is highly concentrated and is becoming more so. Between 1995 and 2001, the combined market share of the ten leading firms rose from 52% to 74% and the market share of the top 20 firms increased from 70% to 89%.

International securities market (Eurobond and Euroequities markets)

Eurobonds

The global international securities market comprises over 60,000 securities with an outstanding value of $9,219 billion at the beginning of 2003. This market is often called the Eurobond market, the name by which it was known during its formative years in the 1960s and 1970s (see Chapter 2). The use of the new name is indicative of the extension of the market from Europe to the whole world and of the broadening of the market from bonds to a wider variety of financial instruments, although bonds remain its bedrock.

The Eurobond market is the largest of a trio of markets in offshore currencies. At the short end of the maturity spectrum is the Eurocurrency market, an interbank market that is a part of the money market. Medium-term lending takes the form of syndicated loans provided by groups of banks, Eurocommercial paper and Euro medium-term notes (MTN). As debt securities, MTNs are generally regarded as forming part of the Eurobond long-term debt securities market. Recent decades have seen the development of Euroequities, which also form part of the international securities market.

Wholesale borrowers, such as major corporations, banks and governments, seeking to raise long-term funds may issue bonds in the domestic bond market, a foreign bond market or the international bond market (Eurobond market). The differences are summarised in Table 3.5.

Since the 1960s, especially from the 1980s onwards, the issuance of Eurobonds has grown faster than domestic and foreign bonds. In 2001 the total outstanding value of international bonds (Eurobonds plus foreign bonds) in the UK was £436 billion, of which four-fifths was Eurobonds. The popularity of international bonds is attributable to the following:

- Eurobond issuance procedures are straightforward and fast, allowing borrowers to take advantage of favourable market "windows".
- Complex structures are common, with issues being tailored to meet clients' requirements.
- Bigger sums can be raised on better terms than are available in the smaller domestic and foreign bond markets.

Table 3.5 **Types of bonds**

Marketplace	Currency	Issuer	Main market	Issuing syndicate	Primary investors
Domestic	Domestic	Domestic	Domestic	Domestic	Domestic
Foreign	Domestic	Foreign	Domestic	Domestic	Domestic
International	Eurocurrency	Any	Domestic	International	International

Source: International Securities Market Association

- Eurobonds are issued in bearer form (unregistered), protecting the identity of investors.
- Interest is paid free of withholding tax and income tax, enabling borrowers to issue at lower yields.
- As offshore instruments, they cannot be frozen as a result of an international dispute.
- International securities issues are denominated in the dominant international trade currencies, especially the dollar. Moreover, the development of swap contracts permits the currency denomination of bonds to be swapped into whatever currency a borrower requires.

The Eurobond market in the UK has the regulatory status of a Designated Investment Exchange. Participants in the international securities market in the City are regulated by the FSA (and overseas banks by their home regulator as well). There are also two important self-regulatory bodies. The International Securities Market Association (ISMA), composed of international banks and brokers, is concerned with all aspects of the secondary trading and settlement of international securities. Formed in 1969 to sort out problems arising from the market's rapid growth, which was overwhelming the paper-based settlement system, it now provides a broad range of services to its hundreds of member firms and represents their collective interest to governments and regulators. It also provides training for the international securities markets, especially through the ISMA Centre at the University of Reading (see Chapter 8). The International Primary Markets Association (IPMA) performs similar services for the primary market. Both bodies promote industry-agreed guidelines designed to protect the market against unethical conduct and activities that could bring it into disrepute and undermine its integrity.

The primary and secondary international securities markets are OTC markets between banks and other participants. In the primary market the standard method of issuance is the bought deal, by which a lead-manager, and perhaps some co-managers, agree to buy an entire issue of securities at an agreed price. The issue is then resold through an international syndicate of banks. Secondary market trading is conducted by dealers on screen and over the telephone. Settlement is made via Euroclear or Cedel, the international securities clearing systems. Eurobond market borrowers include banks, corporations, utilities, governments and government agencies, municipalities and international organisations (such as the IMF, the World Bank and the EBRD). In the early days, individual investors were the bedrock of the market – the "Belgian dentist" was a caricature of a typical Eurobond investor – and individuals are still significant purchasers, many appreciating the anonymity conferred by the bonds' bearer status. But today institutional investors hold an estimated 90% of international bonds.

The principal international securities instruments are as follows:

- Bonds. Issued by all types of borrowers, bonds pay a fixed coupon (rate of interest).
- Floating-rate notes (FRNs). Issued by banks, building societies, governments and government agencies, FRNs are generally medium-term bonds with a typical maturity of 5–15 years and pay a floating-rate coupon fixed to a benchmark such as LIBOR (the London Interbank Offered Rate).
- Medium-term notes (MTNs). Issued by corporations, banks and governments, MTNs generally have a maturity of 1–10 years and pay a fixed coupon. They are issued on a tap (continuous availability) basis.
- Zero-coupon bonds. Issued by all types of borrowers, zero-coupon bonds pay no interest but are issued at a discount and redeemed at par upon maturity.
- Convertibles. Issued by corporations and banks, convertibles pay a fixed coupon and the holder has a right to convert the bond into ordinary shares at a future date.
- Bonds with equity warrants. Issued by corporations and banks, this type of bond is a debt instrument with an attached warrant that confers on the holder the option to buy ordinary shares at a given price in the future. Although the warrants are attached to the bonds, they are securities in their own right and can be stripped from the bonds and sold separately.

Annual primary-market issuance of international bonds increased from $3 billion in the early 1970s to $175 billion in the mid-1980s and to $1,467 billion in 2003. It is estimated that 60% of primary market issuance takes place in London. In 2002 48% of issuance was denominated in euros, 44% in dollars and most of the remainder in sterling. Private-sector borrowers, particularly from the United States and Germany, dominate the market, although governments, international organisations (such as the World Bank) and public corporations are also significant borrowers in the international capital market. Fixed-coupon bonds comprised 78% ($801 billion) of total issues in 2002, FRNs 20% ($209 billion) and equity warrants 2% ($12 billion).

In the Eurobond secondary market, fixed-coupon bonds comprise almost two-thirds of trading volume, FRN one-third and convertibles the rest. Global Eurobond secondary-market trading volume in 2002 was around $31 trillion, of which an estimated 70% was conducted in London. Turnover in the Eurobond secondary market is around five times greater than in the UK gilts market and seven times higher than in UK or international equities.

Securitisation and asset-backed securities
Securitisation has been an important development in the international bond market in recent years. It involves the packaging of loans into asset-backed securities, which are tradable instruments. An asset-backed security is a bond that is supported by income deriving not from an issuing body, such as a corporation or government, but from specific underlying assets. The pioneers in the market were American banks, using income from residential mortgages, credit-card receivables, automobile loans and other loans. The United States is still much the largest market for asset-backed securities, but European issuance has grown rapidly since the launch of the euro, which widened the market. Between 1998 and 2002, issuance of European asset-backed securities rose from $45 billion to $347 billion, not far behind American issuance of $414 billion. European banks have become major issuers of asset-backed securities and the market is expected to expand substantially.

Euroequities
The wholesale Euroequities market developed out of the Eurobond market to provide companies with access to equity capital from institutional investors outside their domestic market. Raising funds from international sources enables companies to broaden their shareholder base

and raise funds on better terms than are available at home. The market is focused on London. Securities are issued using the three-stage American-style public offering method: origination, underwriting, and distribution and marketing (see Chapter 4).

The market began in the 1980s and expanded substantially in the 1990s, when it was promoted by the international investment banks that operate in the Eurobond market. During the 1990s the annual value of Euroequity issues quadrupled from around $20 billion a year to $80 billion, boosted by privatisation issues by European countries: more than $300 billion was raised by the sale of state assets between 1987 and 1997. Large companies also use the market, and as privatisation issues waned in the early 2000s corporate issues became dominant.

The money markets

The money markets comprise a series of closely connected, wholesale OTC short-term financial markets. Their purpose is to borrow and lend spare money for short periods, and they have been described as equivalent to deposit accounts for big financial institutions. Globally, money-market instruments comprise around 20% of total debt securities. The money markets play a crucial role in the transmission of the Bank of England's monetary policy decisions to the UK economy.

There are three conceptually distinct dimensions to the UK money markets:

- the interbank market
- primary and secondary markets for a set of money-market instrument debt securities
- the repo market.

Interbank market

The interbank market involves unsecured lending between banks for periods ranging from overnight to up to three months. Banks with temporary cash surpluses are lenders and banks with temporary deficits are borrowers. Such surpluses and deficits arise in the normal course of business through fluctuations in receipts and payments and through banks' maturity transformation function: borrowing short and lending long. Rather than holding surplus cash balances that generate no interest, banks lend the funds as interest-bearing short-term deposits. Money-market brokers play an important role in bringing together banks with surplus funds and banks seeking funds.

The going rate for borrowings in the interbank market, the London Interbank Offer Rate or LIBOR, is widely used as a benchmark for loans with variable interest rates. In recent decades the market has widened to include non-bank participants as both borrowers and lenders, thus serving as another way in which companies can raise short-term funds and manage their money. The market also allows banks that do not have access to retail deposits to raise funds to finance their lending activities. It was the means by which the so-called "secondary banks" were able to fund their loans to property companies in the early 1970s, leading to the secondary banking crisis of 1973–75 when interbank rates soared (see Chapter 2). This episode demonstrated the interconnectedness of the banking and wider financial system, and the potential of the failure of a significant participant to cause systemic damage.

Money-market instruments

Money-market instruments are debt securities issued by a variety of borrowers. There are two types: those issued at par (face value); and those issued at a discount. Money-market securities issued at par are:

- money-market deposits (MMDs), interbank deposits with a minimum size of £500,000;
- certificates of deposit (CDs), issued by banks to confirm that a deposit has been made with a British bank or building society, or the UK branch of a foreign bank. They are denominated in sterling or dollars with a minimum amount of £50,000 and maturity from three months to five years. CDs are negotiable, so a holder can sell them in an active secondary market if funds are required. Hence the rate of interest paid by CDs is usually a little lower than that paid by non-negotiable MMDs of the same maturity.

A variety of negotiable short-term securities are issued at a discount to their face value, with the extent of the discount constituting the rate of interest paid when the security is redeemed at par at maturity:

- Treasury bills. Issued by the government, mostly in sterling, usually with a maturity of 91 days, although some are for longer periods.
- Local authority bills. Issued by local government bodies, with a maturity of up to six months. Local authorities require short-term

funds because of variations in the timing of their payments and receipts.

- Bankers' acceptances. Issued by companies. The liability of the issuer and repayment are guaranteed (accepted) by a bank of high standing.
- Commercial paper. Issued by companies and banks with a maturity of up to one year. These are unsecured loans, without the additional guarantee of a bank, in sterling or other currencies. Issuing companies must be listed on an authorised stock exchange.

There are also several sterling money-market derivative instruments, including short sterling futures contracts, forward rate agreements (FRAs), options, and sterling overnight index average (SONIA) swaps.

The repo market

The most recent major development in the money markets is the market in gilt repos (sale and repurchase agreements) introduced in 1996. A repo is a contract whereby one party sells securities to another party for cash and gives a commitment to repurchase the securities at an agreed future date and price. In essence, a repo is a device whereby a seller (a cash borrower) can raise cash against an asset, and a buyer (a cash lender) has the security of the loan of the asset in case of default. Thus repos are a form of secured lending. Most repos are short-term arrangements and form part of the money market, although long-term repos form part of the capital market.

Repos are the Bank of England's principal form of open-market operations, by which it sets short-term interest rates in pursuit of its monetary policy objectives. Indeed, since 1997 the UK's short-term interest rate has been known as the repo rate. The Bank's ability to influence money-market interest rates derives from its position as the ultimate provider of funds to the market, which for technical reasons is usually short of liquid funds. The Bank meets the shortfall in liquid funds on a short-term basis, which means that banks and other counterparties regularly need refinancing and are obliged to accept the current rate set by the bank.

In its repo operations the Bank supplies funds to counterparties by purchasing from them a range of "eligible securities" that it agrees to sell back to them at a predetermined date, around two weeks later. The interest rate charged on these two-week repos is the official repo rate. The eligible securities for the Bank's repo operations are:

- gilts
- sterling Treasury bills
- British government non-sterling marketable debt
- Bank of England euro bills and notes
- bankers' acceptances
- local authority bills
- sterling-denominated bills issued by European Economic Area (EEA) governments and major international organisations
- euro-denominated securities issued by the same parties that are eligible for use in the European System of Central Banks' monetary policy operations.

The Bank also offers counterparties the option to sell it certain types of bills on an outright basis. The discount to face value at which it buys the bills is set at a level equivalent to the official repo rate. The types of securities that the Bank will purchase on an outright basis are sterling Treasury bills, bankers' acceptances and local authority bills. The total stock of securities eligible for open-market operations is around £2.5 trillion. At any time the Bank holds £15 billion–20 billion such securities as collateral for its open-market operations.

The Bank keeps a close eye on the money market, as it has done since the 18th century. It maintains relations with market participants through contacts between its dealers and their counterparts and through two market committees. The Sterling Money Markets Liaison Group (MMLG) monitors general developments in the money markets, including monetary conditions and structural and legal issues. The Stock Lending and Repo Committee (SLRC) reviews developments in the repo and stock lending markets. It produces the Gilt Repo Code for market participants and considers issues concerning market infrastructure and regulation.

All the money-market instruments traded in the money markets, including gilts traded in the gilt repos market and the various derivative instruments, are investments as defined by the Financial Services Markets Act 2000. Banks and others that trade in the money markets require authorisation under the act by the FSA, or operate in the UK under the EEA's reciprocal "passport" arrangements. Money-market instruments are not generally listed or subject to prospectus requirements.

Foreign-exchange market

The foreign-exchange market is an OTC market in which trade is conducted via quotes on electronic screens and the telephone. More than

250 banks and securities firms participated in a survey of the UK's foreign-exchange and OTC derivatives markets conducted by the Bank of England in 2001, part of a worldwide survey organised by the Bank for International Settlements (BIS) every three years. The survey revealed that London remained the world's largest centre for foreign exchange, accounting for 31% of the global market. The volume of foreign-exchange trading was roughly equal to that of the United States, Singapore and Japan combined (see Table 12.1 on page 238). In April 2001 total average turnover was $504 billion a day, comprising $151 billion in spot transactions, $53 billion in outright forwards and $300 billion in foreign-exchange swaps. Foreign-owned institutions accounted for 81% of total turnover in London, with North American institutions conducting 46% of business and non-UK EU institutions 21%.

For the first time since the BIS surveys began in 1986, between 1998 and 2001 the volume of UK and global foreign-exchange trading fell. This was partly the result of the introduction of the euro in January 1999, which eliminated cross trading between the former euro-area currencies. But much of the 21% reduction was caused by a decline in interdealer activity arising from consolidation in the global banking industry and the enhanced role of electronic broking systems. A new survey was conducted in April 2004, the results of which were to be released later in the year.

The foreign-exchange market is a continuous dealer's market with four types of participant:

◪ Dealers. These are principally the major international banks. Interdealer activity comprised 68% of foreign-exchange market activity in 2001. Dealers make profits in two ways: from the spread between bid and offer prices; and by speculating on the future course of rates. Activity is concentrated among the largest market participants; the top ten have a combined market share of 58% and the top 20's share is 80%. Mergers between large banks in recent years have boosted the concentration of activity. The elimination of transactions between merged banks contributed to the fall in interdealer volume between 1998 and 2001.

◪ Brokers. These are specialist firms that act as intermediaries, bringing together buyers and sellers. Electronic broking is supplanting direct dealing and voice broking, accounting in 2001 for two-thirds of interdealer spot activity, double the level in 1998. Electronic systems enhance market transparency and efficiency, thereby curbing opportunities for arbitrage. This has contributed to the fall in foreign-exchange turnover.

- Customers. These are large companies and non-bank financial institutions. Customer business grew from 17% of total turnover in 1998 to 32% in 2001. The expansion was attributed to the increased activity and sophistication of asset managers.
- The Bank of England. The Bank supervises the market. Economic policy considerations may lead the Bank to intervene to influence the exchange rate. Intervention is usually executed through a broker, disguising the Bank's role.

The dollar has long been the dominant currency in London's foreign-exchange market, being used on one side of the transaction in 92% of all deals. The euro/dollar is the most actively traded currency pair, comprising 34% of the market. Sterling was involved in 24% of turnover.

The foreign-exchange market features three types of transaction:

- Spot transactions. The exchange of two currencies at a rate agreed on the date of the contract for cash settlement within two business days.
- Outright forward transactions. The exchange of two currencies at a rate agreed on the date of the contract for purchase at a later date.
- Foreign-exchange swap transactions. The exchange of two currencies at a specified date and a reverse exchange of the same currencies at a date further in the future.

In recent years there has been a decrease in the proportion of foreign-exchange business transacted for spot value, from 51% in 1992 to 30% in 2001 (see Table 3.6 overleaf). The principal reason is the expansion of electronic broking. By contrast, foreign-exchange swap transactions grew from 42% of the market to 60% in the same period, and the volume of transactions trebled. The expansion of foreign-exchange swaps has been driven by their use in the management of interest-rate risk. However, the development of new interest-rate derivatives has curtailed the growth in demand for foreign-exchange swaps.

The bullion market

The London bullion market is a wholesale OTC batch market for gold, silver and gold forward contracts. The London Bullion Market Association (LBMA), formed in 1987, has nine marketmaking members, four of

Table 3.6 **Foreign-exchange turnover by transaction type, 1992 and 2001**

| | 1992 | | 2001 | |
	Net average daily turnover ($bn)	%	Net average daily turnover ($bn)	%
Spot transactions	148	51	151	30
Outright forwards	20	7	53	10
Foreign-exchange swaps	123	42	300	60
Total	290	100	504	100

which participate in the daily "Gold Fixing". There are also 51 ordinary members, comprising the leading bullion bankers, brokers and dealers from around the world. London, the traditional outlet for South African gold, is the world's most liquid market for gold and the largest centre for gold trading. The average daily clearing in 2003 was worth $6.3 billion, more than the annual production of South Africa. The average daily clearing of silver is worth $500m. The other major bullion market centres are Zurich and New York, the leading centre for gold futures.

The Gold Fixings began in 1919 in the office of N.M. Rothschild, a merchant bank, which had a long association with the gold market. Clients place orders with the dealing rooms of fixing members, which net off buyers and sellers and then communicate the outcome to their representative at the fixing by telephone. The price is then adjusted up or down depending on demand and supply until an average price is reached at which the market is in equilibrium. When a fixing member is satisfied with the price, he lowers the miniature Union Jack that sits on the table in front of him. When all the flags are down, indicating assent, the price is fixed in dollars and immediately circulated. The fixings take place twice a day at 10.30am and 3.00pm.

The outcome of this somewhat bizarre procedure is a worldwide benchmark price that is used for large-volume gold transactions. Other financial instruments are priced off the fixing price, including cash-settled swaps and options. The fixing is a transparent process and customers are kept informed about price and demand while it is in progress, enabling them to change their orders. An advantage of the fixing process is the narrow spread between buying and selling prices, maximising satisfaction among buyers and sellers. The world's central banks use the London Gold Fixing price to value their gold reserves.

In April 2004 N.M. Rothschild surprised the City by announcing that it was pulling out of the gold market. It explained that metals trading had declined to just 2% of its business and that it was redeploying the capital committed to the bullion business to core activities. The remaining members of the Gold Fixing are Bank of Nova Scotia, Deutsche Bank, HSBC and Société Générale.

The Bank of England provides important forms of support for the London bullion market. Many LBMA members, as well as most of the world's central banks, have accounts at the Bank of England. Many of them also hold a substantial part of their gold holdings at the Bank. The five LBMA clearing members have their own gold vaults, as well as accounts at the Bank. Thus the settlement of trades can usually be made by transfer of title from account to account, minimising the physical movement of gold. The FSA has responsibility for the regulation of participants in the London bullion market.

Trends and issues

- ◪ **Amalgamation of European exchanges.** The creation of the euro and Europe's growing economic and financial integration have led to moves to rationalise the continent's nationally based stock exchanges and derivatives exchanges. Among stock exchanges, the principal moves have been the formation of Norex, a common Nordic stock exchange through a merger between the Stockholm and Copenhagen exchanges in 1998, and Euronext, the amalgamation of the Amsterdam, Brussels, Paris and Lisbon exchanges in 2001. Among derivatives exchanges, there has been the creation of Eurex through the merger of the Swiss and German exchanges in 1996 and the acquisition of LIFFE by Euronext in 2001. There was almost a merger between the London Stock Exchange and Frankfurt's Deutsche Börse, but it fell apart because of opposition among members in London. The consolidation among exchanges is likely to continue and may well involve non-European exchanges in global alliances.

- ◪ **Electronic exchanges.** There have been several attempts to create new electronic pan-European securities marketplaces. Virt-x, a joint venture between Tradepoint and the Swiss exchange, provides a single platform for trading European blue-chip shares, and Euro-MTS trades European government bonds. There will probably be more such start-ups, although the established exchanges are in the game too. There has also been a burgeoning of alternative trading systems (ATS), providing specialist intermediary services that complement the main trading systems.

- **Electronic trading.** Between 1990 and 2004 the volume of exchange trading conducted electronically rose from 3% to more than 50% and the trend will continue. The shift from open outcry to electronic trading began in Europe, where floor trading has almost disappeared. Europe's lead in electronic-trading technology and software has led to opportunities to license its technology around the world, including North America. The spread of common electronic trading platforms, such as LIFFE CONNECT and OM, allows access to new markets and is leading to greater global integration.
- **Clearing and settlement.** In 2002 there were 17 clearing houses in Europe, most of them divisions of national stock exchanges. There is scope for cost savings from economies of scale and performance enhancement from common IT systems and cross-border netting of trades. LCH.Clearnet and Eurex Clearing are leading the rationalisation process.
- **Demutualisation.** Most exchanges have decided to convert from mutual ownership to for-profit corporate status in order to clarify responsibilities, improve services to users and raise additional capital, especially for expenditure on IT but also to acquire other exchanges.
- **Outsourcing.** Many market participants are outsourcing IT and other services in order to concentrate on core activities and cut costs.
- **Contribution to the economy.** In the City an estimated 77,500 people work in securities, 8,000 in foreign exchange and 7,000 in derivatives, constituting almost one-third of total City employment. In 2002 the combined net exports of City securities dealers (£3.1 billion), money-market brokers (£309m) and futures and options dealers (£190m) comprised 20% of total financial sector net exports.

4 The sell-side: investment banking and securities

Selling and buying financial securities is the City's fundamental business. The transactions and the firms that conduct them divide into the sell-side and the buy-side. The sell-side is shorthand for activities concerned with the creation and trading of securities, and with the sale of securities services to the buy-side. The buy-side is shorthand for investors who purchase the securities and the services offered by the sell-side. This chapter focuses on the sell-side.

What investment banks do

The leading sell-side firms are the investment banks. The core activities of investment banks are as follows:

- ◪ The provision of advisory services to large companies, banks and government organisations on financing, mergers and acquisitions (M&A), disposals, privatisation and project finance (known as M&A/advisory).
- ◪ Raising capital for companies through the sale of equities or bonds issued by them in the primary capital markets (see Chapter 3) for an underwriting fee, incurring the risk that buyers cannot be found for the securities at the issue price.

These activities, traditionally the firms' dominant and defining activities, are known as investment banking or corporate finance (the latter term being used on Wall Street in the narrower sense of capital markets activity). They are closely related, with M&A/advisory work often resulting in initiatives that require new financing arrangements.

The major investment banks also undertake a variety of other activities (see Table 4.1). Many investment banks undertake secondary-market securities trading, not because of the intrinsic profitability of the activity (trading for institutional investors may even be loss-making) but because it enables them to distribute the securities created by their profitable investment banking activities and to provide a dealing service that bolsters their relationships with corporate and institutional clients. However,

Table 4.1 **Principal investment bank activities**

Investment banking/corporate finance	Advising large companies and government organisations on financing, mergers and acquisitions, privatisation and other financial matters (M&A/advisory)
	Raising capital for companies in the equity primary markets
	Raising capital for companies in the fixed income (bond) primary markets
Secondary-market securities activities	Securities trading on behalf of retail clients and institutional clients
	Securities trading as principal (proprietary trading)
	Derivatives (structured products) trading
Other activities	Asset management
	Private wealth management/private clients
	Private Public Partnerships (PPP)
	Private equity/venture capital
	Prime brokerage
	Lending (credit)

conducting trades for retail clients, whose small-scale transactions incur much higher commission rates, is generally profitable.

Investment bank traders also conduct proprietary trading (prop trading), in which the bank itself acts a principal and bets on market developments. Plainly this is more risky than acting as an agent for a client, but it can be much more profitable. Investment banks monitor their exposure to proprietary trading risk with value-at-risk (VAR) models, which calculate potential losses on the basis of historical price movements. In the early 2000s proprietary trading, mostly fixed income (bonds), generated more than one-quarter of investment bank profits (compared with one-fifth in the late 1990s), making up for the dearth of investment banking business caused by the stockmarket downturn. Investment banks also originate, market and trade financial derivatives.

The level of activity in both investment banking and equities/securities trading is positively correlated with the stockmarket and earnings generally fluctuate in line with stockmarket conditions. Asset management and private wealth management are not so market driven and generate more stable earnings. For that reason, but also to expand their range of activities enabling them to sell more products to clients, investment and commercial banks have diversified into these buy-side activities (see Chapter 5).

Private Public Partnerships (PPP) were pioneered by City investment banks through the UK's Private Finance Initiative (PFI) as a means of raising private funds for public-sector projects, such as the building of schools, hospitals and prisons (see Chapter 2). Having developed a successful model in the UK, investment banks are seeking to export the technique to other countries.

Private equity or venture capital is the activity of making equity investments in unquoted companies (see Chapter 5). Such investment opportunities arise from an investment bank's corporate advisory work, often from corporate restructuring involving leveraged buy-outs or management buy-outs. Investment banks run buy-out funds that are subscribed by institutional investors and sometimes commit their own funds as well. Private equity is a risky activity as the capital committed is exposed to losses and illiquidity. But the potential profits from acting as a principal, leveraging the firm's expertise and knowledge of the deal, make the business attractive.

"Prime brokerage" services focus on hedge funds, lending them funds to trade and relieving them of administrative and back-office functions, enabling them to focus on making money. Hedge funds use a variety of aggressive investment strategies, such as short selling (betting equities will fall in price), and are often highly leveraged (see Chapter 5). They are managed by professional managers and aim to make an absolute return for investors. Prime brokerage services include lending hedge funds money to provide leverage and liquidity and securities to enable them to cover their short positions. The downturn in equity markets in the early 2000s led to a boom in hedge funds in London and around the world and hence an upsurge in prime brokerage activity at the investment banks. Such was the scramble for prime brokerage business that in January 2004 the Financial Services Authority publicly expressed concern that investment banks might be tempted to relax counterparty credit-risk standards to win clients.

Lending (credit) is the business of clearing (commercial) banks (see Chapter 6). Traditionally, investment banks provided loans from their own resources to clients only for takeovers or other short-term bridging-loan purposes. When major American and European commercial banks entered the investment banking business in the 1990s, credit began to be used as a competitive weapon. With their big balance sheets they were able to offer low-cost credit to help win investment banking mandates from companies. Such credit-led strategies are controversial, particularly as they resulted in heavy losses at major banks when Enron and other companies collapsed with the end of the 1990s bull market.

The conglomeration of global financial services has been taken furthest by Citigroup, the world's largest financial services business. Through a series of bold and controversial moves between 1997 and 2000, a business was constructed that combined bank lending (Citibank) with securities underwriting and M&A/advisory (Salomon Brothers and Schroders) and general and life insurance (Travelers); it also included credit cards, consumer finance, marketmaking in securities, institutional brokerage, retail brokerage, foreign-exchange dealing, derivatives trading and origination, fund management, private banking, proprietary trading in developing-country bonds and private equity investments, both as principal and for clients. The US Congress even lent a hand, repealing in 1999 the Glass Steagall Act of 1933, which imposed a legal separation on the conduct of commercial and investment banking.

By combining commercial banking, investment banking and insurance, conglomerates such as Citigroup are effectively able to use the same capital several times over to back their various activities, enhancing their return on capital. The extent to which they can do so is constrained by the greater risks of simultaneously engaging in several risky business areas. But conglomeration also generates two significant benefits that may outweigh the increase in risk: diversification of revenues and portfolios (losses in one activity being offset by profits in another); and organisational synergies, allowing the cross-marketing of products to clients and the ability to offer a one-stop shop capability for clients. However, conglomeration and cross-marketing can give rise to conflicts of interest between profit maximisation for an investment bank and the interests of clients.

Investment banking industry

The investment banking industry in London is dominated by the same group of nine global investment banks that are pre-eminent worldwide (see Table 4.2). The Wall Street investment banks are "pure" investment banks, in the sense that they do not combine investment banking with commercial banking as do the American and European universal banks. The expansion of the Wall Street investment banks has been largely through organic growth rather than major acquisitions. The commercial

Table 4.2 **Global investment banks**

Bank	Country
Wall Street investment banks	
Goldman Sachs	US
Lehman Brothers	US
Merrill Lynch	US
Morgan Stanley Dean Witter	US
American commercial banks	
Citigroup	US
J.P. Morgan Chase	US
European commercial banks	
Credit Suisse First Boston (CSFB)	Switzerland
Deutsche Bank	Germany
UBS	Switzerland

banks moved into investment banking mainly through mergers and acquisitions in the 1990s and early 2000s (see Table 4.3 overleaf).

There is a set of so-called mid-size investment banks in London owned by major European commercial banks. The leading ones are: Barclays, Royal Bank of Scotland and HSBC from the UK; ING (which bought City merchant bank Barings) and ABN Amro from the Netherlands; Dresdner Bank from Germany (which bought City merchant bank Kleinwort Benson and Wall Street investment bank Wasserstein Perella); and Société Générale (which bought City merchant bank Hambros) and BNP Paribas from France. Lastly, there are three notable British independent firms: N.M. Rothschild and Lazard Brothers, the last of the City merchant banks; and Cazenove, a leading independent broker-dealer, which has developed investment banking activities. There are also many small "boutique" investment banks and broker-dealers.

The trade association of the investment banks in London is the London Investment Banking Association (LIBA). Its origins go back to 1914 when the London merchant banks formed the Accepting Houses Committee to address the crisis in the City caused by the outbreak of the first world war (see Chapter 2). It was reconstituted in 1988, in the wake of Big Bang, as the British Merchant Banking and Securities Houses Association (BMBA). Reflecting the growing importance of American investment banks in London and shifting terminology, the

Table 4.3 **Principal mergers and acquisitions to form global investment banks**

Citigroup	Citibank (US commercial bank)
	Travelers (US insurance company)
	Salomon Brothers (US investment bank)
	Smith Barney (US broker-dealer)
	Schroders (UK merchant bank)
Credit Suisse First Boston	Credit Suisse (Swiss universal bank)
	First Boston (US investment bank)
	Donaldson Lufkin & Jenrette (US investment bank)
Deutsche Bank	Deutsche Bank (German universal bank)
	Bankers Trust (US investment bank)
	Alex Brown (US broker-dealer)
	Morgan Grenfell (UK merchant bank)
J.P. Morgan Chase	J.P. Morgan (US investment bank)
	Chase (US commercial bank)
	Hambrecht & Quist (US specialist investment bank)
	Beacon Group (US asset manager)
	Robert Fleming & Co (UK merchant bank and asset manager)
	Schroders (UK merchant bank)
Merrill Lynch	Merrill Lynch (US investment bank and stockbroker)
	Mercury Asset Management (UK asset manager)
	Smith New Court (UK broker-dealer)
Morgan Stanley	Morgan Stanley (US investment bank)
	Dean Witter (US broker-dealer)
UBS	UBS (Swiss universal bank)
	PaineWebber (US broker-dealer and asset manager)
	Dillon Read (US broker-dealer)
	Philips & Drew (UK broker-dealer and asset manager)
	S.G. Warburg (UK merchant bank)

current name was adopted in 1994. The LIBA promotes the industry's interests to legislators, regulators and opinion-formers in the UK, Europe and worldwide. It has 41 members.

In 2003, global investment banking fee income from the three core activities (M&A/advisory, equity market primary issuance and fixed income primary issuance) was $41 billion (see Table 4.4). This was significantly higher than in 2002, but considerably short of the record $57 billion that the industry received in fees in 2000. Over the decade of

Table 4.4 **Global investment bank fee income, 1993–2003**

	$bn
1993	26
1994	22
1995	23
1996	31
1997	37
1998	39
1999	50
2000	57
2001	42
2002	34
2003	41

Source: IFSL, *Banking*, 2004

the 1990s, worldwide investment banking fee income grew at around 10% per year. The United States generates 56% of the total, Europe 28% and Asia 15%. The UK is the largest source in Europe, producing 27% of the total, followed by Germany (17%), France (15%) and Italy (10%). Around half of European investment banking business is conducted in London.

Each of the three core investment banking activities generated around one-third of global fee income in 2003. M&A/advisory fee income of $14 billion was 34% of the total, a lower proportion than in the 1990s when it constituted over 40%. The total value of M&A announced deals worldwide was $1.3 trillion. M&A fees constituted 59% of total investment bank fee income originating from the UK. Equity-market primary issuance generated $14 billion in global investment bank fee income, and fixed-interest primary market issuance produced $13 billion.

The ten largest investment banks ranked by global fee income are shown in Table 4.5. Seven are American firms, two are Swiss and one is German. Together they received 55% of total global investment banking fee income in 2003. The consolidation of the industry in the 1990s and early 2000s is illustrated by the increase in the share of global fee income received by the leading three firms, which grew from 17% in 1991 to 24% in 2003.

Table 4.5 **Leading investment banks, 2003**

	Global fee income ($bn)	% share
Goldman Sachs	3.5	8.4
Merrill Lynch	3.4	8.2
Citigroup	3.1	7.5
Credit Suisse First Boston	3.1	7.5
Morgan Stanley	2.8	6.7
J.P. Morgan Chase	2.5	6.0
UBS	1.9	4.6
Lehman Brothers	1.6	3.9
Deutsche Bank Securities	1.4	3.4
Bank of America	1.0	2.4

Source: IFSL, *Banking*, 2004

Global investment banks

Global investment banks emerged in the 1990s. The process began with the overseas expansion of the leading Wall Street investment banks, which targeted particularly London and Tokyo. They invested profits from their Wall Street activities to establish a major presence in these global financial centres and then developed operations in the regional financial centres of Europe, Asia and elsewhere.

In London the indigenous merchant banks endeavoured to compete by adopting an American-style "integrated" business model, but they either failed or decided to sell out (see Chapter 2). Two British clearing banks, Barclays and NatWest, also entered into investment banking but withdrew when it became clear that to succeed they would have to purchase a substantial presence on Wall Street and they balked at the risk. The three European global investment banks took the plunge and made substantial acquisitions on Wall Street as well as building up their businesses in London.

The introduction of the euro in 1999 was an ideal opportunity for American investment banks to expand their business in continental Europe. The national currencies had provided a measure of protection for European banks, which dominated their local markets, but the single currency provided a level playing field for all. The euro created a major new capital market almost as big as the dollar market into which innovative American products and investment banking practices could be introduced. As in London and Tokyo, the global investment bankers were able to market their expertise in Wall Street's cutting-edge activities, such as derivatives or securitisation, to gain access to European companies and displace local competitors. The European market is expected to be a fruitful source of future M&A work as businesses become pan-European, since the average European company is around half the size of its American counterparts.

Underlying the rise of the giant investment banks was the longest-ever global stockmarket boom, which began in 1982 and ran to early 2000 (with a temporary correction in 1987). This was associated with rapid and sustained growth rates for the industry's fundamental activities. Over the years 1983 to 2000, global M&A activity grew at an annual compound rate of 23%, debt issuance at 18%, equity-market capitalisation at 14%, equity issuance at 12% and pension-fund assets at 10%. These were substantially faster rates of growth than the 6% rate of expansion of global GDP over these decades, enhancing the investment banking industry's size and significance.

The global investment banks captured a substantial proportion of this growth in activity. In 2001 the top five global investment banks (not the same five firms for each activity) handled 66% of global M&A, 61% of global primary-market equity issuance and 45% of global primary-market debt issuance. In the bull market the leading firms earned formidable rates of return on equity, far higher than those that could be made from commercial bank lending, which prompted commercial banks to enter the investment banking business.

The global spread of the leading Wall Street investment banks was fostered and assisted by several factors. Globalisation (meaning in this context cross-border investment flows) often involved an American company or institutional investor as one party to the transaction, providing Wall Street firms with an entrance. The deregulation of financial markets around the world allowed foreign entrants access to hitherto closed local markets and triggered massive consolidation among both investment banking and securities firms. Global economic growth resulted in greater accumulations of wealth, much of it managed by institutional investors, which purchased the securities intermediated by the global investment banks as well as their asset management services.

Investment banks have also benefited from the spread of securitisation, an American invention and export. Securitisation means the shift in borrowing from banks to borrowing from the capital markets via the issuance of financial securities. It has been driven by several factors, including cheaper finance for borrowers, the need of many banks to reduce lending to strengthen their regulatory capital base, investors' demand for securities and the ingenuity of the investment banking industry in generating innovative securitisation concepts. The increase in securitisation has boosted the debt and equity issuance business of the investment banks at the expense of the lending business of the commercial banks. In the United States, over the years 1980 to 2001 the proportion of loans intermediated by commercial banks fell from 45% to 30%, while the proportion intermediated through the securities markets rose accordingly. In Europe, where bank borrowing has traditionally been a much more important source of funding than in the United States, the proportion is still around 75% but it is falling. The trend was another reason for commercial banks to develop investment banking business.

The outcome has been an increase in the proportion of business handled by the global investment banks around the world, including Europe. Between 1993 and 2001, the six American global investment banks increased their share of the aggregate European investment banking fee pool from 12% to 30%, while the share of the three European global investment banks grew from 12% to 16%. Thus the proportion of the European fee pool received by all the other national banks and investment banks fell from 76% to 54% and was on course to shrink further. The global investment banks dominate the top ten rankings in the league tables for European M&A and equity and debt issuance.

Investment bank business

The cost of entering the investment banking business is high because of the need for heavy investment in state-of-the art information and communications technologies and the expensive compensation packages of their bright and energetic employees. Profitability depends crucially on being able to spread these costs over a large and continuous flow of transactions. This means the achievement of high market share (so-called operational leverage) in the key activities of M&A/advisory and debt and equity issuance, since the leading firms tend to capture a disproportionate volume of revenues. It also means the development of a broad product range in order to be able to take advantage of the possibilities for cross-selling to clients.

Investment banking activities are not equally profitable and cross-subsidisation among products is a feature of the industry. Two activities generate high margins when they are busy: M&A/advisory and equity

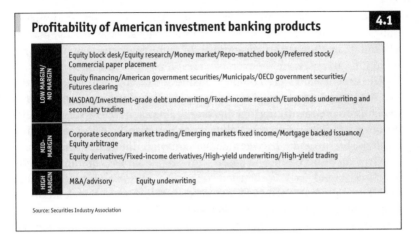

Profitability of American investment banking products **4.1**

LOW MARGIN/ NO MARGIN	Equity block desk/Equity research/Money market/Repo-matched book/Preferred stock/ Commercial paper placement
	Equity financing/American government securities/Municipals/OECD government securities/ Futures clearing
	NASDAQ/Investment-grade debt underwriting/Fixed-income research/Eurobonds underwriting and secondary trading
MID-MARGIN	Corporate secondary market trading/Emerging markets fixed income/Mortgage backed issuance/ Equity arbitrage
	Equity derivatives/Fixed-income derivatives/High-yield underwriting/High-yield trading
HIGH MARGIN	M&A/advisory Equity underwriting

Source: Securities Industry Association

issuance. Both are bespoke services provided by senior investment bankers for top-level company management, so they are relatively unaffected by competitive pricing pressures. In each case, management requires the best available execution and is prepared to pay for it.

Derivatives can also be very profitable. The highest margins are earned from equity derivatives and complex and innovative products. However, much activity comprises low-margin commoditised products, such as interest-rate and currency futures, swaps and options. The underwriting of high-yield debt, private equity and bond-market proprietary trading are generally high-margin activities too. The relative profitability of investment banking products in the United States according to consultants Sanford Bernstein is depicted in Figure 4.1.

There are also so-called "pay to play" products, which are low margin or even lossmaking and are subsidised by the profitable activities. For instance, lossmaking commercial paper issuance is regarded as part-and-parcel of debt-issuance business relationships, which in turn support profitable derivatives trading and secondary-market corporate bond trading. Equity trading for institutional and corporate clients and plain vanilla (commoditised) lending are also generally conducted on a break-even basis because they are considered necessary capabilities to win high-return M&A business and equity primary-market issuance. Equity research was a cross-subsidised activity that became highly controversial because it was produced by Wall Street investment banks not to enlighten investors but to ramp companies' share prices to win investment banking mandates. This corruption of the role of the equity analyst was at the centre of the scandal that rocked the investment banks in the early 2000s and led to various banks being fined a total of $1.4 billion in 2003. Although some of the same practices may have gone on in the City, they were never as widespread or as flagrant.

Investment banks are complex businesses involved in many activities. Maximisation of the overall profit potential of the component parts depends on them working together and selling each other's services. The array of products and personality types can also lead to clashes and rivalries, for instance between suave corporate financiers and aggressive traders or between rule-based commercial bankers and innovative investment bankers. The so-called "one-bank" partnership model, epitomised by Goldman Sachs as a partnership before its public flotation in 1999, is advocated as a solution to these issues. But the model is hard to achieve and sustain, especially for firms that have been put together by mergers, and given the scale and complexity of today's investment banks.

An investment bank's main asset is the ability of its personnel and so the retention of talented employees is crucial. The level of pay is important and so is the bonus scheme, which can be disruptive if it is not administered with great sensitivity. There is widespread agreement that the compensation arrangements of the one-bank partnership model are the ideal solution (even though all the global investment banks are now public companies). The key features are a single bonus pool with allocations from it made on the basis of a subjective, but rigorous, transparent and exhaustive appraisal of the contributions of individuals to the firm as a whole and to the unit, and of their personal achievements. This is difficult to make work in practice.

Reconciling the compensation demands of investment bankers and the maximisation of shareholder value is also a challenge for management. So is keeping control of costs, given the volatility of investment banking revenues. The industry benchmark ratio of employee compensation costs to revenues is 50%, and that of other expenses to revenues is 30%, implying a 20% pre-tax profit margin for shareholders. Of course, given the high minimum costs of entry to the business, the profit performance is crucially dependent on the level of revenues, creating problems for firms that are not industry leaders. A strategy adopted by many firms to align the interests of staff and shareholders and tie talented staff to the firm is for a substantial part of bonuses to take the form of share options and equity lock-ups. At Lehman Brothers, for instance, in 2004 employees held 35% of the firm's shares, compared with 4% in 1994, and it is a strategic goal of management to raise the proportion even higher.

M&A/advisory

Advisory work is profitable in its own right, but it also affords an opportunity to market an investment bank's other products to a company's senior management. Companies may seek advice on their financial structure or on raising funds for expansion or making acquisitions. Alternatively, they may be seeking to sell a business unit or to protect an incumbent management team from a hostile takeover bid. Often investment banks themselves come up with ideas for acquisitions or divestments that they pitch to chief executives. In such strategic matters, it is the quality of the advice and execution that is of crucial importance rather than the level of the fee (within reason). A survey of American chief executives by Greenwich Associates found that "lower fee" ranked 11th out of 13 among the factors determining the award of an M&A mandate, behind the bank's historic relationship and credibility with the company's management, the capability and track record of its M&A staff, the creativity of its ideas and its ability to arrange financing.

Advisory work and associated primary-market securities issues are the basis of the so-called "single product" strategy of N.M. Rothschild, Lazard Brothers and new advisory boutiques, which do not undertake securities secondary-market trading or many of the other businesses conducted by the global investment banks. Their advice is prized by company chief executives because their focus on advisory work eliminates the possibility of a conflict of interest with the promotion of an investment bank's other products. The growing use of multiple advisers for M&A work may ensure that there is a niche for small specialist advisers as well as the global investment bank titans.

Primary-market securities issues

Investment banks raise funds for companies and other borrowers through the issuance of securities either by a public offering or by a private placing. There are three basic types of public offering:

- Initial public offering (IPO). For a company new to the stockmarket to raise funds (traditionally known in the UK as a flotation).
- Follow-on (secondary) equity offering. For an already listed company to raise additional funds.

■ Bond offering. For companies, governments, local authorities and other borrowers.

An "offer for sale" was the traditional way in which City merchant banks sold shares to the public on behalf of a company, offering the shares to both individual and institutional investors at a fixed price. However, in recent years, with the global expansion of American investment banks, the American-style public offering has become common practice internationally. Essentially the same procedure is used for IPOs and follow-on equity offerings, and for both equities and bonds. A public offering proceeds in three stages:

■ **Origination.** A company wanting to raise funds through the securities market conducts a "beauty contest" among investment banks and chooses one to act as lead manager to the issue. The lead manager has overall responsibility for arranging the issue, for which it receives a management commission. Its duties include advising on the type and structure of the offering, conducting a due diligence investigation to establish that the borrower's presentation of its financial and commercial position is accurate, and the writing of the issue prospectus. For an IPO, a listing is arranged with the London Stock Exchange (LSE), the Alternative Investment Market (AIM) or OFEX.

■ **Underwriting.** The lead manager, in consultation with the issuer, puts together a syndicate of other investment banks and securities firms to underwrite the issue. The underwriters guarantee that the issuer will receive an agreed amount of money, irrespective of developments in the market. Other firms that assume responsibility for a substantial proportion of an issue may be appointed co-lead managers, and those taking lesser parts are made co-managers. The role of the underwriter involves a risk of financial loss if the securities cannot be sold to investors at the anticipated price. The underwriters receive a commission for assuming this risk and for providing a guarantee to the issuer.

Before the marketing phase, the lead manager takes soundings from institutional investors to appraise the buy-side's likely reception of the issue. These pre-marketing inquiries provide the basis for determining the volume of securities that the market can absorb and for setting upper and lower price limits.

◪ **Distribution and marketing.** The distribution syndicate comprises the members of the underwriting syndicate and a "selling group" of financial firms that take no underwriting risk. The members of the underwriting syndicate may decide to undertake all the selling, in which case the underwriting and distribution syndicates are identical. Invariably, the underwriters account for a high proportion of sales; the members of the selling group are invited to participate on account of their ability to broaden the market for the securities. Members of the distribution syndicate receive commissions based on the sales for which they are responsible.

The lead manager and the company then embark on a road show to market the securities to institutional investors. Important potential investors are invited to one-on-ones, that is, private presentations by the company and the lead manager. The lead manager performs the role of "bookrunner" to the issue, entering in the "book" indicative orders received for the securities. The bookbuilding process permits the lead manager to appraise demand for the issue among institutional investors and to adjust the size of the issue and price accordingly. However, it cuts individual investors out of the picture unless some securities are set aside for retail investors. For large international issues, with tranches of securities being sold in several markets, the lead manager may appoint regional bookrunners and act as global co-ordinator, merging the regional books into a single global book. At the end of the marketing exercise the lead manager fixes the issue price, securities are allocated to investors and trading begins in the market.

For a typical offering, the "gross spread" of fees and commissions amounts to 3–4% of the sum raised, although for IPOs fees may be higher (in the United States they are as high as 7–8%, which explains the eagerness of investment bankers for mandates). The lion's share of the fees goes to the lead manager, with other firms receiving payments proportionate to their underwriting and sales contributions. Invitations to rival firms to participate in offering syndicates ensure that when rivals are awarded mandates the lead manager is invited to participate in their syndicates.

Multinational corporations and governments use the wholesale Euroequities market to raise large sums through the sale of securities or privatisation issues. Small and medium-sized companies are likely to use the cheaper and faster method of a private placing. The investment bank that has been engaged to conduct the fundraising negotiates the sale of the securities to one or more large institutional investors. Both the seller and the buyers benefit from the cost savings of a private placing. A potential disadvantage for purchasers is lack of liquidity in the securities, but this can be mitigated by trading private placings among institutional investors. The privatisation issues in the UK in the 1980s and 1990s generally used a mixture of offer for sale to retail investors and private placings with institutional investors. A variant of the placing is the "bought deal", in which a new issue of shares is purchased en bloc by an investment bank, which then sells them to clients.

Traditionally, the method by which British companies raised additional equity funds was through a "rights issue". Existing shareholders are offered additional shares, usually at a discount to the market price, which can be either taken up or sold. This "pre-emption right" allows existing shareholders to avoid a dilution of their ownership interest. Despite hostility from some institutional investors, companies now also use private placings and American-style follow-on public offerings to raise additional funds.

Trends and issues

- **Consolidation.** Industry analysts expect further consolidation among the global investment banks, perhaps resulting in four or five truly global, fully integrated firms.
- **Middle-sized European banks.** Many predict that competition from the global investment banks will further erode the market share of middle-sized European banks, prompting some to pull out of investment banking. However, some see a role at the national level to service the requirements of small and medium-sized firms.
- **Employee shareholdings and options.** These are expected to continue to increase, helping to resolve the conflict of interest between those working in a business and outside shareholders. Options help keep staff and also encourage talented staff to firms; shareholdings do not as staff simply sell when they leave.
- **Focus on Europe.** The pan-European restructuring of the European economy has a long way to go and investment banks anticipate strong demand for their services in coming years. Much of this business is likely to be done in London, which should increase the share of European investment banking business conducted there from the current 50%.

- **European Takeover Directive.** After 14 years of wrangling, the European Takeover Directive was approved by the European Parliament in December 2003. Its goal is to create a single market for European mergers and acquisitions. A previous draft directive was rejected in 2001 because Germany feared takeovers of major German companies. Economic liberals are disappointed that the watered-down directive allows countries to retain anti-takeover obstacles.
- **Equity research.** The scandals in the United States in the early 2000s when equity research was used to ramp stock prices have led to the separation of equity research from investment banking. Without funding from investment banking revenues, equity research is likely to continue to decline at the investment banks.
- **Conflicts of interest.** The conglomeration of financial services has increased the potential for conflicts of interest between the company and its clients at the integrated investment banks. Further scandals, particularly if they affect retail clients, may lead politicians to seek to eliminate conflicts of interest by imposing restrictions on the range of activities that banks can undertake, as they did in the United States in the 1930s.
- **Legal challenges in the United States.** Some of the major investment banks in the United States face years of uncertainty about claims arising from the securities fraud and scandals of the early 2000s. Court awards could cost investment banks damages running to billions of dollars.
- **Largeness dangers.** Global investment banks may have become too big and too complex to be managed effectively. Some analysts foresee promising prospects for "human-sized firms", especially in the provision of independent and impartial advice to company chief executives.

5 The buy-side: investors and asset management

The buy-side of the financial-services industry has three components: investors, investment products and asset management. The leading investors are insurance companies, pension funds, unit trusts and investment trusts, known collectively as "institutional investors". However, banks, companies, charities, overseas financial institutions and individuals are also significant investors. Investors' money is invested mostly in financial securities, the instruments through which borrower-spenders – the users of capital – raise funds.

The asset management industry provides investment products and investment services to investors of all sorts, although institutional investors are the most important clients. The asset management function is to invest the flow of money from savings, pension contributions and insurance premiums in financial assets in ways that minimise risk to capital and maximise returns so as to meet clients' financial requirements. Some institutional investors conduct the asset management function in-house, but others use outside professional asset managers.

"Asset management" is in origin an American term, but it is now commonly used in the City, along with "investment management" and "fund management", the traditional City terms, and "portfolio management". In narrowly focused City and Wall Street everyday usage, "the buy-side" is shorthand for professional institutional asset managers.

Individual investors and institutional investors

In the 19th and well into the 20th century, most investment was undertaken directly by prosperous individual investors. They turned to accountants, solicitors and bank managers for investment advice, and to stockbrokers, who executed their buy and sell orders and might pass on the latest City tips.

The rise of the institutional investors began in the 19th century when insurance companies and investment trusts started to become significant investors, followed by pension funds from the 1920s and unit trusts from the 1930s. Yet in the mid-1950s, individual investors still owned two-thirds of UK equities and institutional investors owned less than

Table 5.1 **Ownership of UK equities, 1963–2002 (%)**

	1963	1981	1992	2002
Individuals	54	28	20	14
UK institutional investors	28	57	61	50
of which:				
Insurance companies	10	20	20	20
Pension funds	6	27	32	16
Unit/investment trusts[a]	2	10	9	14
Overseas	7	4	13	32
Others[b]	11	11	6	4

a Includes other financial institutions.
b Charities, companies, public sector, banks.
Source: Office for National Statistics

one-fifth (the rest was owned by companies and banks). It was in the 1960s that the march of the institutional investors really got under way, driven particularly by the growth of pension fund assets and the transformation of the life insurance industry into a savings medium. The development of the professional asset management industry was largely a response to the growing requirements of institutional investors.

The shift away from individual investors to institutional investors as owners of UK equities since the 1960s is shown in Table 5.1. Over the four decades from the early 1960s to the early 2000s, the proportion of UK equities owned directly by individuals dropped from 54% to 14%. The decline happened despite the boost to individual share ownership in the 1980s and 1990s provided by privatisation issues and the demutualisation of building societies. From the time of Margaret Thatcher's election in 1979 to the end of the privatisation programme in the mid-1990s, the number of individual shareholders rose from 3m to 12m. However, 9m of them owned shares in three or fewer companies.

Between 1963 and 1992 the proportion of UK equities owned by institutional investors more than doubled, rising from 28% to 61%. In the 1990s the share of equities owned by UK institutional investors fell to 50%, largely as a result of a shift from equities to bonds in the asset composition of the portfolios of UK pension funds. Even so, overall institutional ownership of UK equities reached new heights in the 1990s and early 2000s because of the increase in overseas ownership

Table 5.2 **Assets of UK institutional investors, end-2002**

	£bn	%
Insurance companies	951	52
of which:		
Long-term insurance funds	853	47
General insurance funds	98	5
Self-administered pension funds[a]	621	34
Unit trusts[b]	203	11
Investment trusts	41	2
Total	1,816	100[c]

a Insurance company managed pension funds included with long-term insurance funds.
b Includes property trusts and OEICs.
c Percentages may not add up to 100 because of rounding.
Source: Office for National Statistics

(predominantly institutional investors), which soared from 13% in 1992 to 32%.

The total assets of UK institutional investors are shown in Table 5.2, which provides a general indication of their relative size and significance as investors.

Insurance companies

Insurance companies are the source of over half of the assets of UK institutional investors (see Table 5.2). Their activities are covered in Chapter 7, but their role as institutional investors is dealt with in this chapter.

There are two types of insurance business: long-term and general (see Chapter 7). Long-term insurance is mainly concerned with life insurance, and the companies that conduct it are often referred to as life insurance companies (or simply life companies). General insurance provides cover against losses from accident, fire and theft and includes motor and marine insurance. This business is conducted by general insurance companies and Lloyd's of London. Some insurance companies, known as composite companies, conduct both types of insurance, but the different categories of funds are kept separately.

The growth in the value of insurance industry investment funds is shown in Figure 5.1. More than 90% of the total comes from long-term insurance activities, which include life insurance proper, unit-linked life

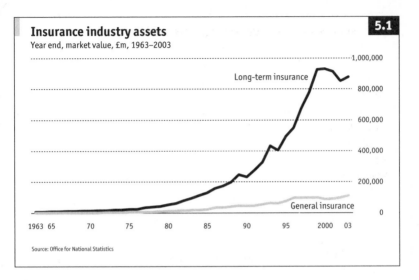

Insurance industry assets
Year end, market value, £m, 1963–2003

5.1

Long-term insurance

General insurance

1,000,000

800,000

600,000

400,000

200,000

0

1963 65   70   75   80   85   90   95   2000   03

Source: Office for National Statistics

insurance savings policies and insurance industry managed pension funds.

In return for providing insurance cover, insurance companies are paid a fee (known as a premium) by customers. General insurance policies are purchased for a short period, usually a year, and most claims arise within that period or soon after. Claims outflows diminish the volume of funds available for investment, so the assets of general insurance companies account for less than 10% of total insurance industry assets (see Table 5.2). To meet claims, which fluctuate considerably, almost two-thirds of the assets of general insurance companies comprise short-term and highly liquid assets (see Table 5.3 overleaf). Moreover, the holdings of company securities are generally the sort that are readily realisable for cash.

Long-term insurance (traditionally known as life assurance) originated in the 18th century when advances in actuarial science, the calculation of mortality risks, made it possible for companies to offer policies that paid out on someone's death. Usually these were "term life" policies, pure insurance policies that provided cover against death during a specified period but made no payment if the purchaser lived longer. Such cover was taken out by relatively prosperous people on a long-term contractual basis, generating stable income flows for the insurers. These funds were invested to meet actuarially estimated pay-out obligations. Thus from early days, the life assurance industry was

Table 5.3 **Insurance company assets, general funds, end-2002**

	%
Highly liquid	63
of which:	
current assets and balances	44
UK public-sector securities	19
Less liquid	37
of which:	
company securities	25
loans, mortgages & fixed assets	12

Source: Office for National Statistics

a significant investor in financial securities and asset management was a basic activity.

A mass-market form of life insurance known as "industrial life" insurance, paid for by weekly home collections, developed from the mid-19th century. The cheapest policies provided just for burial expenses, but for higher payments cover was available against ill health and unemployment. It was estimated that in the late 1930s a staggering 75–90% of working-class families had some form of private insurance policy. This was because there was no welfare state or National Insurance tax. The driving force in the development of mass-market industrial life insurance was the Prudential, then based in its gothic revival chateau in the City at Holborn. Premiums were collected from door to door by an army of "men from the Pru". At the peak in 1948, there were 18,000 Prudential collectors who made collections from 5m homes, providing life insurance cover to one-third of all households.

Life insurance becomes a savings medium
As people became more prosperous, a market developed for life insurance products with a savings element. For the payment of a higher premium, purchasers could buy the payment of a sum at death whenever that occurred (whole-of-life policy), thus making provision for dependants. Or they could buy the payment of a capital sum at the end of a specified period of time (endowment policy). The amount paid to purchasers could be defined at the outset, or alternatively it could be on a "with-profits" basis. With-profits policies supplement a basic sum

assured with a bonus declared by the insurer based on the performance of the fund into which premiums are paid. They are attractive if equity prices are rising and provide some protection against inflation, although they have the effect of transferring part of the performance risk to the policyholder. With-profits policies were first introduced by the Prudential in 1950, and in the 1960s as inflation gathered pace they became the most popular type of life insurance policy.

The life insurance industry was reinvented in the 1960s through the linkage of with-profits endowment life policies to unit trusts. The retention of an insurance element allowed such "unitised" insurance policies to qualify for tax relief, making them attractive savings vehicles. Most policies involved a contract by which policyholders paid regular premiums out of income and in return received life cover and a holding of unit-trust units. A further development was the single-premium bond to meet the requirements of investors with a capital sum to invest. Under this type of policy investors paid a lump sum which secured both life insurance cover and an investment that could be cashed in later. Again it was a tax feature that made such policies popular with investors: the proceeds were exempt from capital gains tax (introduced in 1962).

Unit-linked life insurance policies, which first appeared in the late 1950s, developed into a major form of saving in the 1960s and 1970s. Their early growth owed much to the vision and drive of Mark Weinberg, who made Abbey Life and later Hambro Life the leading players in the life insurance industry and introduced millions of people to life insurance as a way of saving. In particular he promoted single-premium policies, which were not subject to the restrictions on commission payments to salespeople that applied to regular-premium policies, providing a powerful incentive for the salesforce.

Tax relief on life insurance was abolished in 1984, eliminating that competitive advantage of life policies. Nonetheless, life insurance continues to be a popular form of saving. One reason appears to be the so-called "halo effect" on investment products bearing the word "insurance" (or assurance), with its associations with prudence and protection. Another is aggressive marketing, including high up-front commissions for salespeople and independent financial advisers, which has been a feature since the outset. Moreover, the dynamic development of new products – including personal pensions, which inadvertently led to the mis-selling scandal of the 1980s and 1990s (see Chapter 13) – has enabled the industry to retain its role as a leading provider of retail savings products.

Table 5.4 **Insurance company assets, long-term funds, end-2002**

	%
Highly liquid	25
of which:	
current assets and balances	10
UK public-sector securities	15
Less liquid	75
of which:	
company securities	64
property	6
loans, mortgages, fixed assets, etc	5

Source: Office for National Statistics

Premiums paid by the holders of long-term policies are invested in a range of assets that enable the companies to meet their long-term liabilities (see Table 5.4). Company securities, mostly equities but also some corporate bonds, both UK and overseas, make up almost two-thirds of long-term insurance company assets. Since the 1960s, equities have been the favoured asset class for long-term investors as a hedge against inflation and because generally they generate higher returns than bonds (although at higher risk). British insurance companies own one-fifth of quoted UK equities. Property is also a significant asset class: long-term insurance companies are major commercial landlords and developers. Cash and public-sector securities (mostly British government obligations) make up one-quarter of the assets of long-term insurance companies.

Pension funds

From the 18th century, members of the middle class made provision for their retirement and old age by purchasing an annuity – a contract between an individual and a life insurance company whereby in return for a sum of money the latter undertakes to provide a defined income for the individual from retirement to death. Annuities were often purchased with a lump sum, but endowment policies also provided a means of saving for them. In the first half of the 20th century, consumer expenditure on life insurance in the UK increased from 2% of total expenditure to 4%, mainly because of savings through endowment policies for old age. The number of people covered by life policies tripled from 2m to 6m. Many private pension policies were purchased on behalf of individual staff members by employers, constituting the earliest form of occupational pension.

Insured pension schemes

In the early 20th century, American insurance companies began to devise group insurance schemes for corporations, covering the whole of their workforce (subject to qualification criteria). Such schemes had the advantages of economies of scale and pooled risk, enabling the insurance companies to offer cover at attractive rates. Group insurance schemes were introduced in the UK in 1927 by Metropolitan Life, an American insurance company. Initially, its clients were American multinationals, such as Kodak, Woolworth and General Motors, which had subsidiaries in the UK, but indigenous firms soon also became clients. Metropolitan Life sold its UK group pension operation to Legal & General in 1933, making it the leading provider of so-called "insured pension schemes" (run by insurance companies). By the mid-1950s insurance company administered group pension schemes covered 2.3m people, the majority of those in private-sector pension schemes.

Self-administered pension schemes

Around the beginning of the 20th century some large British companies began to establish funded staff pension schemes which they ran themselves. These came to be known as "self-administered" pension schemes. They were based on the concept of the legal trust, which became the standard form for such schemes. A trust is a legal entity that separates the control of assets from the right to benefit from them. It is administered on behalf of beneficiaries by a set of trustees, whose prime duty is to safeguard the interests of beneficiaries. Assets purchased with contributions from the sponsoring employer and from staff to pay pensions are placed in a ring-fenced pension fund (hence the term "funded") administered by trustees and separate from the employer's finances. However, it was common for members of the board of directors of a sponsor company to serve as trustees. Today self-administered pension funds account for one-third of the total assets of institutional investors (see Table 5.2 on page 114).

The creation of self-administered funded occupational pension schemes was boosted by a government decision in 1921 to exempt from taxation both contributions to pension schemes and the investment

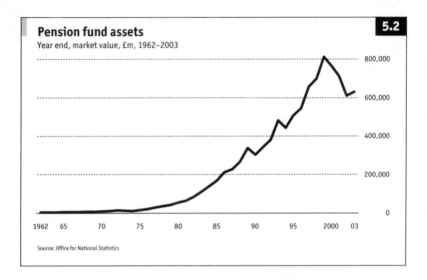

Pension fund assets
Year end, market value, £m, 1962–2003

5.2

Source: Office for National Statistics

income flowing from them. Funded occupational pension schemes were also established by local government authorities (although the pensions of other government workers are financed out of current taxation on a non-funded, pay-as-you-go basis). By the mid-1950s, 8m British workers were covered by funded occupational pension schemes: 3.7m in public-sector schemes, 2.3m in insurance company group schemes and 2m in self-administered private-sector schemes. There were 37,500 funded schemes covering one-third of the workforce.

The formation of occupational pension funds accelerated in the 1960s, and by the early 2000s there were 200,000 in existence, although three-quarters of them had fewer than six members. Total UK pension fund assets multiplied more than 150-fold between the early 1960s and the early 2000s (see Figure 5.2), by which time occupational pension schemes and private pensions provided around 40% of retirement income in the UK, the rest coming from basic state benefits paid out of taxation.

The asset holdings of self-administered pension funds have a similar pattern to those of long-term insurance companies and similar long-term liabilities (see Table 5.5). Corporate securities, mostly equities of British and overseas companies, constitute around two-thirds of the total. Property and other illiquid (but hopefully high-yield) assets roughly balance the high liquidity (but low-yield) holdings of short-term and UK public-sector assets.

Table 5.5 **Self-administered pension fund assets, end-2002**

	%
Highly liquid	19
of which:	
current assets and balances	5
UK public-sector securities	14
Less liquid	81
of which:	
company securities	65
property	5
others	11

Source: Office for National Statistics

Competition for self-administered pension fund mandates

Before the 1950s, the asset portfolios of self-administered pension funds mostly comprised investment grade bonds, making the selection of securities reasonably straightforward. But rising inflation after the second world war meant that the returns from fixed-interest securities were insufficient to meet obligations to scheme members. The solution was the adoption of a bolder investment strategy: investing in equities. This necessitated greater investment expertise than most self-administered pension schemes had in-house, creating an opening for City merchant banks and stockbrokers, as well as some large insurance companies, to provide asset management services for a fee. Increasingly, the trustees of self-administered pension funds opted to have them managed as "segregated funds", independently of other funds, by a City fund manager.

In the 1960s, believing that they would achieve a better investment performance, many firms switched from insurance company group pension schemes to self-administered schemes, assigning the asset management function to City asset managers. In response, the larger insurance companies, led by Legal & General in 1971, launched "managed funds", which were, in effect, tax-exempt unit trusts for self-administered pension funds. Managed funds gave pension fund trustees a degree of control over investment strategy through their ability to switch funds. They were also much more transparent than traditional group insurance company schemes, in which asset allocation and valuation were entirely a matter for the insurance company.

Table 5.6 **Leading UK pension funds, 2001**

	Assets under management (£bn)
British Telecom (BT)	28.9
Coal Pension Trustees Services	26.4
Electricity Pensions Services	21.4
Universities Superannuation Scheme	20.0
Royal Mail	16.0
Railways Pensions Management	15.1
BP	12.5
Lattice Group	12.2
Scottish Public Pensions Agency	12.0
Lloyds TSB Group	11.7

Source: IFSL, *Fund Management*, 2003

Today the management of the assets of smaller pension funds is generally conducted on a pooled basis, either through a managed fund run by an insurance company or a pooled fund run by an investment bank or stockbroker. Pooled funds are cheaper than funds managed on a segregated-fund basis. Some of the largest self-administered pension funds, which include some of those in Table 5.6, remain self-managed and have their own in-house asset management team, but this is now unusual. BT, the UK's largest pension fund manager, owns Hermes, the UK's third largest pension fund manager.

Pension fund trustees, many of whom are not investment specialists, engage pension fund consultants for assistance with the selection and monitoring of outside asset managers. There are around 20 firms of pension fund consultants, many of them firms of actuaries whose traditional business was advising life insurance companies and undertaking the valuation of life funds. (The actuarial profession, so the old joke goes, is for those who find accountancy too exciting.) The leading firms are Watson Wyatt, an Anglo-American entity, Bacon & Woodrow and Hymans Robertson, two UK partnerships, and two firms owned by American insurance brokers William M Mercer, part of Marsh & MacLennan, and Aon Consulting. Consultant actuaries play an important role in appointing asset managers. They draw up a shortlist of firms that will make presentations to fund trustees and assist the trustees with their choice.

Types of pension fund mandate

Traditionally, asset management firms were appointed to run segregated pension funds on what is known as a "balanced" basis. Under a so-called "balanced appointment", the asset allocation decision – the key strategic decision about the proportion of the fund that should be invested in equities, bonds and other asset classes – is delegated to the asset manager. Having determined the asset allocation, the asset manager assigns tranches of the fund to the management of in-house experts in the respective UK and overseas asset classes.

"Specialist" pension fund management, the prevalent form in the United States, is an alternative to balanced management. Under a specialist arrangement, it is the trustees, assisted by pension fund consultants, who make the asset allocation decision. The trustees divide the fund into a variety of asset classes, such as domestic equities, foreign equities, bonds or property, and award mandates to the leading managers in each asset class from a variety of asset management firms.

Proponents of specialist management argue that it gives trustees more control and allows managers to be set more demanding performance targets. However, it is more expensive than balanced management, in terms of both fees and demands on trustees. The debate about the merits of balanced as against specialist fund management became quite heated in the UK in the 1990s and early 2000s, in part because American asset management firms and pension fund consultants were trying to break into the UK market and promoted their approach as superior to the UK model. Nonetheless, specialist fund management caught on, and between 1998 and 2002 specialist pension fund mandates as a proportion of total mandates rose from 37% to 47%.

This shift has been associated with another trend: the growth of "passive management". Traditional asset management was "active", in the sense that fund managers used their judgment to buy and sell securities to enhance performance. However, as funds grew bigger it became increasingly difficult to move in or out of many shares without turning prices against an active manager. Moreover, the 2002 Sandler Review and other studies criticised the poor performance of UK actively managed funds. Sandler reported that the average UK unit trust under-performed the equity market by 2.5% a year because of high fees and poor share selection, and an FSA study in 1999 found that an investor would have to put £1.55 into an actively managed retail fund to get a return equivalent to £1 invested directly in the market. Although there were active managers who consistently outperformed the market, it was difficult for retail investors to identify them because of the plethora of subjective marketing material issued by asset management firms.

Since one of the benchmarks against which fund managers' performance is assessed is a prescribed share price index, it became more and more tempting simply to track the index. Funds that track an index are called "passive" or "tracker" funds. One virtue is that they are cheap to run since they require no costly research or analysis and in theory can virtually be handed over to a computer. (In practice, tracking an index is a lot trickier than it sounds.) However, some supposedly actively managed funds closely replicate an index and are therefore labelled "closet indexer" or "index hugger".

The index mostly used for benchmarking purposes in the UK is the FT Actuaries All-Share Index. Launched in 1962, the All-Share Index encompasses the largest 800 or so British companies that account for 98% of the total capitalisation of the London stockmarket. For asset managers, it is the performance of their pooled fund (or managed fund for insurance companies) against the All-Share Index that is the basis of performance ratings.

Specialist management often features a combination of tracker funds and specialist mandates. This is known as the core-satellite model. A portion (the core) of the fund is assigned to tracker funds and the rest is divided among 10–20 specialist mandates for investment in promising asset classes. The lower cost of passive fund management is offset against the higher fees paid to specialist managers.

Peer group comparison is an alternative benchmark used to assess the performance of pension fund managers and unit trusts. Industry performance data are collected and published by two UK pensions industry ratings agencies, CAPS, which is owned by three firms of consultant actuaries, and WM Company, a subsidiary of Deutsche Bank. The ambition of asset managers is to achieve consistently a position in the upper quartile (top 25%) or at least the top two quartiles (that is, above the average).

How a pension fund is managed is heavily influenced by the fund's age. Younger funds are generally biased towards equities to maximise long-term growth, whereas more mature funds have heavier weightings of bonds and cash to provide greater predictability of income and liquidity to pay pension entitlements. Pension funds have tax advantages for savers compared with other types of funds, although they have to wait until retirement to benefit.

Defined benefit to defined contribution

An important development in funded pensions in the UK in the 1990s and 2000s was the shift from the traditional "defined benefit" basis to a "defined contribution" basis, mirroring a similar trend in the United States. In defined benefit schemes, the employer guarantees beneficiaries a pension related to final salary and years of contributions. In defined contribution schemes (also known as money purchase schemes), the contributions are fixed but retirement benefits depend on the performance of the fund. Upon retirement, the amount in an individual defined contribution plan is converted into an annuity, making the value of the pension dependent upon the performance of the fund at the point of retirement.

Between 1999 and 2001 the proportion of pension scheme sponsors in the UK offering defined contribution schemes rose from 26% to 45%, and it was predicted that they would soon become the prevalent type of funded pension scheme. In most cases, companies set up a defined contribution scheme in parallel with an existing defined benefit scheme, which was then closed to new entrants. The impetus behind the shift to defined contribution schemes was legislative and regulatory changes that potentially increased companies' exposure to defined benefit pension claims:

◪ The Pensions Act 1995 imposed a new solvency test for defined benefit schemes which increased an employer's exposure to the risk of having to make top-ups. This legislation was a response to Robert Maxwell's raiding of the Mirror Group pension fund to shore up his tottering media empire (see Chapter 13).

◪ Accounting standard FRS17, issued in June 2001, changed the basis on which companies report pension assets and liabilities, making them wary of commitments that might undermine their profits performance (and share price).

◪ The removal by the chancellor, Gordon Brown, of dividend tax credits for pension funds in 1997 (a so-called "stealth tax") diverted £5.5 billion annually from pension schemes to the Treasury, increasing the likelihood of underfunding and again raising the potential burden of defined benefit schemes to their sponsors.

A new form of pension, a "stakeholder pension", was introduced by the government in April 2001 with the aim of encouraging pension saving by individuals who do not have access to a conventional occupational scheme. Stakeholder pensions combine elements of occupational schemes and retail private pension products. There is a government-imposed cap on charges of 1% of funds under management, which is one reason why they have not proved an attractive proposition for pension providers. However, the tax advantages for wealthy people who can invest in stakeholder pensions for their children, grandchildren and even friends have given stakeholder pensions a boost.

The ageing of the UK's population and the long-drawn-out pensions mis-selling scandal (see Chapter 13) pushed pensions and savings up the political agenda, prompting the government to commission several reviews that reported in the early 2000s:

- The Myners Review (2001) on the asset management industry recommended greater transparency of charges and simplification of procedures to promote competition.
- The Pickering Review (2002) on private pension legislation proposed a radical simplification of pensions legislation and of the administrative burdens on schemes and employers.
- The Sandler Review (2002) on the savings industry criticised the poor performance of retail savings products and recommended the introduction of cheaper and simpler savings products that could be sold to private investors directly, without the cost of an independent financial adviser.

Collective investment institutions

Investment through a professionally managed collective investment institution has many advantages over direct investment by individuals. The pooling of investors' funds allows a greater degree of diversification of assets, affording increased security for capital. Professional asset management provides more skilled and better researched investment, enhancing performance. Moreover, professional asset managers are better able to achieve the investment objectives of savers regarding income, growth, risk, liquidity and tax. There are three main types of collective investment institution: unit trusts, open-ended investment companies (OEICs) and investment trusts.

Unit trusts

Unit trusts are the most popular type of collective investment vehicle, their aggregate assets comprising 11% of the total assets of institutional investors (see Table 5.2 on page 114). A unit trust is a fund made up of contributions from individual investors or companies. Investors receive a share of the returns generated by the fund. Unit trusts are trusts in the legal sense, with a trustee, usually a bank or insurance company, acting as guardian of the assets on behalf of investors. A separate management company is responsible for investment decisions, but generally it has close ties with the trustees. A unit trust operates under a trust deed that specifies the terms and conditions of its activities. Unit trust units are predominantly held directly by individuals, although they are also held on behalf of individuals by life insurance companies that run unit-linked life insurance policies.

Unit trusts are "open end" funds, meaning that the number of shares (units) is not fixed but expands (or contracts) depending on investor demand. There is no secondary market for units; purchases and sales of units are made with the trust management company (although other intermediaries may act as an agent in the transaction). The price at which investors buy and sell units is determined by the value of the underlying assets divided by the number of units outstanding. The price of units is calculated daily.

Unit-holders often regard their holdings of unit trusts as more akin to a deposit account than a long-term investment. Whereas life insurance companies, pension funds and investment trusts are long-term holders of securities, unit trusts are much more active buyers and sellers, driven by inflows and outflows of funds. They thus have a considerable impact on the equity market. The performance of unit trusts is under constant scrutiny in the financial press, subjecting them to pressure for short-term results. Largely for this reason they hold around 90% in equities, mostly the securities of major British and overseas corporations.

The first UK unit trust was established in 1931 by M&G (now owned by Prudential). Based on the example of American mutual funds, it was intended as an investment vehicle for investors of modest means; buyers and sellers had no need for a stockbroker and units were available in small denominations. Unit trusts proved to be a successful innovation and by 1939 there were 96 of them with total assets of £80m, already about a quarter of the volume of the assets of the longer-established investment trusts.

The growth of unit trust business came to a standstill for a generation in 1939 with the outbreak of war, and the high post-war levels of taxation and inflation left little disposable income for personal saving. The removal of capital market controls in 1958 led to an upsurge in unit trust formation and investment: unit trust assets, which had fallen to £60m in

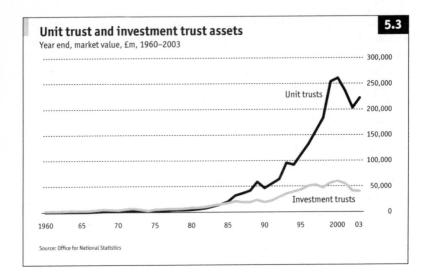

5.3

Unit trust and investment trust assets
Year end, market value, £m, 1960–2003

Unit trusts

Investment trusts

300,000
250,000
200,000
150,000
100,000
50,000
0

1960 65 70 75 80 85 90 95 2000 03

Source: Office for National Statistics

1957, surged to £200m in 1960. By 1972 unit trust assets had increased 13-fold to £2.6 billion.

Driving the growth of the unit trust industry in the 1960s and 1970s was the marketing of its products by life insurance companies as tax-efficient savings products. Expansion resumed after the stockmarket slump of the mid-1970s and continued with only temporary setbacks until the market downturn that began in 2000 (see Figure 5.3). A new stimulus was the extension of the scope of Personal Equity Plans (PEPs) to include unit trusts and investment trusts in 1989. (PEPs, which had been introduced in 1987 as a tax-free saving mechanism for small savers, were replaced by Individual Savings Accounts – ISAs – in 1999.) Unit trust assets overtook those of investment trusts in 1985 and by the early 2000s were four-times greater (see Figure 5.3). In 2003 the 1,950 UK unit trusts had total assets of £222 billion, which were owned by 19m unit-holder accounts.

Unit trusts are mostly managed on a group basis, with management companies running a number of unit trusts with a range of investment strategies. This provides managerial economies of scale in infrastructure and research. Some management groups are independent specialists, but many are linked to insurance companies, stockbrokers, investment banks and clearing banks. In the 1960s, 1970s and 1980s there was an influx of new entrants to the unit trust management business and the number of management groups rose from 13 to a peak of

Table 5.7 **Leading unit trust management groups,[a] 2003**

	Funds under management (£bn)
Fidelity Investments	18.5
Scottish Widows Unit Trust Managers	10.6
Invesco Perpetual	10.5
Threadneedle Investments	10.5
Legal & General Unit Trust Managers	9.4
M&G Group	8.5
Schroder Investments	8.2
Halifax Investment Fund Managers	6.4
Gartmore Investment Management	6.3
SLTM	5.6

a Includes unit trusts, OEICs, PEPs and ISAs.
Source: Investment Management Association

162 in 1989. In the 1990s and early 2000s there was consolidation in the industry and by 2002 the number of management groups had fallen to 130. The industry is represented by the Investment Management Association (IMA), the trade body for the UK's asset management industry.

The UK's leading unit trust management companies in 2003 are shown in Table 5.7. The performance of actively managed retail funds has come in for considerable criticism. In 2002 the Sandler Review reported that the average UK unit trust underperformed the equity market by 2.5% a year because of high charges and poor investment selection. Yet over nine-tenths of retail investors chose actively managed funds rather than tracker funds, probably, the review suggested, because they pay higher commission rates to so-called independent financial advisers. Hedge funds offered the prospect of higher returns, but at greater risk, and with minimum investments of £30,000 were not an option for most retail investors.

Open-ended investment companies

An OEIC (pronounced "oik") is a hybrid of an investment trust and a unit trust. OEICs came into existence in 1997 as a result of European legislation to create a single European market for investment products. They are based not on trust law but on a specially framed company law, and

Table 5.8 **Principal features of unit trusts, OEICs and investment trusts**

	Unit trusts	OEICs	Investment trusts
Legal structure	Trust	Company	Company
Nature of fund	Expands and contracts on demand	Expands and contracts on demand	Fixed number of shares in issue
Investor's holdings	Units	Shares	Shares
Independent supervision	By trustee	By depository; optional independent directors	Stock exchange; requires independent directors
Investment restrictions	Clearly defined rules on what investments the manager may make	Clearly defined rules on what investments the manager may make	Almost unlimited investments allowed subject to approval by board
Stock exchange listing	Not listed in practice	Not listed in practice	Listed
Price system	Dual price: different buy and sell prices	Single price	Dual price: different buy and sell prices
Frequency of valuation	Normally daily	Normally daily	Normally once a month
Price	Reflects value of investments in fund (net asset value) with changes in spread	Reflects value of investments in fund (net asset value) with changes shown separately	Varies according to market sentiment and charges are shown separately

Source: Association of Unit Trusts and Investment Funds

like investment trusts they are listed on the stock exchange. However, OEICs function in a similar way to unit trusts, expanding and contracting in response to purchases and sales by investors. Again like unit trusts, the shares reflect the value of the fund and do not trade at a discount or a premium. In common with European practice, OEIC units have a single price rather than the separate buying and selling prices of unit trusts, so money is made through commission. The principal features of unit trusts, OEICs and investment trusts are summarised in Table 5.8.

All new unit trusts are structured as OEICs, and unit-holders can vote to convert existing unit trusts to OEICs. Around one-third of aggregate unit trust and OEIC assets is held by OEICs, and it is expected that traditional unit trusts will disappear by the end of the first decade of the 2000s.

Investment trusts

Investment trusts, the original collective investment institution, now have assets only one-fifth as large as those of unit trusts, although this comparison under-represents their importance as City investment vehicles. Investment trusts are quoted companies that invest in the shares and securities of other companies, raising funds for investment through the issue of shares. (Despite the name, in the legal sense they are companies not trusts.) Investors may subscribe for a new issue of shares by an investment trust, or they may buy (or sell) existing shares on the stockmarket. Because the number of issued shares is finite, investment trusts are referred to as "closed-end funds". As companies, investment trusts are able to raise additional funds by borrowing, usually through the issue of bonds, with the aim of enhancing returns to shareholders (though also increasing risk).

The price of investment trust shares is set by demand and supply for these securities in the stockmarket. Usually the quoted share price is at a significant discount to the net asset value – the quoted value of the investment trust's investments in the securities of other companies. One reason for this discount is the risk engendered by the trust's borrowing or "gearing". The level of discount varies considerably, but the wider the discrepancy the more tempting it is for someone to mount a takeover bid for the shares to capture the value of the discount; to pay 60p or 70p for assets worth £1 is, as they say, "a no-brainer".

Traditional investment trusts were so-called "general" trusts, which sought to optimise a blended total return of income and growth. Most investment trusts formed since the 1980s have specialised in a particular market sector, size or type of company, or geographical region. They are suitable vehicles for investments with a long-term pay-back, or for investments in assets with poor liquidity but exciting growth prospects, such as emerging markets and private equity. The stability of their funding means that they have no need to be active traders and their impact on stockmarket activity is small.

Investment trusts are run by boards of directors, who have a legal responsibility to pursue the interests of shareholders. Most investment trusts are managed by an external asset management firm, which is appointed by the board and makes the investment decisions. City and Scottish asset management firms typically serve a cluster of connected investment trusts. Trusts that employ in-house asset managers are known as "self-managed". The industry is represented by the Association of Investment Trust Companies, formed in 1932.

The first investment trusts were set up in the 1860s, just a few years after legislation that limited the liability of shareholders for a company's debts to the extent of their shareholdings, thereby ushering in modern company finance and equity investment. They became popular investment vehicles in the 1880s because interest rates fell below dividend yields and it became profitable to borrow money and reinvest it in shares. At the start of the first world war there were 65 City-based investment trust companies and 35 Scottish ones; Edinburgh remains to this day an important centre for investment trust management. They focused on foreign bonds and UK equities, asset classes that required professional investment skills.

There was further expansion in the 1920s and 1930s, the latter also a decade of low interest rates; by the mid-1930s there were 123 City and 76 Scottish investment trusts. Growth was interrupted by the second world war but resumed in the 1950s. The 1960s were a high point: the number of trusts peaked in 1964 at almost 350 and their assets multiplied almost fourfold over the years 1960–72 (see Figure 5.3 on page 128). Investment trust asset managers were early converts to the "cult of the equity", and by the mid-1950s their portfolios had 90% equity weightings. This is still the case, with the difference that the proportion of shares of overseas and private companies has grown.

The expansion of investment trusts in the 1950s and 1960s was driven by demand for their securities from the rapidly growing life insurance companies and pension funds, many of which were still managed in-house. Post-war price inflation necessitated higher holdings of equities, but in-house fund managers lacked the expertise and resources required for equity research. Investment trusts provided them with a ready-made means of diversification into equities and overseas securities. At the same time, private investors were selling investment trust shares and putting their savings into unit trusts and unit-linked life insurance policies. The outcome was that by the early 1970s, institutional investors owned three-quarters of investment trust shares.

Investment trusts languished in the 1970s, and total assets in 1980 were lower than in 1972. The losses inflicted by the slump in share prices in 1973–74, exacerbated by gearing, were a factor. More fundamental was the waning interest of institutional investors, who were developing their own in-house investment expertise or assigning the asset management function to outside asset managers. The latter were eager to justify their fees by making their own portfolio decisions, rather than buying somebody else's through an investment trust (although it was often the same City merchant banks and stockbrokers that managed many of the investment trusts). The abolition of exchange controls in the UK in 1979, allowing institutional investors freely to buy foreign securities, further diminished the investment trusts' market niche.

Weak demand for investment trust shares from both individual and institutional investors led to discounts to net asset value as high as 40% in the mid-1970s. The discounts made investment trusts vulnerable to takeover bids by financial predators seeking to capture the discrepancy in values. In the 1970s and 1980s many investment trusts succumbed to unwelcome takeover bids. Two of the most active bidders were the British Rail and British Coal pension funds, for which the acquisition of an investment trust was a discount device for making substantial share purchases without moving the market against them. To forestall such plunder, many investment trusts were liquidated or converted into unit trusts to secure the discount for all shareholders. By the early 1990s the number of investment trusts had fallen to 230, and many believed that it was an institution that had had its day.

But during the 1990s there was a revival because investment trusts were found to be suitable vehicles for investment in emerging markets, new technologies and private companies, which provided some of the potentially most lucrative (and risky) investment opportunities of the 1990s and early 2000s. The number of trusts rose from 232 in 1991 to 358 in 2003, and total assets grew from £24 billion to £56 billion. These totals were made up of 258 conventional trusts with assets of £48 billion and 100 split capital trusts with assets of £8 billion.

In the 1990s there was a boom in the formation and marketing of split capital investment trusts, many of which ran into difficulties when the stockmarket turned down in spring 2000 (see Chapter 13). In summer 2003 the Association of Investment Trust Companies (AITC) established the AITC Foundation to provide financial assistance to people suffering severe financial hardship as a result of having lost money in split capital investment trusts (see Chapter 13).

Investment clubs

Investment clubs enable their members to pool their funds, share their knowledge, intuition and the responsibility for buying decisions, and save money on dealing costs. The formation of investment clubs is correlated with rising markets. During the first boom in the 1960s, imitating a fashion in the United States, more than 2,000 clubs were formed. There were further upsurges during the bull markets of the 1980s and 1990s.

Asset management

Professional asset managers invest funds on behalf of institutional investors and private clients to obtain a better investment performance than their clients could achieve themselves. Their investment skills, superior research capabilities, specialist knowledge and experience enable them, in theory at least, to build diversified investment portfolios that fulfil the investment objectives of their clients.

It is estimated that 39,000 people worked in asset management in London at the beginning of 2004, 80% of the industry's UK workforce. There are also around 6,000 asset management jobs in Edinburgh and Glasgow and 2,000 elsewhere. A further 14,000 people are employed around the country by retail stockbrokers in the management of private client funds. Among participants in a 2000 survey of member firms by the IMA, the largest asset management firm had 1,360 London staff and the average size was 322. Typically, half of each firm's staff was engaged in the management, administration or selling of investment products, and the other half worked in support capacities. Respondent firms employed 3,700 fund managers, the elite of the industry and the principal investment decision-makers.

In 2004, assets under management in the UK totalled £3,000 billion, more than ten times the £284 billion-worth of assets under management in 1989. Institutional investors account for 86% of the assets managed by the industry in the UK: UK institutional investors for 58% and overseas institutional investors for 28% (see Table 5.9).

Institutional assets consist of funds managed on behalf of pension funds, unit trusts, investment trusts, OEICs, insurance companies, central banks, charities and colleges. Retail and private client funds are investments owned directly by individuals or managed by their financial adviser or stockbroker.

It is estimated that in 2001 the asset management industry's revenue from fees was £7.6 billion, of which £6.2 billion came from institutional clients and £1.4 billion from private clients. The sector's contribution to

Table 5.9 **Assets under management in the UK, 2003**

	%
UK institutional investors	58
Overseas institutional investors	28
UK retail and private clients	11
Overseas private clients	3

Source: Corporation of London, *The City's Importance to the EU Economy 2004*, 2004

the UK economy was equivalent to 0.6% of GDP, about one-tenth of the financial sector's total 5.3% contribution to GDP. Net exports of UK asset management reached £600m in 2001, three times as much as in 1990 (£202m). UK asset management also contributed £12.1 billion in net exports from portfolio investment by financial institutions. However, the overseas ownership of many asset management firms means that there was also a net outflow of profits and dividends to overseas parents and shareholders.

Equities are the largest asset class held by UK asset managers, accounting for 54% of the total (34% overseas and 20% UK equities). The others are bonds (24%), money market assets (12%), and property, venture capital funds and hedge fund investments (10% – see Table 5.10).

Development of the asset management industry

The development of the UK's asset management industry is complex and fragmented. Asset management expertise evolved simultaneously in several different contexts in the 19th and early 20th centuries. It

Table 5.10 **Asset allocations of UK asset managers, 2002**

	%
Overseas equities	34
UK equities	20
Bonds	24
Money markets	12
Property, venture capital, hedge funds, etc	10

Source: Corporation of London, *The City's Importance to the EU Economy 2004*, 2004

developed in life insurance companies, which were managing the investment of revenues from life and endowment policies. Accountants, solicitors and bank managers were also sources of investment know-how, assisting clients with the management of personal fortunes and tax matters. Investment expertise developed, too, in City stock-brokers and merchant banks, initially in connection with the management of the money of the partners and their families and friends. In the City, and in Scotland, investment expertise was deployed in the formation and management of investment trusts, the earliest collective savings institutions.

The early corporate pensions industry was heavily reliant on asset management and administration services provided by the insurance industry. Insurance company group schemes were attractive to small and medium-sized firms for several reasons: economies of scale cut administration costs; the pooling of funds reduced risk; and experienced asset management produced, in theory, better investment returns than could be achieved by the asset managers' clients. However, larger firms increasingly opted for self-administered pension funds, taking advantage of tax concessions granted to this form of pension provision in 1921. To do so they hired actuaries, accountants and brokers to undertake asset management in-house.

After the second world war the surge in inflation led self-administered pension funds to engage the services of professional City asset managers. City firms also developed mass-market unit trusts, often linked to a life policy to gain tax relief. Life insurance companies diversified, reinventing life insurance as a tax-efficient retail savings medium and entering the unit trust business. They also competed for pension fund mandates through their managed funds and developed new products such as personal pensions.

The abolition of exchange controls in the UK in 1979 opened up new opportunities in overseas asset management for City merchant banks and securities firms, which serviced the international diversification of the portfolios of UK institutional investors. Even more important was the flood of money from American pension funds in pursuit of diversification into overseas investments, the so-called ERISA (Employee Retirement Income Security Act) funds. An ERISA boom started in 1980 and over the following two decades the volume of American holdings of overseas securities grew from almost nothing to around $500 billion. Much of this build-up was handled by specialist mandates awarded to London-based asset managers.

Structure of the asset management industry

The asset management industry today can be broadly divided into two parts: in-house "captive" investment departments or subsidiaries and outside providers that undertake asset management services for a fee. Captive investment departments or subsidiaries service parent institutional investors: insurance companies and self-managed pension funds.

There are three main external fee-earning providers of asset management services:

- Financial conglomerates, such as investment banks and commercial banks, conduct asset management as one of a number of financial services activities (see Chapter 4). They are required to maintain internal barriers ("Chinese walls") between their asset management and their securities and investment banking activities. This means that there is little in-firm synergy between asset management and other activities. Financial services conglomerates play a prominent role in asset management because of its profitability, the stability of earnings (in contrast to the volatility of investment banking revenues) and the importance of reputation and brand for marketing asset management products.
- Insurance companies, which offer asset management services for outside clients, as well as providing them for their parent company. The work may be undertaken either by an investment department or a by separate specialist subsidiary. The provision of pension fund management services to outside clients spreads the cost of research and administration over a larger volume of business and provides an external check on performance.
- Independent asset managers, in the form of specialist firms not linked to any banking, securities or insurance group. As well as large independent firms such as Schroders, there are a number of smaller independent "boutiques", such as Liontrust in London and Baillie Gifford in Edinburgh.

Asset management activity is evenly divided between the three principal providers (see Table 5.11 overleaf).

The UK asset management market is highly concentrated, with the top five firms accounting for no less than 60% of the pool of assets managed by the 30 largest asset managers. The level of concentration has increased because of mergers and acquisitions in the global asset

Table 5.11 **Asset managers' share of UK assets under management, 2001**

	%
Financial conglomerates	35
Independent asset managers	34
Insurance companies	29
Self-managed pension funds	2

Source: Corporation of London, *The City's Importance to the EU Economy 2004*, 2004

management industry. Consolidation has been driven by the pursuit of more funds under management, broader management skills, greater marketing reach, better distribution channels and new clients on an international basis, as well as the need to develop costly administrative and information technology systems. The leading UK-owned asset management firms are shown in Table 5.12.

A survey in 2000 of Investment Management Association (IMA) members (in which 69 out of 76 participated) revealed that 35 firms were British-owned, 32 were foreign-owned and two were joint UK-foreign owned. A significant distinction exists between firms that form part of an international group, which conducts asset management both in the UK and overseas, and firms that are active only in the UK. In the IMA

Table 5.12 **Leading UK-owned asset management firms, 2001**

	Assets under management (£bn)
Barclays Global Investors	530
Amvescap	274
Aviva	209
HSBC Holdings	196
Prudential M&G	152
Legal & General Group	122
Schroders	110
Standard Life Assurance	82
Lloyds TSB Group	78
HBOS Group (Insight)	63

Source: IFSL, *Fund Management*, 2003

Table 5.13 **Ownership of UK asset management firms, 2000**

	Number of firms	Assets managed by UK firms		Assets managed worldwide, incl UK
		£bn	%	£bn
International group of which:	36	1,338	66	6,273
UK-owned	8	572	28	1,230
foreign-owned	28	766	38	5,043
UK-only business of which:	33	682	34	
UK-owned	27	583	29	
foreign-owned	4	81	4	
joint UK/foreign	2	18	1	
Total	69	2,020	100	6,273

Source: IMA, *Fund Management Survey 2000*

survey the international group firms, comprising 8 UK-owned and 28 foreign-owned firms, managed 66% of UK assets under management, double the amount managed by the 33 firms active only in the UK (see Table 5.13). The £1,338 billion of assets managed by the international group in the UK constituted one-fifth of the total of £6,273 billion funds under management by the international group worldwide.

The international group is headed by the world's leading wealth managers (pension fund assets and private banking business). Globally, the industry has consolidated into a league of very large firms and a host of smaller firms. Each of the ten leading global wealth managers has assets under management worth at least €500 billion and totalling €8,066 billion, which constitutes 38% of the €21,376 billion of assets managed by the world's wealth managers (see Table 5.14 overleaf).

In the late 1990s and early 2000s there was an acceleration in several related trends, leading to a fundamental restructuring of the asset management industry in London. First, there was a big increase in the volume of funds allocated by pension fund trustees to tracker funds to deliver benchmark returns far more cheaply than could be achieved by active management. The principal beneficiaries were a set of UK tracker-fund managers led by Barclays Global Investors and Legal & General, whose assets under management grew by 40% and 21% respectively in

Table 5.14 **Leading global wealth managers, 2002**

Firm	Country	Worldwide assets under management (€bn)
UBS	Switzerland	1,404
Allianz Group	Germany	989
Fidelity Investments	United States	831
Credit Suisse Group	Switzerland	821
AXA Group	France	742
State Street Corporation	United States	726
Deutsche Bank	Germany	725
Barclays Global Investors	UK	706
Vanguard Group	United States	565
Mellon Financial Corporation	United States	553
Total		8,066
Total all firms		21,376

Source: *Financial Times*, February 16th 2004

2003. Second, there was substantial expansion in pension fund portfolio weightings for hedge funds and private equity funds in the hope of achieving higher performance (though at higher management fees). The outcome was the emergence of a so-called "barbell" effect – as in weightlifting – with money flowing to both ends of the bar, tracker funds at one end and hedge funds at the other. This left the middle ground, the traditional core of the industry focused on balanced mandates and active management, being steadily drained of funds. The outcome was a scramble by asset management firms to develop new products to offer clients to meet the changes in the marketplace.

The economics of asset management

Fees paid to asset managers are based on the market value of their clients' portfolios at the end of a set accounting period. Overhead costs for asset management firms are substantial and include the expenses of fund management, research, marketing and back-office administration. But having incurred the costs necessary to deliver a competitive professional quality of service, the marginal cost associated with additional business is minimal if not zero. Thus higher levels of funds under management generate higher profit margins. As an industry consultant says:

"It's a scale game. The more money you manage, the more profitable you can be. It is a fact that a fund with €1m is as hard to run as a fund with €100m."

The basis of remuneration of asset management firms means that they benefit from rising equity prices. Although share prices do sometimes fall substantially, as in 1973–74, 1987 and 2000–02, the long-term trend since the second world war has been for prices to rise (see Chapter 2). The increase in market values generates higher fees for asset managers with no additional costs, meaning that the increase should flow directly to profits. As long as costs are kept under control, this market effect (also called the endowment effect) alone ensures profits growth. Winning additional mandates is a bonus. Conversely, a downturn in share prices will lead to a reduction in fee income, as will a loss of clients to rival asset managers.

In the 1990s, a decade in which the FTSE 100 index rose from 2,200 to 6,720, asset management was a highly profitable industry. Estimates suggest a gross profit margin of 20–25% for the industry overall in most of these years. These returns were achieved despite cost increases at an annual compound rate of 8% in the years 1993–97 and 18% in 1998–2000. The principal causes of the cost inflation were increased marketing expenses and higher levels of remuneration, particularly for key fund managers and analysts. The increase in costs left the industry vulnerable to a market downturn, which when it arrived in 2000 caused problems for many firms.

The profitability of the asset management industry in the 1990s was the outcome of not only the rising stockmarket and substantial flows of new business but also the existence of barriers to entry into the business. The process by which firms are admitted to the selection process for pension fund mandates has been one such hurdle: generally, only established firms are considered. A related factor, it has been argued, is the importance of reputation in asset management. Clients prefer familiar and highly regarded asset managers, in the hope of buying high-quality performance (and also, no doubt, as a way of covering their backs if investment performance is not so good). The acquisition of reputation requires time and resources, protecting established firms against new entrants.

There are two sorts of reputation in asset management: performance and trust. Performance means beating, or at least matching, whatever benchmark is used to judge investment return. It is the key to winning and retaining (and losing) institutional clients and is keenly monitored by trustees and consultant actuaries. Changing asset managers is a costly and disruptive process for all concerned and performance is judged over a three-year or five-year rolling period. In the case of balanced manage-ment mandates, changes of asset managers are infrequent, with the result that the composition of the industry's leading firms changes slowly, almost regardless of how they perform in the short term.

Trust – meaning a reputation for soundness, security and reliability – is particularly important for attracting business from retail savers. Unlike other major items of expenditure, such as a house or a car, pur-chasers of investment products are unable to judge exactly what they are buying since the outcome lies in the future. Historic performance potentially sheds some light, but differentiating between competing per-formance claims is difficult for ordinary people.

Paradoxically, the importance of trust for the retail market has allowed companies with brand names associated with trustworthiness by consumers, but no experience in asset management, to enter the unit trust or personal pensions markets, such as retailers Marks & Spencer, Sainsbury and Tesco, and Virgin (a conglomerate). These non-financial firms have used their powerful brand names and convenience to market their financial products to retail customers. However, their involvement is cosmetic since the asset management function and administration are contracted out to professional asset management firms.

With the exception of these high-street brands, vertical integration between savings products and asset management is the norm. Most life insurance companies that sell life insurance products and banks that market unit and investment trust products undertake the asset manage-ment of the revenues generated by these sales in-house. Thus competi-tion among providers of asset management services to win funds to manage focuses principally on self-administered pension funds, over-seas institutional investors and private clients.

Asset management products
Wholesale, retail and private clients purchase products they believe are appropriate to their requirements, taking into account regulatory and tax factors. The principal products offered by asset management firms are as follows:

- Segregated fund. Assets belonging to a single client are managed independently from those of other funds under a fund manager's control.

- Pooled fund. A tax-exempt unit trust for pension funds in which a number of funds hold units.
- Life fund. Long-term savings products that provide purchasers with a lump sum at the end of a defined period and include life insurance cover (see page 117). These are still going strong, despite the abolition of tax relief on such products in 1984.
- Endowment policies. Long-term savings products purchased with the aim that they will more than pay off a residential property mortgage at the end of its term.
- Insurance fund. The management of a pool of premiums paid by clients (see page 121). The fund manager must maximise investment returns and ensure that cash is available to meet claims.
- Index tracking funds. "Passive" funds that track an equity index (see page 124). They have been increasingly popular because of strong performance relative to "active" management and lower management fees. Since it is impossible to replicate an index entirely, the management skill is to minimise deviation (tracking error) between the returns to the fund and the index it is tracking.
- Unit trusts. Collective investment vehicles that allow small investors to benefit from diversification of risk and professional asset management (see pages 126–29). Specialist unit trusts are also used by segregated fund managers to gain exposure to a range of markets, using a "fund of funds" approach to fulfil a market strategy.
- OEICs. Recent collective investment entities that are replacing unit trusts (see pages 129–31).
- Investment trusts. Collective investment companies (see pages 131–33).
- Hedge funds. Investment funds that assume a high degree of risk in the hope of achieving high returns (see below).
- Private wealth management. Investment and money management services for high net worth (rich) private clients (see pages 146–47).
- Private equity/venture capital funds. Funds subscribed by investors to finance privately owned businesses (see pages 147–49).

Hedge funds
There is no legal definition of a hedge fund. A common characteristic is that they aim for an absolute return, unlike asset managers who

measure their returns against a benchmark. Other common characteristics are incentive-based fees – typically a hefty 20% of profits above a threshold plus a 1.5–2% annual management fee – and shared risk, with the hedge fund itself subscribing some of the fund's capital. Hedge funds use a number of high-risk investment techniques that are unavailable or inappropriate for asset managers running unit trusts or pension funds and are closer to the activities of investment banks' proprietary trading desks. The latter have been described as "the mothers of hedge funds", and the early 2000s boom in proprietary trading and prime brokerage have given some investment banks risk profiles increasingly resembling those of hedge funds (see Chapter 4).

Hedge funds attempt to make money out of price inefficiencies, adopting a variety of strategies from buying commodity futures to betting on currencies. Operational techniques include the following:

- Short selling. The sale of securities or currencies not owned by a fund that are predicted to fall in value. Aggressive short selling may itself lead to the anticipated fall in price, coming close to market manipulation.
- Leverage (gearing). The use of borrowing to enhance the scale and profitability of operations, particularly through derivatives. Since a fund needs only to cover a derivatives exchange's margin requirements (a fractional down payment) it can build up a large position based on limited capital.
- Arbitrage. The simultaneous buying and selling of a financial instrument in different markets to profit from the difference in price. Such opportunities are increasingly rare and transient in developed-world markets, but there is plenty of scope in emerging markets.

Hedge funds hit the headlines in 1992 when George Soros bet $10 billion that sterling would be forced out of the EU's Exchange Rate Mechanism, and made $1 billion profit when his prediction came true (see Chapter 2). They were back on the front pages in 1998 when Long-Term Capital Management, a giant American hedge fund, supposedly run by some of the most brilliant brains on Wall Street, collapsed. So large were its potential liabilities that the Federal Reserve deemed it a threat to the international banking system and obliged its shareholders to recapitalise it to the tune of $3.6 billion to allow an orderly unwinding of its positions.

Hedge funds boomed in the early 2000s following the downturn in the major equity markets that led to poor returns from conventional asset managers and an increase in portfolio weightings for hedge funds and private equity funds by pension fund trustees. Industry analysts estimated that 1,000 hedge funds were formed worldwide in 2003 alone, bringing the global total to 7,500 with aggregate assets of $775 billion. Since 1999 the European hedge fund industry has grown sixfold. The biggest increase has been in London, which by 2004 was home to three-quarters of the European total, controlling $100 billion of assets and emerging as the industry's global capital.

It is estimated that around three-quarters of hedge-fund investors – a mixture of private clients, family investment vehicles and pension funds – are from North America. Outside the United States investors have traditionally been wealthy individuals, but since 2000 pension funds and insurance companies have begun to allocate funds to hedge funds. The low returns from conventional asset management led pension funds to increase the asset weighting allocated to hedge funds. In early 2004, it was reported that American and other pension funds were taking steps to raise their weighting from 0.2% to 5% of assets, implying a global flow into hedge funds of $710 billion, almost doubling the size of the industry in a few years. But as the sector becomes more crowded, the likelihood of the achievement of high absolute returns becomes more remote.

As mostly private entities that accept business only from professional investors, hedge funds are not obliged to be open about their trading techniques and the sector is shrouded in secrecy. It is also little regulated, with funds usually domiciled in offshore centres such as the Cayman Islands or Bermuda. The regulatory authorities in the UK and the United States fear that greater regulation would only drive funds offshore and entirely beyond their oversight. However, the high level of failure is a cause of concern: each year around one-fifth of hedge funds fail.

Hedge funds are mostly small operations that rely on the ability of a star trader or two and a few high-calibre support staff. Some have been set up by traders from investment banks' proprietary trading desks and others by fund managers from the conventional asset management industry. Talented people have been lured to the sector by the prospect of escaping the politics and bureaucracy of large organisations and making a lot more money if trades go right. The boom has stripped asset management firms of some of their best people, in a way reminiscent of the dotcom boom of the late 1990s, which depleted the corporate finance departments of investment banks.

The principal location of European hedge funds is St James's in London's West End. Around 100 hedge funds have their offices in this area of expensive clothes shops, art galleries and gentlemen's clubs, including some of the most famous, such as Soros, KKR and Blackstone. It has been estimated that the St James's cluster manages around $150 billion, which through leverage would amount to assets of at least double that amount, meaning that more money is managed in St James's than in Frankfurt.

Private wealth management

As institutional investors became larger and increasingly dominant in the 1960s and 1970s, many asset management firms ran down their private client activities. However, a group of London private banks that had for centuries catered for wealthy clients, as well as Swiss banks and some banks in offshore financial centres, continued to specialise in meeting their requirements. They then complemented their traditional private banking services with specialist asset management services, and the combination became known as private wealth management.

The upsurge in private wealth in the 1990s, driven by economic growth and buoyant stockmarkets, generated new interest in private clients on the part of asset management firms and other City services providers, notably lawyers and accountancy firms. Many formed (or revitalised) private banking operations in an endeavour to get a piece of the booming market in private wealth management.

In 2001 the global private wealth management market, defined as those with financial assets in excess of $1m, comprised 7.1m high net worth individuals with combined assets of $26.2 trillion, a larger sum than the assets of the global insurance industry. High net worth individuals may be classified as either "old money" (inherited), or "new money" (earned), of which the principal sources were the technology and telecoms, financial services, and media and publishing sectors. By region, 35% of these millionaires live in North America, 32% in Europe and 24% in Asia.

The investment of private wealth is undertaken in both onshore and offshore financial centres. London is a leading centre for onshore private wealth management, along with New York, Tokyo, Singapore and Hong Kong. The UK has 1.1m high net worth individuals, a number that doubled between 1997 and 2001. Private banks have a 35% share of the UK's private wealth management market, asset managers and stockbrokers 25%, retail banks 25% and investment banks 10%. London also has a

15% share of the offshore market, although this is a lot less than Switzerland, the leading offshore centre, which has 33% of the market.

Private equity/venture capital funds

Private equity and venture capital funds provide finance for new, expanding or reorganised privately owned businesses. In recent years the original name for the industry in the UK – venture capital – has increasingly been supplanted by the term private equity. In the UK and Europe the two terms are now used synonymously and encompass all aspects of the industry's activities. In the United States, however, a distinction is drawn between venture capital, which refers to the funding of start-ups and early-stage development, and private equity, which means the financing of management buy-outs (MBOS – the acquisition of a company by its management) and management buy-ins (MBIS – the acquisition of a company by an outside team of managers).

Private equity is an alternative to public equity or debt as a means of financing companies. It is appropriate when the perceived level of risk or the payback time horizon is too great for providers of debt or for public equity markets. Thus it is, in theory, particularly applicable to technology companies and growth-oriented start-up businesses. But it has also become a common means of financing the divestiture of non-core assets by large companies, the facilitation of management succession in family-owned firms and the de-listing of companies from public stock exchanges (public-to-private transactions).

Private equity providers become co-owners of the companies in which they invest. They take an active managerial interest in the development of these companies, and their ability to provide hands-on expertise is a crucial complement to the provision of finance. Profits are generated by the sale of firms in which investment has been made (an "exit"), either to a trade buyer or through an offering on a public stockmarket. Most private equity firms are independent and owned by their partners, although some are owned by the banks or insurance companies that provide the bulk of their investment funds. Some are based in the City, but many have their offices in London's West End.

Private equity firms put together funds, which provide the resources to finance their activities. Participants in the funds are wholesale investors, such as pension funds, insurance companies, banks and high net worth individuals. Pension funds allocate up to 5% of their funds to this asset class. Private equity funds are usually structured as limited partnerships between a private equity firm, known as the general partner, and outside investors (typically 10–30), which constitute the limited partners. Limited partnerships, which usually have a fixed life of ten years, are run by the general partner; it selects investments, structures deals, monitors investments and designs and executes appropriate exit strategies. The rewards are a management fee and participation in the overall returns of the fund (known as the carried interest).

Private equity activity has existed since the 18th century in the form of rich patrons backing entrepreneurs with enterprising ideas or new technologies. A formal venture capital industry emerged in the UK in the late 1970s and was nurtured with tax breaks by Margaret Thatcher's Conservative government in the 1980s. The formation in 1983 of a trade association to represent the industry's interests, the British Venture Capital Association (BVCA), was testament to its coming of age. Over the following two decades a total of £28 billion was invested by private equity firms in around 18,000 companies, and the annual level of private equity investment rose over the period from £190m to £5.5 billion. Today the BVCA has 165 members encompassing most of the industry. These firms have investments totalling £60 billion in 11,000 companies, which between them employ almost 3m people, 18% of the UK's private-sector workforce. Member firms account for 50% of total private equity investment in Europe, and the UK industry is the second largest after the United States.

A report by London Business School in 2002 showed that since the stockmarket crash of 1987, the private equity asset class had outperformed all other major UK asset classes. However, it stressed the importance of diversification between funds and managers for the protection of capital. One way of achieving this diversification is investment in a private equity "fund of funds", with participation in a diversified portfolio of private equity funds.

The BVCA's annual report shows that in 2002 member firms made investments in 1,196 UK and 263 overseas companies. Among the UK companies, 398 were start-up or early-stage investments, 675 were expansion-stage investments and 179 were MBO or MBI investments. However, the distribution of funds by value was very different: 87% went to MBOs or MBIs, 10% to expansion and a mere 3% to start-up or early-stage investments. The latter pattern supports the criticism that, "despite its nomenclature, the venture capital industry is distinctly unadventurous". Most of its energies and resources are focused on MBOs and MBIs, which are established businesses (reducing risk) being disposed of by their owners because they do not fit a company's new strategic plan.

Often they are sold to management, backed by venture capital firms, at a discounted exit price.

Since the 1930s there have been a number of initiatives to assist start-ups and small companies to find equity funding. 3i, a leading private equity firm, is the legacy of one such endeavour in the 1940s. The principal source of start-up and early-stage financing in the UK is rich individuals, so-called "business angels". The formation in 1999 of the National Business Angels Network (NBAN) was a new attempt to facilitate their activities, bringing together potential investors and businesses seeking finance through the NBAN's Bestmatch website. FISMA, created in 2004 by a former 3i executive, was another web-based initiative to match people looking for investment opportunities with impecunious entrepreneurs.

Asset management operations

Although each asset management firm has its own organisational structure, certain roles and functions are common to most. A fundamental distinction exists between the front office and the back office. Front-office functions focus on winning clients and managing funds, including making decisions on asset allocation and risk management, investment analysis, dealing and cash management. Back-office functions comprise a range of support activities, including the processing of transactions, information technology, accounts and administration. (See Table 5.15 overleaf.)

Fund managers are the key figures in every asset management firm. They have responsibility for the investment performance of funds in their charge, which means beating the benchmark. Generally, the bigger the client, the more senior is the assigned fund manager. Fund managers may also have ultimate responsibility for dealing on clients' behalf, ensuring that the fund has cash available to meet obligations and that all clients receive equal treatment. Senior fund managers often have a senior managerial position in the firm, reporting directly to the chief executive. Day-to-day contact with clients is usually handled by a client service team. Effective marketing, selling the firm's product range and developing new products, is also crucial.

Regulation and reform

Institutional investors and the asset management industry are regulated by the Financial Services Authority (FSA), the UK's unitary financial regulatory body responsible for the regulation of deposit taking, insurance and

Table 5.15 **Functions of asset managers**

Front office

Fund management	Strategic fund management: long-term asset allocation, currency and risk management
	Operational fund management: stock selection decision making and implementation
	Research: fundamental and technical economic and quantitative analysis
	Dealing: buying and selling investments. Pre-trade broker liaison
	Cash management: placing deposits, foreign exchange
Marketing	New business and product development

Back office

Transaction processing	Transaction processing and settlement: deal administration and control, post-trade liaison with brokers and custodians
	Safe custody: security, safekeeping and control
	Stock lending: arranging and processing loans
Information technology	Systems maintenance: operational and technical maintenance of existing IT
	Systems development: planning and implementation of new IT and major improvements to existing systems
Accounting and administration	Investment accounting: provision of valuations and client reports, tax reclaims, management information
	Performance measurement: provision of investment performance reports, attribution analysis of returns
	Unit trust administration: client dealing and associated administration including contract notes, distributions and trustee liaison
General administration	Compliance: regulatory reporting and in-house monitoring activities
	Financial accounting: corporate accounting and reporting
	Corporate management: training, human resources, staff and premises management

Source: IFSL, *Fund Management*, 2003

investment business (see Chapter 11). The FSA's Investment Firms Division regulates around 7,500 investment firms, ranging from City-based investment banks, stockbrokers and asset management firms to independent financial advisers, both large and small. The investment advisory aspects of the activities of accountants and lawyers also fall within its remit. The FSA is empowered to take a range of measures to remedy and penalise regulatory breaches, including compensation for consumers, fines for firms and, ultimately, termination of a firm's authorisation.

The government-commissioned Myners Report on institutional fund management, published in spring 2001, criticised secretive market arrangements between stockbrokers and asset managers known as "softing" and "bundling", for which institutional investors picked up the tab through inflated dealing commissions. Softing (short for soft commissions) is the practice of brokers paying for the supply of a service received by an asset manager, for instance a Reuters screen, in return for an agreed volume of dealing business at a set commission rate. Bundling is the provision by brokers of additional in-house services, such as research, together with dealing in a single commission charge. In both cases, the costs of these services are passed on to clients in commission charges.

The FSA agreed with Myners that these practices were harmful to the interests of investors, estimating that approaching half of commission payments to brokers were for services on top of dealing. In a paper published in spring 2003, the regulator called for the end of soft commissions and for fund managers to itemise the services that they buy in addition to dealing and to obtain the approval of clients. The Myners Report and the FSA's paper provoked howls of protest from the industry and complaints that ending these practices would put the UK asset management sector at a competitive disadvantage to rivals in other financial centres. Concern that asset management firms might simply decamp to New York caused the FSA to stay its hand in resorting to compulsion.

In the meantime, the mutual fund (unit trust) industry in the United States was being accused of graver shortcomings. Eliot Spitzer, New York's attorney general, revealed that he was looking into practices known as "market timing" and "late trading", which allowed brokers to profit at the expense of investors from the process by which mutual fund units are priced. On top of this came allegations of excessive fees and inadequate disclosure, which prompted Peter Fitzgerald, head of the Senate banking oversight committee, to call mutual funds "the world's largest skimming operation".

Thus in the early 2000s the asset management industry on both sides of the Atlantic found itself the focus of unwanted attention from regulators and politicians. The issues were technical, but largely boiled down to conflicts of interest between asset managers and investors as to which of them would shoulder the burden of a contested set of costs.

Links between asset management and other City activities

There are substantial links between asset management and other City activities, notably life insurance, which both buys and sells asset management services. Property advisers and marketmakers in securities provide services to asset managers. The expansion of their international asset management activities has been particularly important for the development of the London Stock Exchange's international equities business and for the over-the-counter market in Eurobonds (see Chapter 3). Asset managers are the principal buyers of new securities issues, and the presence of a substantial asset management industry in London reinforces the City's role as a centre for primary-market securities issuance (see Chapter 4). Perhaps more than any other financial activity, asset management relies on high-quality information about companies and economic indicators. It thus supports a variety of consultants and other information providers, including a sophisticated financial press (see Chapter 8).

Trends and issues

- **The EU Financial Services Action Plan.** The single currency and the drive to complete the EU single market in financial services are likely to generate increased buy-side pan-European mergers, acquisitions, joint ventures and strategic alliances.
- **The EU market.** The growth of funded pension schemes in Europe should present opportunities for UK-based asset managers to sell their expertise. The expanded EU market means more customers and opportunities to introduce cross-border products and services. It also means more competition in the home market.
- **Global consolidation.** It is predicted that the industry will continue to consolidate globally along the lines of a league of global businesses and smaller national or regional boutiques.
- **Costs.** Pressure on profits in the market downturn of the early 2000s led to an increased concentration on costs. Even as markets recover, competition is likely to necessitate continued attention to costs, including further outsourcing of support services such as

custody, accounting, valuation and shareholder record keeping. Between 1998 and 2001 outsourcing grew from 4% of total costs to 13%.

- **New services.** The expansion of specialist investments, such as hedge funds and private equity, has led to an increase in demand for investment consulting services, and this is likely to increase further.
- **Benchmarking under deflation.** Some economists believe that the world has entered an era of stable or even falling prices (deflation). In periods of inflation with rising equity prices, benchmarking against an equity index is an appropriate measure of asset management performance. But in a deflationary environment with falling share prices, as in Japan in the 1990s and early 2000s, it makes little sense. Some argue that benchmarking against cash is a more appropriate industry yardstick in today's economic environment.
- **Equity research.** Traditionally, asset managers relied largely on research provided free by the sell-side. Will they now be prepared to pay for independent research or generate more of their own research in-house?
- **Broker-dealer commissions.** How far will they fall?
- **Shareholder activism and corporate governance.** In recent years there has been a proliferation of challenges to corporate management by institutional shareholders, particularly over executive remuneration. Following the publication of the Myners Report on institutional investment, institutional shareholder activism received encouragement from the government, which went as far as considering legislation requiring institutions to intervene actively in companies in which they invest. A statement of best practice on the responsibilities of institutional shareholders was published in October 2002, with a review scheduled for two years later to determine whether legislation is required. In keeping with the Higgs Report, the government is also keen to strengthen the role of non-executive directors to keep a check on executives and strengthen corporate governance.

6 Banking, payments and specialist financial institutions

The fundamental business of banking is receiving deposits from savers and making loans to borrowers. For their services as intermediaries banks receive the difference between the rate of interest paid to depositors and the rate charged to borrowers (the spread). Lending is conducted in a variety of ways, depending on the type of borrower and the purpose for which the loan is to be used. Banks may also undertake a wide range of other financial activities, such as foreign-exchange dealing, asset management, insurance and the provision of personal financial advice.

There is a difference between UK domestic retail banking, serving the requirements of households and small businesses, and City-based wholesale and international banking. The banking activities discussed in this chapter are known as commercial banking (clearing banking is the traditional UK term). Investment banking is discussed in Chapter 4 and private wealth management in Chapter 5.

There were 686 banks authorised to take deposits in the UK in 2003. They comprise 185 banks incorporated in the UK and 501 incorporated elsewhere (see Table 6.1). The presence of a substantial number of foreign banks has been a feature of the City for many decades. In recent years there has been a big increase in the number of European Economic Area (EEA – comprising the EU countries as well as Iceland, Liechtenstein and Norway) authorised banks operating in the UK, partly on account of the European Commission's Banking Consolidation Directive, which allows home country supervision of branches of EEA incorporated banks throughout the EEA.

The total assets of the British banking sector at the start of 2004 were £4,165 billion, the third largest in the world after Japan and the United States. Because of the large number of foreign banks undertaking business in the wholesale markets on behalf of foreign clients, foreign currencies comprise more than half of the British banking sector's assets.

City commercial banking
The City's commercial banking sector comprises the head offices of five

Table 6.1 **Banks in the UK, end-March 2003**

Incorporated in the UK	185
of which:	
UK-owned	95
foreign-owned (1)	90
Incorporated outside the UK	501
of which:	
EEA located in the UK (2)	94
other EEA	304
outside the EEA (3)	103
Total authorised banks	686
Foreign banks with physical presence in the UK	
Branches and subsidiaries (1) + (2) + (3)	287
Representative offices (4)	160
Total (1) + (2) + (3) + (4)	447

Source: IFSL, *International Financial Markets in the UK*, May 2004

major British banks, and branches, subsidiaries and representative offices of 447 foreign banks. The five British banks employ around 22,000 people in the City. In 2001 foreign banks employed 113,000 people in the UK, compared with only 41,400 in 1990. It is estimated that international banking generates 56,500 City jobs while others who work for foreign banks undertake foreign-exchange trading, derivatives business, securities dealing, asset management and other activities.

The five British banks are Barclays, HSBC, Lloyds TSB, NatWest (owned by Royal Bank of Scotland) and Standard Chartered. Each has a City headquarters that looks after board-level administration and support, group strategy, treasury operations (management of the bank's balance sheet), human resources and IT. Their City operations also handle much of their wholesale and international banking operations, such as foreign-exchange dealing, Euromarket activities, sterling lending and securities trading.

The 447 foreign banks, from more than 70 countries, comprise 287 branches or subsidiaries of foreign banks which are authorised to conduct a full range of banking business, and 160 representative offices which are not authorised to take deposits or lend. The largest contingent is from the EU, accounting for 50% of overseas banks' assets. American banks, the second largest group, account for 16% of overseas banks' assets. The international orientation of their activities is reflected in the denomination of their assets, with three-quarters being in foreign currencies. Nearly 20% of global cross-border lending is conducted from London, the world's largest market for international banking business.

Overseas commercial banks established City branches and subsidiaries in the second half of the 19th century. One group, including the forerunners of HSBC and Standard Chartered, served the British Empire. The first foreign bank, a forerunner of BNP (Banque Nationale de Paris), arrived in 1867, followed by Credit Lyonnais and Société Générale in 1870, Deutsche Bank in 1873, Bank of Tokyo in 1884 and Swiss Bank Corporation in 1898. By 1914, 26 foreign banks had offices in the City. The principal reason was to participate in the London money market, where they were able to invest in interest-bearing liquid assets on a scale that was not possible in their home markets. Between the two world wars there were some departures and a few new arrivals. In 1947, when they formed a trade association, the Foreign Banks Association (now the Foreign Bankers and Securities Association), 21 were eligible for membership, including seven French, six American and three Belgian.

In the 1960s the number of foreign banks in London rose substantially, from 77 in 1960 to 163 in 1970. The reason was the rapidly growing Euromarkets, which were soon dominated by the City branches of foreign banks. American banks were the leaders, with their number rising from 14 in 1964 to 51 in 1973. The expansion continued in the 1970s, when much of the petrodollar recycling was done in London through the Eurocurrency market. By 1980 there were 403 foreign banks in the City (including 50 representative offices). The 1970s and 1980s saw the rise and decline of the "consortium bank", a bank owned by other banks to operate in the Euromarkets, which provided a toehold in London for even more of the world's banks. By the 1980s virtually every major bank in the world undertaking international activities had established a presence in London. Indeed, having a presence in London is a hallmark of a bank's status as an international bank, as a 2003 survey of international bankers confirmed.

The presence of an unrivalled number of foreign banks is one of London's key strengths as an international financial centre. They give depth and liquidity to the markets and increase the diversity of the City's players and activities. It is widely agreed that they greatly enhance financial innovation, importing cutting-edge techniques from New York or elsewhere and generating new products and services through their interaction with other market participants. They provide the City with worldwide ties and help to engender a truly global outlook. They send some of the brightest banking talent to the City from all over the world – a posting to London is a coveted career move in most banks. Lastly, through example and commercial competition they have obliged domestic banks to sharpen their performance.

The banking industry makes a substantial contribution to the UK's balance of payments. The net overseas earnings of City-based international banks were £3.2 billion in 2002, almost twice the amount in 1996. Commitment fees, credit and bill transactions and derivatives transactions generate 51% of the total. Securities transactions and asset management account for 36% and foreign-exchange dealing 13%. The United States is much the most important source of overseas net earnings (32%), followed by Germany (6%) and France (5%).

International banking

There are two types of international banking in the City: lending in sterling to foreign borrowers (a relatively minor part of the business); and lending in currencies other than sterling, known as Eurocurrency lending (see Chapter 3). A Eurocurrency is a deposit or loan denominated in a currency other than that of the country in which the transaction takes place. The bulk of transactions are conducted in offshore dollars (known as Eurodollars), though any other currency (apart from sterling) may be involved, such as Euroyen, Euro-Australian dollars and (confusingly) Euro-euros. Around 80% of the world's total international bank lending is Eurocurrency lending.

The Eurocurrency market is a wholesale market in which transactions are measured in millions. Deposits are mainly short-term, with an average maturity of around three months. The principal depositors and borrowers are major banks, multinational corporations, governments and international institutions. There is a large volume of short-term interbank Eurocurrency lending.

Longer-term Eurocurrency lending often takes the form of syndicated loans – loans for which a number of banks, often a score or more, subscribe. Maturity ranges from 3 to 15 years, averaging 6–8 years. Interest rates are floating, based on a benchmark reference rate such as LIBOR (London interbank offered rate). Syndication techniques resemble those used in the bond market (from which they were borrowed), with the bank that gets the client mandate acting as lead-manager of the syndicate and receiving a fee for its management services.

Syndicated loans can be arranged for huge amounts because the risk is spread among a large number of lenders. The dispersion of risk means that lenders require a lower-risk premium, which for borrowers increases the price competitiveness of syndicated loans over single bank borrowings. Despite their size, syndicated loans can be arranged rapidly, often within a few days. Since the 1980s a secondary market has developed in syndicated loans, particularly less-developed country debt. One stimulus was the Basel Accord of 1988, which set a common capital-adequacy standard for banks operating in the major industrial economies. This required some banks either to raise additional capital or to reduce their balance-sheet assets, which was done by securitising debts and selling them to other parties.

The major international commercial banks and investment banks are also the leading players in the Eurobond market, the international long-term debt (capital) market. The Eurobond market began in London in 1963 and was a further reason why so many foreign banks flocked to the City in the 1960s and 1970s. This is a much bigger market than Euro-syndicated lending; in 2003 worldwide Eurobond issues totalled $1.5 trillion. It is estimated that 60% of Eurobond primary issuing business and 70% of secondary market trading take place in London.

Custody

A set of major international banks dominates the global custody market. Custody is the function of safeguarding securities on behalf of institutional investors and asset managers. This activity has grown and become global in recent years, driven by the expansion of institutional asset holdings and cross-border investment flows. Custodians also provide a range of essential administrative services for owners of securities, such as settlement, income collection, reporting, proxy voting, tax reclaims, cash management and fund administration.

Global custodians are appointed by institutional investors to provide custody services for all their assets, irrespective of how many asset managers are engaged to handle specialist tranches of their investment portfolio (see Chapter 5). Asset managers focus solely on investment performance and the specialist custodian carries out the administrative duties. The major global custodians provide clients with worldwide services. In the UK, custody was traditionally in the hands of clearing banks and asset management firms. But the major American global custody firms, whose European operations are based in London, have captured a significant proportion of the market. There are substantial

Table 6.2 **Leading global custody banks, end–December 2002**

	Worldwide assets ($bn)	% share
J.P. Morgan Chase	6,700	16
Bank of New York	6,613	16
State Street	6,200	15
Citibank NA	5,400	13
Mellon Group	2,800	7
BNP Paribas Securities Services	1,783	4
Northern Trust	1,720	4
SIS Segaintersettle AG	1,200	3
HSBC Bank	1,060	2
RBC Global Services	872	2
Others	7,880	17
Total	42,228	100

Source: IFSL, *Securities Trading*, 2003

economies of scale in custody work which means the market is highly concentrated, with the top five global custodians controlling two-thirds of it (see Table 6.2).

UK commercial banking

The British banking industry employs around 460,000 people, accounting for 1.6% of total UK employment. Most of them work in branches and offices around the country, servicing the requirements of domestic individual and small business customers. This is typically a large-volume, low-value activity. In the UK, 94% of adults have some form of bank or building society account and 83% have a cheque facility. Banks incorporated in the UK are authorised to take deposits by the Financial Services Authority under the Financial Services and Markets Act 2000. Depositors with authorised banks are protected under the UK's deposit protection scheme. Customers' deposits comprise 90% of British banks' liabilities, with the remainder composed of shareholders' capital, reserves and debt. Reflecting the client base, British banks' deposits are mostly denominated in sterling.

Two-thirds of British banks' assets comprise loans to individuals and business customers. The remainder is made up of financial assets, divided roughly equally between cash and short-term interbank loans, and marketable securities such as government bonds. The bulk of British banks' assets are denominated in sterling. Since the 19th century, retail banking services have been delivered through extensive networks of high-street branches. Cost cutting and bank amalgamations have led to the closure of more than a quarter of bank branches in the UK in recent years, with the number falling from 15,700 in 1990 to 11,200 in 2002. The growth of telephone and internet banking services and ATMs (cash machines) has reduced the need for branch visits. The role of the remaining branches has been expanded beyond the traditional money transmission function to include the selling of a variety of financial products. The face-to-face contact between buyers and sellers available at branches makes them suitable venues for the marketing of relatively complex financial products, including mortgages, insurance and investment products.

Technology is transforming the delivery of many banking services. There are 41,000 automated teller machines (ATMs) for cash withdrawal, double the number in 1995 and almost four times the number of bank branches. In 2002 there were 2.3 billion withdrawals from ATMs totalling £110 billion, three times more than a decade earlier.

There were 178m plastic bank cards of all sorts in issue in the UK in 2002, comprising 123m multifunction payment cards, 22m ATM-only cards and 22m store cards. Around 90% of adults hold one or more cards. There were 4.8 billion card purchases in the UK in 2002, double the 2.4 billion transactions conducted by cheque. The entry of American banks and credit-card companies such as MBNA and BankOne into the market in recent years has expanded the number of cards on offer to British consumers. Business payments by BACS (see page 163) have contributed to a decline in the use of cheques and cash, and the introduction of chip and PIN technology to all UK credit- and debit-card transactions by 2005 is expected to lead to a further decline.

Internet banking has expanded rapidly in recent years, with 6m British adults accessing their bank account online. Banks have developed online services to complement their branches and some have created new internet-only banking entities, such as Cahoot (Abbey National), Smile (Co-operative Bank) and Virgin One (Royal Bank of Scotland), or telephone and internet banks, such as Egg (Prudential) and First Direct (HSBC). With a low cost base relative to the high street banks, these virtual banks compete by offering cheaper credit or higher interest.

Another source of competition has been the conversion of building societies into banks. In the 1970s and 1980s these mutual savings soci-

Table 6.3 **Leading British banks, end-2002**

	Tier-one capital ($bn)	Assets ($bn)	Global rank
HSBC	39	759	3
Royal Bank of Scotland	28	649	7
HBOS	24	512	13
Barclays	23	638	14
Lloyds TSB Group	15	334	29
Abbey National	12	284	42
Standard Chartered	10	182	47
Alliance & Leicester	3	66	134
Northern Rock	3	53	138
FCE Bank	2	26	172

Source: *The Banker*, July 2003

eties (owned by depositors and borrowers), with the specialist function of funding house purchases through mortgages, began to compete for retail deposits by offering accounts similar to bank current accounts. The Building Societies Act 1986 and further legislation in 1997 permitted them to offer a full range of banking services and financial products such as insurance and investment services. Deregulation paved the way to a wave of consolidation through mergers and acquisitions in the 1980s and 1990s and to demutualisation (conversion to public limited company status).

Conversion into a bank with public limited company status provides both an escape from restrictions on business activities imposed by building society legislation and access to capital for growth and diversification. Abbey National, the biggest building society, was the first to demutualise in 1989. Between 1995 and 1998 nine of the ten largest building societies converted into banks, including Alliance & Leicester, Bradford & Bingley, Halifax, Northern Rock and Woolwich; the notable exception was Nationwide. Some have been acquired by traditional banks, including Halifax by Bank of Scotland (HBOS), Cheltenham and Gloucester by Lloyds TSB and Woolwich by Barclays. Banks have also diversified through the acquisition of insurance companies, notably Scottish Widows by Lloyds TSB and Scottish Provident by Abbey National.

The ten largest British banks are listed in Table 6.3. The top six, with tier-one or core capital (equity capital plus disclosed reserves) of £12 billion or more, constitute a league of their own and dominate the provision of retail banking services and mortgage provision. Standard Chartered and HSBC were originally British Empire banks and have extensive overseas branch networks in countries of the Commonwealth. HSBC used to be based in Hong Kong but became a major British bank through its acquisition of Midland in 1992. It is the third biggest bank in the world, and five of the UK's leading banks rank among the world's top 30.

In recent years a variety of non-banks have entered the retail banking market. Retailers such as Tesco and Sainsbury, through partnerships with established banks, offer own-brand banking services alongside baked beans and soap powder in their extensive store networks, and in future they may decide to go it alone.

The Post Office, with 16,500 branches throughout the UK, is a significant distribution channel for retail banking services and is the country's largest handler of cash. It is the biggest provider of foreign currency and 500m household bills are paid over Post Office counters each year. It is also the leading distribution channel for the financial products offered by National Savings and Investments, a British government agency, which offers Premium Bonds (UK government bonds that are entered in a monthly prize draw) and a variety of state-guaranteed savings products. To capitalise on its extensive branch network, in 2003 the Post Office launched an extensive range of personal banking services, including personal loans.

Payment and settlement

A robust payment and settlement system is crucial for the functioning of the banking system and for general financial stability. The UK's bank payment and settlement mechanisms are run by APACS (Association for Payment Clearing Services), a body set up in 1985 as a non-statutory association of major banks and building societies to undertake money transmission. APACS has three companies which manage different aspects of payments clearing.

High-value wholesale payments are handled by CHAPS (Clearing House Automated Payments System) via a private payments network between banks. CHAPS is a Real-Time Gross Settlement (RTGS) system, which means that payments are processed individually and continuously during the day as they occur. Settlement takes place through settlement accounts at the Bank of England. Before the introduction of CHAPS, payments were processed as a single net transaction at the end of the day. This exposed banks to the risk of losses should a counter-party bank fail during trading hours, the fate that befell counterparties to Bankhaus Herstatt when it was hastily closed down during trading hours by the Bundesbank in 1974. Since then this type of risk has been known as "Herstatt risk". CHAPS has two component parts, one operating in sterling and the other in euros. To enable large real-time cross-border payments to be made, CHAPS euro is linked to TARGET, the pan-euro RTGS system. TARGET links euro RTGS systems in all the EU central banks with each other and the European Central Bank. CHAPS euro is the second largest component of TARGET.

CHAPS is one of the largest RTGS systems in the world. There are 20 direct members as well as around 400 other financial institutions that make use of its facilities via agency arrangements with direct members. To be eligible for membership, firms must:

- hold a sterling and/or euro settlement account at the Bank of England for the purpose of settling CHAPS payment obligations;
- be able to comply with the operational requirements of the CHAPS systems;
- be a shareholder of the company;
- pay a £100,000 joining fee.

APACS also runs two retail-oriented payment-clearing services: BACS (Bankers' Automated Clearing Services), which provides facilities for automated direct credits and debits; and the Cheque and Credit Clearing Company, which oversees paper clearing and handles around 2.6 billion cheques a year.

Several payment-card arrangements operate in the UK. Credit cards are predominantly issued through the Visa and MasterCard schemes. The principal debit-card issuers are SWITCH and Visa. ATMs are connected via the LINK system, a reciprocal agreement allowing customers to access their accounts from any of the participating institutions.

Regulation

The Financial Services Authority (FSA) is responsible for the authorisation and supervision of banks in the UK under the Financial Services and Markets Act 2000 (see Chapter 11). The Bank of England provides banking services to the government, other central banks and commercial banks that hold accounts with it (see Chapter 10). It also has responsibility for the stability of the financial system as a whole, including the banking system.

The Bank keeps a close watch for potentially destabilising economic and financial market developments. It plays a crucial role in the provision of safe and efficient payment and settlement services, being the overseer of UK payment systems under the EU Settlement Finality Directive. The Bank stands ready, if necessary, to act as lender of last resort to banks should the failure of one institution threaten to bring down otherwise sound firms. In 1973–75 it organised a consortium of City firms to act as a "lifeboat" in resolving the secondary banking crisis and in 1984 acted alone to rescue the failed Johnson Matthey Bankers (see Chapter 13). However, when Barings got into trouble in 1995 it was allowed to fail because the Bank judged that this posed no systemic risk (threat to the financial system).

Basel Accords

The international co-ordination of bank regulation is the reason for the Basel Committee on Banking Supervision's existence. It was formed in 1975 in the wake of the collapse the previous year of Bankhaus Herstatt in Germany and Franklin National Bank in the United States. These shocks prompted the central-bank governors of the Group of Ten (G10) leading industrial countries to work towards better, internationally co-ordinated standards for banks. Based at the Bank for International Settlements in Basel, the committee serves as a forum for discussion of problems and new developments in banking.

The Basel Accord of 1975 established guidelines for international banking supervision, defining the responsibilities of home and host countries and setting up mechanisms for information sharing and compliance with common standards. The guidelines have been reformulated and updated several times. In 1988 the Basel Committee agreed on common minimum capital-adequacy standards for banks. The agreement defined two tiers of capital: tier one – equity and published reserves; and tier two – current year's profit, general provisions and subordinated debt. A target 8% ratio of capital to risk-weighted assets was established, with tier-one capital constituting at least half. The Basel Accord has been implemented in more than 100 countries and applies to both domestic and international banks.

The controversial New Capital Adequacy Framework (Basel II) was agreed in 2001 and is scheduled for introduction in 2005. It has three principal elements:

- Minimum capital requirements. The aim is to ensure that banks' capital is proportionate to the scale of risks undertaken.

- ▱ Supervisory review. This seeks to ensure that regulators set capital requirements higher than the bare minimum and outlines how banks should make their own internal assessments of capital adequacy.
- ▱ Market discipline. Proposals regarding capital structure, risk exposure and capital adequacy are intended to improve market discipline.

EU developments

It is an objective of the EU to create a single market in banking services. The 1985 European Commission White Paper on the Completion of the Internal Market established that trade in financial products should be governed by three principles: mutual recognition, home-country control and minimum co-ordination of individual national rules. A trio of European Commission directives has established a "passport" for banks to operate throughout the EU without further authorisation from host countries. This means that banks authorised in other EU countries do not need FSA authorisation to take deposits in the UK. These arrangements have been extended to all countries in the EEA.

The Financial Services Action Plan (FSAP) issued by the European Commission in May 1999 contains a range of measures aimed at achieving full financial integration across the EU. An important component is a review of capital-adequacy provisions for banks and investment firms to complement Basel II. The FSAP is scheduled to be implemented by the end of 2005.

Specialist financial institutions

Several specialist banking or capital market institutions form part of the wholesale financial services landscape.

European Bank for Reconstruction and Development

The London-based European Bank for Reconstruction and Development (EBRD) was established in 1991 to assist former communist countries from eastern Europe to central Asia with the transition from a command economy to a market economy. It is owned by 60 countries and two international financial institutions. Most of its €20 billion capital is subscribed by the United States and members of the EU, and voting power is proportional to capital subscriptions. The bank has 33 offices and operates in 27 countries.

The EBRD provides project financing for banks and industries, both new ventures and existing companies. It also works with publicly owned enterprises, promoting privatisation, and state-owned firms, assisting in restructuring. It is the largest single investor in the region and mobilises substantial private-sector investment as well as its own financing. It funds its lending activities by borrowing in the international capital markets. With its AAA credit rating, it can borrow at the lowest market rates and pass on the low cost of funding to its clients. EBRD securities are purchased by major investors such as central banks, pension funds, insurance companies and global asset managers.

CDC
Originally called the Commonwealth Development Corporation, the London-based CDC (Capital for Development) was founded in 1948 as an agency of the British government for investment in the private sector of developing Commonwealth countries. Today the CDC invests in the private sector of all developing countries and has an investment portfolio totalling $1.6 billion. It focuses on equity investment, a critical funding constraint in many developing countries. It does not invest directly, channelling funds through specialist private equity fund managers in its target markets. The CDC expects to achieve returns "appropriate to the opportunities and risks in the relevant market".

3i
Originally called the Industrial and Commercial Finance Corporation, 3i (Investors in Industry) was formed in 1945 by UK clearing banks and the Bank of England to supply long-term finance to the UK's small and medium-sized businesses, a sector previously starved of investment capital. It is now a leading venture capital and private equity investor with an international portfolio of investments in more than 2,000 business in Europe, Asia Pacific and the United States. 3i invests in start-ups, buy-outs and buy-ins with strong management and high growth potential. Its headquarters are in London and it operates in 14 countries. It is a member of the FTSE 100 share index, although its worldwide staff numbers a mere 900.

Trends and issues
- **Development of pan-Europe banks.** The creation of a single European market in financial services and the euro are expected to lead to the emergence of banks operating throughout the EU. However, although there has been consolidation within national

banking systems and a number of banks have taken minority shareholdings in each other to forge alliances, there has been little cross-border merger or acquisition activity among European commercial banks. One inhibiting factor is that banking cultures, practices and systems vary widely from country to country, presenting formidable problems for institutional integration. So do the banking habits and expectations of customers, which creates further difficulties. Moreover, the quest for cost savings through economies of scale and the elimination of duplication, which has driven bank mergers in the United States and in national markets, is not achievable on a pan-European basis because of either lack of overlap or European labour legislation, which makes substantial redundancies almost impossible. Nevertheless, it appears likely that at some point in the not too distant future Europe's (including the UK's) commercial banks may reconfigure as European rather than national entities.

◪ **Competition.** The distinctive role of the established banks will continue to be eroded by the provision of banking services by new players, such as internet banks, credit-card companies, insurance companies, supermarkets and others. Simultaneously, the banks will continue to make inroads into the provision of other financial services.

◪ **Transferring functions offshore.** In recent years technological advances have made possible the transfer of a variety of labour-intensive and routine retail banking functions, such as customer support and accounting work, to low-wage offshore locations, notably India, Malaysia, the Philippines, Sri Lanka and China. Software and hardware development is also being transferred offshore, particularly to India. Deloitte Consulting estimates that 2m jobs will be transferred from the industrial economies by 2008, with three-quarters of leading banks and financial institutions shifting jobs offshore.

◪ **Distribution.** The growth of internet and telephone banking will continue. There may be some further closures of bank branches, but most will be reoriented as points of sale for a range of retail financial services. It is estimated that European banks will spend $1 billion on making this transformation by 2005.

◪ **Challenge of American mega-banks.** Mergers between major American banks in the late 1990s and early 2000s resulted in the creation of a set of mega-banks. Three of them – Citigroup,

J.P. Morgan Chase and Bank of America – emerged with capital of over $100 billion, far more than any European bank apart from HSBC. This presented a challenge to European banks because it made American banks increasingly competitive in servicing global corporations and it was predicted that they would next look to Europe to make acquisitions. Some analysts commented that European banks were being left behind and that their share of corporate and capital markets business was destined to grow smaller and smaller.

7 Insurance

The City-based wholesale sector of the UK insurance industry supports 40,000 City jobs plus a further 10,000 in back-office activities around the country. The insurance industry is the UK's biggest institutional investor (see Chapter 5). It is also the largest single contributor to UK net financial exports, generating two-fifths of the total.

Insurance has been an important City activity for more than 300 years, beginning with the provision of cover for sailing ships and their cargoes in the informal market that operated in City coffee houses, notably that run by Edward Lloyd which became Lloyd's of London. Marine insurance is part of general insurance, an insurance activity concerned with providing cover for specific contingencies, such as accident, fire and theft, over a relatively short period of time, usually 12 months. Long-term insurance, the other insurance activity, is mainly concerned with life insurance (traditionally known as life assurance). Life insurance not only provides cover against death and ill health but is also a significant form of saving. Furthermore, life insurance companies are important pensions managers (see Chapter 5).

The fundamental characteristic of all forms of insurance business is the spreading of risk, either over time or between policyholders (or both). Individuals and companies require insurance for protection against risks that may potentially have adverse financial consequences. They obtain cover by paying a fee (called a premium) to an insurer, which takes on the risk of undertaking to make payment in specified circumstances. The funds to make payments to claimants are derived from premium income and from investments, premiums being invested in the financial markets.

The UK is Europe's leading insurance market and the third largest in the world after the United States and Japan, accounting for 9% of total worldwide premium income. In total the UK insurance industry, both wholesale and retail sectors, employs 360,000 people, who work for insurance companies, in the Lloyd's of London market and in support capacities. Proprietary companies with shareholders undertake most insurance business. In addition, a number of mutual offices that are owned by policyholders are significant in life insurance, as are Lloyd's syndicates in general insurance. Most of the UK's 808 insurance companies undertake

Table 7.1 **UK insurance industry, premium income, 2002**

	£bn
London Market	25
of which:	
Lloyd's of London	13
Companies, P&I clubs	12
Non-London Market	14
Total general	39
Total long-term	122
Total premium income	161

Source: IFSL, *International Financial Markets in the UK*, May 2004

either general or long-term insurance, but many of the largest insurance companies are "composites", meaning that they conduct both types of business (regulation requires them to keep general and long-term funds separately). Although many UK insurance companies have their head-quarters in the City, most of their staff are based in less costly places, nearer to their domestic retail market.

The structure of the UK insurance industry, classified by premium income, is shown in Table 7.1. Long-term insurance generates three-quar-ters of total premiums and general insurance a quarter. On the general insurance side of the business, around two-thirds of premiums derive from the "London Market" and the rest from domestic business.

The London Market is the generic term for the wholesale and inter-national insurance business conducted in the City. It comprises three types of insurance-cover providers – Lloyd's of London, insurance com-panies, and protection and indemnity (P&I) clubs – as well as insurance brokers who act as agents for parties requiring insurance.

General insurance

There are five main classes of general insurance ("property/casualty" is the more helpful American term):

- Transportation, such as motor, marine, aviation, railway
- Property, such as damage to property, including fire and natural forces
- Pecuniary, such as theft, credit, legal expenses

- Liability, such as protection against harm to others from accidents, product failure
- Personal accident, health and travel, such as temporary disablement and disruption of plans

For general insurance policyholders, the purchase of insurance cover substitutes a modest certain loss – the premium – for a large potential loss. For the providers of general insurance cover, the commercial risk is that claims may be more frequent and more costly than anticipated and that investment and premium incomes are insufficient to meet them, as occurred at Lloyd's of London in the late 1980s and early 1990s (see Chapter 13). General insurers may decide to limit their risk exposure by laying off part of their liability to another insurance company, paying a premium for this reinsurance facility. General insurance contracts are in force for a specified period, usually 12 months. In the UK, the insurance industry pays out £16 billion a year in general insurance claims.

Long-term insurance
Long-term insurance is mainly concerned with life insurance (traditionally called life assurance), but it also includes permanent health insurance. Life insurance is aimed at providing for dependants in the event of the policyholder's death or saving for the future. In the UK it is divided by legislation into two types: "industrial" life insurance and "ordinary" life insurance. The defining legal feature of industrial life business is that premiums are paid at regular intervals of less than two calendar months (traditionally they were collected weekly by agents who called door-to-door at millions of working class homes). Industrial life premiums are small and benefits correspondingly modest and simple. Ordinary life business is all life insurance that is not industrial life business, encompassing the bulk of modern long-term insurance activity.

There are three main types of ordinary life policy:

- Term life insurance. The oldest and simplest form of life insurance, providing for the payment of the sum insured if the policyholder dies within a specified period. No payment is made if the insured survives the specified period.
- Whole life insurance. A capital sum is paid on the death of the person insured, whenever that occurs.
- Endowment life insurance. As with a term policy, a payment is

made if the policyholder dies within a specified period. However, benefits are also paid to policyholders who are still alive at the end of the term of the policy. An endowment policy thus comprises a term policy and a lump sum paid on survival.

Each type of life policy may be organised according to three criteria: the frequency with which the premium is paid; the basis on which benefits are calculated; and whether the contract is for an individual or a group:

- Renewal and single premiums. Renewal premiums are paid in regular instalments over the term of the policy. A single premium is a lump-sum payment at the start of a policy.
- Non-profit, with-profit and linked benefits. Non-profit policies pay the exact sum insured. With-profit policies have higher premiums because they provide policyholders with the right to receive a bonus based on financial market performance on top of a basic sum insured. With linked policies the benefits paid to policyholders are directly tied to the performance of defined assets. The most common form of linkage is to a unit trust, the value of the benefit being dependent on the performance of the unit trust or mutual fund.
- Individual and group schemes. Life insurance and pensions are purchased both by individuals and on behalf of groups of people, the latter usually by employers.

There are three main methods of providing a guaranteed income on retirement:

- Life annuity purchased by an individual. An annuity is a contract that pays a guaranteed income, usually for life, in return for a lump sum or series of payments.
- Personal pension. Premiums paid by individuals (which are eligible for tax relief) accumulate in a fund, administered by an insurance company, which is used at retirement to purchase an annuity. Part of the accumulated fund is often taken as a tax-free lump sum.
- Occupational pension. Pension contributions by employees and employers are either paid into a fund independent of the employer and run by trustees, known as a self-administered

fund, or are invested in an insurance policy run by an insurance company, known as an insured pension scheme (see Chapter 5). Retirement pensions are paid out of the income generated by the professional investment management of these funds.

The liabilities of life insurance companies are long-term and generally predictable and can be calculated from actuarial tables compiled from decades of data on life expectancies. The commercial risk of the life insurance business lies on the revenue side: the hazard that anticipated returns from invested premiums are insufficient to meet payments due on life and annuity contracts. This is a particular problem for products that promise to pay fixed rates, as Equitable Life found out (see Chapter 13). The UK insurance industry pays out £88 billion a year in life insurance and pension claims.

The business of insurance involves three distinct activities: underwriting (bearing risk for a price), selling and advisory work (the provision of risk-management services to major clients). The principal participants in the industry conduct all or some of these activities in different mixes. General insurance companies combine underwriting and selling. Advisory work is often important for life insurance companies, which also conduct underwriting and selling. Insurance brokers typically combine selling and advisory work. Reinsurers are principally underwriters, although some provide advisory services. Lloyd's syndicates are simply underwriters.

Each activity has a different market geography. Selling, which still has a substantial human dimension (the adage in the industry is that "life insurance is sold, not bought"), means primarily face-to-face contact with customers, although telesales (sales over the telephone) have grown. Advisory work requires access to the corporate clients that make up the market for risk-management services. Underwriting is conducted in a thoroughly international marketplace.

The London Market

The London Market focused on the City is the leading international market for wholesale insurance and reinsurance business, and it generates the bulk of the UK insurance industry's export revenues. It specialises in covering high-exposure (large) and complex risks that other insurance markets are unable to handle. It also provides large-risk cover for UK-owned companies and reinsurance facilities for domestic insurers.

Table 7.2 **London Market participants, 2003**

Insurance companies (IUA members)	112
Lloyd's syndicates	71
P&I clubs	39
Insurance brokers	142

Sources: International Underwriting Association; Lloyd's of London

Participants in the London Market are insurance and reinsurance companies, Lloyd's of London and P&I clubs, which provide insurance, and insurance brokers who act on behalf of those seeking insurance (see Table 7.2). The insurance companies active in the London Market are mostly large, composite undertakings. Most are members of the International Underwriting Association (IUA).

Risks are covered in the London Market on a subscription basis, with, usually, wholesale insurance brokers acting as intermediaries between parties wishing to buy insurance cover (their clients) and insurers that want to sell it. The subscription process begins with a specialist underwriter (known as a lead underwriter), who determines the terms on which cover will be provided and subscribes for part of a risk offered by a broker, typically around 5%. Then other insurers – companies, Lloyd's syndicates, P&I clubs and insurers in other markets – subscribe for further portions of the business on the same terms as the lead underwriter until the whole risk is covered.

Insurance business comprises both direct insurance and reinsurance. There are two kinds of reinsurance: proportional reinsurance, which is a form of risk-spreading by direct insurers; and non-proportional reinsurance, which, in essence, provides a direct insurer with a guarantee against loss.

The number and variety of insurers operating in the London Market give it unrivalled depth, ensuring that brokers are able to find cover for virtually any type of risk. The concentration of insurers and intermediaries in close physical proximity helps brokers to know the specialisms, strengths and shortcomings of the insurers they deal with and to tap the underwriting capacity of the various sectors of the market. Many insurance firms have offices close to the Lloyd's building.

The premiums set on the London Market are global benchmarks. The intensity of competition for business leads to innovative solutions, a

Table 7.3 **London Market gross premium income, 1995–2002 (£bn)**

	1995	2000	2001	2002
Lloyd's of London	5.6	8.5	10.4	12.8
Insurance companies	6.2	8.5	8.6	11.1
P&I clubs	0.6	0.7	1.0	0.7
Total	12.4	17.7	20.0	24.6

Sources: IFSL, *Insurance*, 2001; *International Financial Markets in the UK*, November 2003

crucial factor that sustains the City's leading position. Thus companies seeking cover for previously unquoted risks turn first to the London Market.

The London Market is bolstered by the services provided by a pair of trade associations: the International Underwriting Association of London and the London Market Insurance Brokers' Committee. There are also several professional bodies, notably the Chartered Insurance Institute, the Insurance Institute of London, the Institute of Actuaries and the Institute of Risk Management, which represent members and help to keep them abreast of developments in the marketplace.

The London Market is thoroughly international in both the origins of business and the nationalities of its participants. Three-quarters of the insurance companies active in it are foreign-owned and many of the brokers are too. It is the only location in which all the world's 20 largest international insurance and reinsurance companies are active.

Premium income

The London Market is the principal market for internationally traded insurance and reinsurance. Gross premium income in 2002 was £24.6 billion. This was almost twice the level of 1995, a healthy rate of expansion. Lloyd's of London accounts for 52% of total London Market business, insurance companies 45% and P&I clubs 3% (see Table 7.3). A 2000 survey of London Market operators indicates that North America generated 38% of total business, the UK domestic market 25% and Japan 3%. Continental Europe accounts for 18% and is of growing importance, stimulated by the integration of the new market economies of eastern Europe.

The business of the London Market comprises three principal types of insurance:

Table 7.4 **International insurance premium income, 1999 (% share)**

	Net marine	Net aviation
London Market	19	39
United States	13	23
Japan	14	4
Germany	12	3
France	5	13
Others	37	18

Source: Lloyd's of London

- ◪ Marine, aviation and transport (MAT)
- ◪ Home-foreign
- ◪ Non-MAT treaty reinsurance

The London Market's MAT business has developed from the centuries-old marine underwriting conducted at Lloyd's. Lloyd's does 59% of the business, insurance companies 29% and P&I clubs 13%. The London Market has the largest share of global net premiums for marine and aviation insurance, 19% and 39% respectively (see Table 7.4).

Home-foreign business involves writing risks abroad from London. Lloyd's undertakes 63% of home-foreign activity and insurance companies 37%. Non-MAT treaty reinsurance means general risks (non-transport) reinsured on the London Market. Insurance companies conduct 64% of this business and Lloyd's 36%. The London Market has a 60% share of the market for the insurance of offshore oil and gas rigs. It has a 10% market share of total worldwide reinsurance and accounts for 25% of internationally available reinsurance business. Its market share of large industrial insurance business is 10–15%.

Despite its leading position and substantial expansion, the London Market's share of international wholesale insurance business has been eroded since the 1990s by several factors over which it has little control. Consolidation within and between the insurance and reinsurance sectors has resulted in much larger and more international insurance companies, which have internalised business flows, cutting out recourse to the London Market. The growth of rival financial centres, notably in Bermuda and Ireland, is another factor. The establishment of "captive" insurance companies by large multinational corporations, effectively taking their insurance business in-house, and the international diffusion of risk-management activity have also been adverse developments for the London Market.

Insurance companies

There has been a substantial insurance-company sector of the London Market for more than a century, although it was overshadowed by Lloyd's until the 1970s. Initially, the City offices of domestic general and composite insurance companies focused on marine insurance, subsequently developing aviation, energy and other non-marine business. The "company market" (the term for the non-Lloyd's sector of the London Market) expanded from the 1970s as most major European and North American insurers and reinsurers opened offices in the City. Mergers reduced the number of participant companies in the 1990s, resulting in significant increases in their average size and capacity to do business. The company-market sector accounts for almost half of the business of the London Market.

Virtually all the insurance companies active in the London Market are members of the International Underwriting Association of London (IUA), the world's largest representative organisation for international and wholesale insurance and reinsurance companies. It has 57 ordinary members based in London or Europe and 35 associate members from 20 other countries, with the largest group of associates coming from the United States. The total capital of these companies is more than $300 billion. The IUA represents its members' interests to politicians and regulators in the UK and abroad, and it works jointly with Lloyd's to promote and develop the London Market. A recent benefit of this co-operation was the merger of the accounting and settlement systems of the company market and Lloyd's to provide improved and more economical back-office services for the whole market.

Protection and indemnity clubs

The London Market includes a number of insurance mutual associations that provide some of the same services as the insurance companies but whose capital is subscribed by policyholders, not outside shareholders. P&I clubs furnish cover for their members against risks not covered by policies written by Lloyd's and the insurance companies. Originally devised to meet the needs of the marine industry, in recent years P&I clubs have been established by doctors and lawyers to provide professional indemnity. London is the world's leading centre for P&I insurance.

Table 7.5 **Leading insurance brokers, 2000**

Company	Country	Revenue ($m)
Marsh & McLennan Co	US	6,915
Aon Corp	US	5,137
Willis Group	UK	1,305
Arthur J Gallagher & Co	US	716
Wells Fargo Insurance	US	610
Jardine Lloyd Thompson Group	UK	462
HLF Insurance Holdings	UK	406
Alexander Forbes	South Africa	385
USI Holdings Corp	US	360
Hilb, Rogal & Hamilton	US	260

Source: IFSL, *Insurance*, 2001

For the marine sector, cover may include risks such as collision liability, loss or damage to cargoes, pollution, loss of life and personal injury aboard ships (see Chapter 9).

Insurance brokers

Most of the insurance and reinsurance risks placed in the London Market are handled for clients by insurance brokers. There are around 140 firms of brokers that are regulated by Lloyd's, as well as a group of large international firms that direct business to the London Market from their offices around the world. Through the pursuit of the best terms for their clients in the London Market or elsewhere, brokers stimulate competition among insurance underwriters. Most of the world's leading insurance-broker firms are based in London or have London offices. Their interests are represented by the London Market Insurance Brokers Association.

Mergers between firms in the early and mid-1990s led to a contraction in the number of brokers and the emergence of some very large companies. American companies dominate the industry league table with six out of the top ten companies; three of the remainder are UK companies. The two largest brokers, Marsh & McLennan and Aon, operate on a global basis and dominate the international insurance-broking business; they account for three-quarters of the revenues of the leading brokers (see Table 7.5).

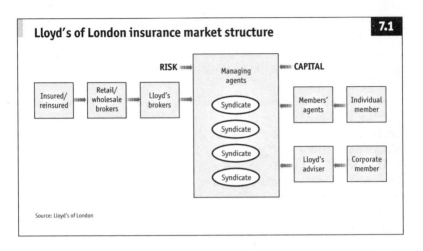

Lloyd's of London insurance market structure 7.1

Source: Lloyd's of London

Lloyd's of London

Lloyd's of London is a membership insurance market that focuses on high-risk wholesale international insurance business. It receives a little over half of the London Market premiums (the insurance companies and P&I clubs get the rest), amounting to 8% of total UK premium income (wholesale and retail combined). Brokers bring business to the Lloyd's market on behalf of clients requiring insurance cover, which is provided by the members of Lloyd's (also known as "capital providers"). Members pool resources in groups known as "syndicates" to underwrite insurance risks. Syndicates are run by firms of professional managing agents. The structure of the market is shown in Figure 7.1.

The membership of Lloyd's comprises:

- individual members ("Names") – wealthy individuals whose exposure to the insurance risks they underwrite extends to their total personal wealth;
- corporate members – limited liability companies formed specifically to underwrite insurance business at Lloyd's;
- NameCos, Scottish Limited Partnerships and Group Conversion Vehicles – limited entities owned by former individual members that serve as a mechanism for the conversion of their unlimited underwriting liabilities into limited liabilities.

Syndicate members receive income from the premiums paid by clients, but they are liable for claims arising from risks insured. Individual members are often members of several syndicates, but corporate members generally underwrite through a single syndicate. Syndicates are annual ventures in which the members participate on an independent basis for their own profit or loss, meaning that they are not responsible for each other's losses.

Many syndicates specialise in particular types of risk. There are four main areas of business: marine; motor; aviation; and "non-marine", an industry term for a cocktail of risks including catastrophe (such as hurricanes and earthquakes), professional indemnity, product liability, fire, theft and disease. Lloyd's underwriters also create bespoke policies for big corporate clients, including 96% of FTSE 100 companies and 93% of Dow Jones Industrial Average companies. Innovation is a feature of the market; for instance, in the 1990s following Nick Leeson's bankrupting of Barings (see Chapter 13), Lloyd's underwriters were the first insurers to offer "rogue trader" cover.

Syndicates are run by firms of specialist managing agents, which are either public or private companies. Some provide capital to the syndicates they manage, assuming a hybrid role as managing agent and corporate syndicate member. Clients insured by Lloyd's have multiple safeguards. Premiums received are held in trust for policyholders. Individual members are liable to the full extent of their assets, and corporate members are required to commit capital to back their commitments. Lloyd's central fund is available to meet claims that are not paid from other sources.

Accredited Lloyd's brokers place risks on behalf of clients with Lloyd's syndicates, using their expertise to negotiate competitive terms. Many of them specialise in particular risk categories. Traditionally, only brokers regulated by Lloyd's could deal with Lloyd's syndicates, but since 2001 membership of the General Insurance Standards Council and fulfilment of Lloyd's accreditation requirements have allowed other UK-based brokers to do so too. Equivalent arrangements apply to brokers based in other EU countries and elsewhere.

Consolidation and profits at Lloyd's

As in the global insurance industry, consolidation has been a feature of Lloyd's business in recent years. In 1990 there were 401 Lloyd's syndicates, but by 2003 the number had fallen to 71. Over the same period the number of Lloyd's brokers decreased from 245 to around 150. The number of managing agents has also decreased, standing at 45 in 2003. The consolidation process resulted in larger syndicates and firms with bigger capital bases.

Table 7.6 **Lloyd's membership and capacity, 1990–2003**

	1990	1995	2001	2003
Number of members				
Individual	28,770	14,744	3,317	2,198
Corporate	–	140	853	768
Total	28,770	14,884	4,170	2,966
Number of syndicates	401	170	108	71
Gross allocated capacity (£bn)				
Individual members	10.7	7.8	1.8	1.8
Corporate members	–	2.4	9.3	12.6
Total	10.7	10.2	11.1	14.4

Source: Lloyd's of London

Following two decades of profitable trading, in the years 1988 to 1992 the Lloyd's market experienced heavy losses of around £14 billion. This was the result of a conjunction of adverse factors, including an unprecedented series of major catastrophes and an upsurge of asbestos and pollution claims arising on policies underwritten many years earlier. The losses prompted a major reconstruction of the market, including the admission of corporate capital for the first time in 1994. Between 1990 and 2003, the number of individual Names slumped from 28,000 to 2,000, while the proportion of corporate capital-backed insurance capacity soared from zero to 87% (see Table 7.6). An acrimonious dispute over liability for the losses between Lloyd's and many of the Names was eventually resolved in August 1996, relieving the Names of £3.2 billion of losses and allowing a renewal plan for the Lloyd's market to be fully implemented (see Chapter 13). The Society of Lloyd's continues to administer the market, its authority to do so being renewed by a new act of parliament in 2000.

Lloyd's returned to profit in 1993. However, in the later years of the 1990s there was a deterioration in profitability and there were losses in 2000 and 2001. The poor performance was caused by a downturn in the international general insurance industry, a cyclical business that was suffering from excess capacity, fierce competition and low premium rates, exacerbated by some heavy catastrophe insurance losses including the September 11th 2001 terrorist attacks in the United States.

Because of higher premiums, stemming partly from September 11th, and low catastrophe losses, performance was strong in 2002 and 2003, with profits of £834m and £1,892m respectively.

The volume of business that can be underwritten by Lloyd's in any year is the aggregate capacity of all the syndicates. The capacity of particular syndicates depends on the amount of capital support allocated by members. During the 1990s the total capacity of Lloyd's was around £10 billion. In the early 2000s there was an upsurge in capacity, reflecting increased investment by market members and the impact of higher premiums in a more robust market; in 2003, stimulated by the resumption of profits, capacity soared to a record £14.4 billion.

Development of Lloyd's of London

The history of Lloyd's goes back to 1688, when Edward Lloyd opened a coffee house in the City, which became a popular gathering place for merchants, shipowners and ships' captains to arrange the insurance of ships and their cargoes. Cover was provided by wealthy individuals, each of whom assumed a portion of a risk in return for a portion of the premium that was paid by a ship's owner. These individuals became known as "underwriters" because they signed their names, along with the amount that they agreed to cover, at the foot of the policy. To meet claims, underwriters were liable to the full extent of their personal wealth.

Publication of *Lloyd's List*, a weekly bulletin giving details of ships seeking insurance, began in 1734 and continues today. *Lloyd's Register of Shipping*, the shipping industry's bible, was first published in 1764 to provide underwriters and merchants with information about the condition of the vessels they insured and chartered (see Chapter 9). Such initiatives made Lloyd's the fount of up-to-date marine intelligence, which explains why the market was focused there. In 1774, spurred by scandal, a group of underwriters who frequented Lloyd's coffee house formed a membership association and moved to their own exclusive accommodation in the Royal Exchange, retaining the name Lloyd's. Henceforth the Lloyd's market was run as a club, supervised by a committee of members that controlled admission. Another scandal a century later led to the strengthening of the control of the Lloyd's committee by an act of parliament in 1871, which bestowed on Lloyd's the legal status of an incorporated society and empowered the committee to make bylaws to regulate members.

The dynamic expansion of the international economy in the late 19th and early 20th centuries led to a rapid expansion of international trade and shipping. Naturally, Lloyd's marine business boomed, but these prosperous decades also witnessed a diversification into insurance risks of new types: the first motor policy was issued in 1906 and the first aviation policy in 1911. A key episode was the San Francisco earthquake and fire of 1906; the prompt payment of claims by Lloyd's underwriters greatly enhanced the market's reputation in the United States and confirmed its position as the world's leading wholesale insurance market.

In the 20th century, Lloyd's faced mounting challenges from insurance companies at home and abroad that sought to capture its underwriting business. Its continued success was based on several factors:

- Its "first mover" advantages, particularly its traditional ties with the shipping industry.
- The security of a Lloyd's policy, resting on the entire personal fortunes of the underwriter members backed by the market itself.
- The entrepreneurial initiative of individual Lloyd's underwriters, in contrast to the more sluggish and bureaucratic conduct of rival company insurers.
- Its relatively modest cost base compared with the heavy overheads of an insurance company.

But Lloyd's also had weaknesses relative to the insurance companies which contributed to the long-term decline of its share of the global insurance market:

- Inadequate capital. Until the admission of corporate underwriters in 1994, the market's capacity was limited to the collective commitment of individual underwriting members and it was unable to tap the capital market.
- Marketing. As a market made up of individual underwriters, it was difficult to establish sales and marketing operations that matched those of the big insurance companies.
- Poor management. This applied to both the market as a whole and to some syndicates.
- Scandals. A series of scandals began in the late 1970s, tarnishing Lloyd's reputation (see Chapter 13).

By the early 2000s Lloyd's share of the total world insurance market was well below 1%, although that statistic does not do justice to its importance in the international wholesale segment of the insurance market.

Lloyd's remained in the Royal Exchange until 1928 when it moved to its own premises in Leadenhall Street. The expansion of business led to the acquisition of a second building in Lime Street in 1958. Two decades later, renewed overcrowding led to the redevelopment of the Leadenhall Street site. The controversial new building in glass and gleaming metal by Richard Rogers, an avant-garde architect, was opened in 1986. It was not to everyone's taste. "We began in a coffee house," remarked a Lloyd's traditionalist, "and we have ended up in a coffee percolator."

The UK insurance industry

There were 808 companies authorised to conduct insurance business in the UK in 2003: 592 for general insurance; 160 for long-term insurance; and 56 "composites", which undertake both types of business. Most insurance companies operating in the UK are members of the Association of British Insurers, which represents member's interests. It has a staff of 120 people.

The companies are predominantly (79%) UK-owned. However, the proportion of foreign-owned companies is increasing as a result of mergers and acquisitions and the establishment of a presence in the UK by European and American companies. Between 1990 and the early 2000s, foreign-controlled companies' share of UK premiums increased from 20% to 29%. Almost 25% of UK insurance companies' net premium income derives from overseas business, including revenues from UK companies' overseas subsidiaries (see Table 7.7).

During the 1990s the worldwide premium income of the UK insurance industry (including the London Market) increased from £66 billion to £175 billion. The economic slowdown in the early 2000s led to a downturn, and by 2002 the total had fallen to £161 billion (see Table 7.7). Although the volume of general insurance business grew over these years, most of the increase was the result of the rapid expansion of long-term business, its proportion of total premium income rising from 60% in 1990 to 75% in 2002.

Long-term insurance

Long-term premiums trebled between 1990 and 2002, increasing from £41 billion to £122 billion. Life insurance business generated 40% of long-term premiums, occupational pensions 31% and individual pensions 25%. Domestic business accounted for 80% of long-term premium income and it was domestic factors that propelled the expansion. Pen-

Table 7.7 **Net worldwide premiums generated by the UK insurance industry, 1990–2002 (£bn)**

	1990	1995	2000	2001	2002
UK risks					
Long-term	34	45	117	93	97
General	16	21	23	26	28
Total	50	66	140	119	125
Overseas risks					
Long-term	7	11	20	24	25
General	9	15	15	13	11
Total	16	26	35	37	36
Total long-term	41	56	137	117	122
Total general	25	36	38	39	39
Grand total	66	92	175	156	161
% of premiums written by foreign-controlled companies	20	25	26	29	na

Source: IFSL, *International Financial Markets in the UK*, May 2004

sion premium income tripled in the 1990s as the number of people with a private pension expanded to 11m, stimulated by the spread of personal pension plans (and in spite of the scandal over the mis-selling of pensions – see Chapter 13). A further stimulus was provided by the introduction of the stakeholder pension in 2001. This low-charge, portable and flexible pension scheme was principally aimed at those not in occupational schemes. Despite its attractions, take-up has been less than expected. Single premium (lump sum) life business also increased rapidly, boosted by savings vehicles with tax advantages such as PEPS, TESSAS and ISAS, which have grown more than sixfold since the early 1990s. As regards the 20% of long-term premiums that derived from overseas business, the most important markets were the EU (40%) and North America (35%).

The long-term insurance industry has been consolidating in recent years through mergers and acquisitions that have boosted the size of the leading firms. The industry restructuring is a reflection of mounting international competition as companies diversify into new markets and seek economies of scale to increase efficiency. Industry experts predict that the number of UK life insurance companies is likely to contract to around 20 main competitors over the next decade. Notable combinations have been those between Norwich Union and CGU, creating the UK's largest composite insurance company (renamed Aviva); Barclays Bank and Woolwich, to form the UK's biggest long-term insurer, Barclays Life Assurance; Abbey National and Scottish Provident; Lloyds TSB and Scottish Widows; and Cheltenham & Gloucester and Abbey Life. The outcome has been greater market concentration: the five leading companies account for more than 30% of total long-term premium income and the ten leading companies for more than 50% (see Table 7.8).

General insurance

General insurance business generated a quarter of total UK premium income in 2002 (see Table 7.7 on the previous page). In the first half of the 1990s there were substantial increases in general insurance premium income, but thereafter the pace slowed, reflecting downward pressure on premiums because of intense competition in the market. Two-thirds of total general insurance premiums is generated by the London Market and one-third by domestic business (see Table 7.1 on page 170). In the London Market, around half of the business is handled by insurance companies and half by Lloyd's underwriters. Insurance companies dominate the domestic market in general insurance. The largest sources of domestic general insurance premium income are motor policies (about a quarter) and property policies (about one-fifth). Premiums from accident and health business have grown steadily over the last decade, the latter boosted by reforms in the provision of private medical insurance as an employee benefit. More than a quarter of general insurance premiums originate overseas, the most important markets being the United States and the EU, which each generate about one-third of such overseas business.

As a result of recent mergers, the UK's general insurance market is one of the most concentrated in Europe. The ten leading firms account for as much as 78% of the business conducted by insurance companies (domestic plus the company market sector of the London Market). The leading player is Aviva, followed at some distance by Royal & Sun Alliance, Zurich and AXA (see Table 7.9 on page 188).

Insurance distributors, loss adjusters and actuaries

Insurance companies market their products to customers through their own salesforces and tied agents, and through independent intermediaries. Traditionally, much insurance business has been done

Table 7.8 **Leading long-term insurers, UK premium income in 2002**

Group/company	Net premium income (£bn)
Barclays Life Assurance	11.8
Standard Life	9.6
Aviva (formerly CGNU)	8.6
Prudential (incl Scottish Amicable and M&G)	8.4
Halifax (incl Clerical Medical)	6.2
Lloyds TSB (incl Scottish Widows and Abbey Life)	5.5
Legal & General	4.2
American Life	3.9
Zurich Financial Services (incl Eagle Star, Allied Dunbar and Sterling)	3.7
AXA Insurance	3.5

Source: Association of British Insurers

through independent insurance brokers who act on behalf of clients, placing their business with the insurance companies and negotiating on price and policy terms. The British Insurance Brokers Association has around 2,500 member firms. Despite competition from rival sales media, independent intermediaries still handle two-thirds of general insurance premium income. Independent financial advisers are the most important distribution channel for long-term insurance business, handling 60% of new single-premium business and 45% of new regular-premium business. Company salesforces generate 43% of new regular-premium business and 30% of new single-premium long-term insurance business.

For general insurance, direct selling generates one-sixth of premiums and company agents account for one-eighth. Direct selling by telephone of general insurance policies to retail consumers has grown rapidly in recent years and now produces 15% of business. The most rapid growth of telesales has been in the motor, household property, accident and health sectors. By 2002, the firm that pioneered this form of distribution, Direct Line, had risen from nowhere to number six among the ten leading general insurance companies (see Table 7.9). Banks and building societies, which market insurance products to their established customer bases, are also growing distribution channels, accounting for around 10% of premium income.

Loss adjusters are independent specialists who verify the liability of

Table 7.9 **Leading general insurers, UK premium income in 2002**

Group/company	Net premium income (£bn)
Aviva (formerly CGNU)	5.0
Royal & Sun Alliance	3.3
Zurich Financial Services (incl Eagle Star)	2.4
AXA Insurance (incl PPP Healthcare and Equity & Law)	2.2
Churchill Group (incl Winterthur and NIG)	2.0
Direct Line Group	1.8
BUPA Insurance	1.3
Allianz Cornhill	1.2
NFU Mutual	0.8
Co-operative Insurance Society	0.6

Source: Association of British Insurers

an insurer for a claim. After inspecting or investigating a claim the loss adjuster reports to the insurance company; both the insurer and the policyholder rely on the loss adjuster's skill and impartiality. The Chartered Institute of Loss Adjusters, to which most people working for independent loss-adjusting firms belong, has around 2,300 members.

Actuaries are experts in the mathematics of life expectancy. They compute life insurance risks based on mortality statistics and probability theory to determine rates for life insurance and pension policies, reserves against death claims, annuity rates and other premiums. They are employed by insurance companies and Lloyd's syndicates to make such calculations. With the increasing availability of detailed statistics for non-life insurance business, actuaries are also playing a greater role in determining general insurance premiums. The two professional bodies of actuaries, in London and Edinburgh, have a combined membership of 5,500, of whom around two-fifths work for firms of actuarial consultants and one-third for insurance companies, the rest being employed by government or other companies. The consultant firms play an important role in the pensions industry, acting as advisers to pension fund trustees in the appointment of asset managers and in making asset allocation decisions (see Chapter 5).

Regulation

Responsibility for the authorisation and regulation of insurance companies lies with the Financial Services Authority (FSA), the UK's unified financial services regulator (see Chapter 11), based on the Insurance Companies Act 1982. The FSA monitors and supervises the regulatory compliance of insurance companies operating in the UK. New companies applying for authorisation must satisfy the FSA that they are financially sound, submit a coherent business plan and demonstrate that their directors are fit and proper persons to run an insurance company. The sale of life and investment products by independent financial advisers is regulated by the FSA. In November 2001 the FSA's regulatory remit was extended to the whole of the insurance industry when it became responsible for the regulation of Lloyd's of London.

General insurance intermediaries are regulated by the General Insurance Standards Council (GISC), which was established in 2000 to ensure the fair treatment of general insurance policyholders. It is an independent, non-statutory organisation that regulates the sales, advisory and service standards provided by its 4,000 members, which include most insurance brokers and underwriters. GISC rules provide a common framework for supervision of the sale of general insurance products by insurers and intermediaries.

The FSA, in common with regulators in other major financial markets and in consultation with the industry, is developing a more risk-based (as opposed to rule-based) approach to capital adequacy for the financial-services industry including insurance (see Chapter 11). This will involve new financial monitoring practices and reporting requirements to ensure effective supervisory oversight.

As a result of an EU directive of July 1994 designed to create a European single market for insurance, insurance companies with a head office in another EU country are allowed to operate in the UK under a licence from their home country's supervisory authority. The underlying aim is to allow companies based in one EU country to undertake business in other member countries and to allow consumers access to products regardless of their origin. Several measures affecting the insurance industry are being pursued by the European Commission, principally new directives on insurance intermediation, reinsurance and financial conglomerates, as well as the Solvency II Project, which will determine the future framework for solvency and other regulatory requirements.

Insurance industry's contribution to the UK's economy

It is estimated that insurance and pension fund activity generates around 1.4% of the UK's GDP. The 360,000 people who work in the insurance sector account for over one-third of total financial services employment. The London Market and other wholesale insurance activities generate around 50,000 of these jobs (40,000 in the City and 10,000 elsewhere).

The insurance industry gives rise to overseas earnings in several ways:

- Through the sale by UK companies of cross-border insurance and reinsurance cover.
- Through the commissions earned by brokers through the placement of cross-border risks.
- From the remittance of interest, profits and dividends by the overseas subsidiaries and affiliates of UK insurance companies.
- From income from overseas investments, both general reserves and policyholders' life insurance and pension funds.

For years, the insurance industry has made an important positive contribution to the UK's balance of payments, generating higher net exports than banking, securities dealing or any other financial sector activity. Between 1990 and 2000, insurance industry net export earnings trebled from £1.4 billion to a £4.3 billion (see Table 7.10). Claims resulting from the destruction of the World Trade Centre in September 2001 totalling an estimated £2.5 billion led to a downturn that year. However, in 2002 net earnings soared to a record £6.9 billion.

The insurance industry is the UK's largest institutional investor, accounting for 40% of total institutional investor assets. Insurance company shareholdings amount to around 20% of UK equities. More than 90% of insurance investment funds arise from long-term policies, the premiums being invested in assets appropriate for meeting the liabilities at maturity (see Chapter 5).

Insurance industry financial assets (long-term and general combined) expanded rapidly in the 1990s, rising fourfold between 1990 and 2002, from £240 billion to £980 billion. This was mostly because of the rising volume and value of life insurance assets, which grew by 170% during the 1990s, while general insurance assets increased by about 30%. Rising equity prices were a significant contributory factor. Falling share prices in the early 2000s led to a 10% shrinkage of insurance-industry funds

Table 7.10 **UK insurance industry net exports (£bn)**

1990	1.4
1995	2.3
1997	3.1
1999	3.9
2000	4.3
2001	3.8
2002	6.9

Source: IFSL, *World Invisible Trade*, 2003

from the peak in 1999. The stockmarket price falls obliged some insurance companies to review their portfolio asset allocations and increase their holdings of other asset classes in order to increase their solvency ratios.

Trends and issues

- **Consolidation.** In many European countries there has been significant consolidation in the insurance industry in recent years through mergers and acquisitions, driven by pressures to reduce costs through economies of scale and to develop distribution channels. In the UK there is likely to be further consolidation on the long-term side of the industry. But there is limited scope in the general insurance market, which is already the most concentrated in Europe.

- **Bancassurance.** The selling of insurance services by banks has grown rapidly over the last decade. Some banks have acquired insurance companies, and vice versa, and others have diversified their product range to sell to their client base. The trend is likely to continue with insurers seeking distribution through bank customer networks, while banks strive to extend their financial products.

- **New distribution channels and e-insurance.** The development and diffusion of information technology are presenting new opportunities for product distribution.

- **Pension provision.** There will be further expansion in private saving for retirement, especially in Europe where pension provision has mostly been financed out of taxation. With their broad expertise in handling a diverse range of assets – international as well as domestic, equities as well as bonds – British asset managers, life insurance companies among them, are well placed to benefit from the swelling tide of funds (see Chapter 5).

■ **Internationalisation.** As with other financial services, the insurance industry is becoming increasingly international in its organisation and orientation. In the 1990s some large pan-European insurance companies were formed through cross-border mergers and acquisitions, notably AXA of France and Allianz of Germany. In the next few years some truly global players may well emerge.

■ **The euro.** The UK's decision not to join the euro zone does not seem to have damaged the London Market. The Bank of England is co-ordinating preparations by the wholesale industry for possible entry to the euro, while the Association of British Insurers, the domestic industry's market association, is advising members on what it will mean in practice should the UK adopt the euro as its currency.

■ **EU directives.** The EU's Financial Services Action Plan comprises a series of measures designed to create a single market for financial services, including insurance, by 2005. The Action Plan has three objectives: the creation of a single European market for wholesale financial services; open and secure retail markets; and state-of-the-art prudential rules and supervision. The European Commission is also working on new directives on the environment, consumer protection, corporate governance, takeovers and many other matters that affect the insurance and pensions industries.

■ **Global liberalisation.** The 1997 Financial Services Agreement, by which more than 100 countries belonging to the World Trade Organisation (WTO) made commitments to liberalise trade in financial services, was a significant milestone in the liberalisation of trade in insurance. The commitments offered guarantees on market access and other matters. In 2001 the WTO Doha Ministerial Conference launched a new round of negotiations on the liberalisation of trade in services and set a deadline of January 1st 2005 for their conclusion. However, many practical barriers remain, and in general trade in insurance is less liberalised internationally than banking and is particularly prone to the erection of new regulatory obstacles. But the trend towards a more liberalised global marketplace appears set to continue.

8 Professional and support services

The activities of City financial firms generate demand for a host of professional and other support services. Foremost are the City's specialist law, accountancy and management consultancy firms, which employed 71,000 people at the start of 2004, 23% of total wholesale financial services employment in London (see Table 1.2 on page 6). Other support services include specialist financial public relations, recruitment, education and training, publishing and information provision, IT, economic consultancy and trade associations. There are even specialists such as master printers, who can run off a prospectus within hours, and expert banknote, bond and share certificate designers.

Legal services

London is the world's leading centre for international and financial legal services, specialisms that have grown substantially since the early 1990s. Between 1993 and 2002, the number of solicitors employed by the largest 100 London law firms, many of them undertaking City work, rose from 10,000 to 16,000. Fee income grew even faster than the head count, trebling from £2.8 billion to £8.4 billion. International commercial law is the area of expertise of the 1,000 members of the Commercial Bar Association. Many cases are heard in the Commercial Court, where procedures are geared to accommodate the needs of international business. The UK's law firms generated net exports of £1.4 billion in 2002.

The growth of demand for international legal services was driven by the expansion and globalisation of City business, and the increasing concentration of European wholesale financial services activity in London. In response, a number of leading City law firms merged with European and (in some cases) American counterparts to enhance their international presence, mirroring that of the global investment banks that were among their most important clients. (It was a development that echoed the internationalisation of the banking sector in the 1960s, following in the footsteps of their multinational corporation clients.) Competition for the City's legal business has intensified. There are now more than 200 foreign law firms with London offices. The Big Four accounting firms have also set up significant legal practices, and the leading Scottish law firms have established a presence in London. Half the

Table 8.1 **Leading global law firms, 2002**

	Headquarters	Number of lawyers	Lawyers outside home country (%)
Clifford Chance	UK – international	3,322	63
Baker & McKenzie	US – international	3,094	83
Freshfields, Bruckhaus Deringer	UK – international	2,430	61
Allen & Overy	UK – international	2,197	48
Linklaters	UK – international	2,000	52
Eversheds	UK – national	1,776	4
Skadden, Arps, Slate, Meagher & Flom	US – New York	1,653	10
Jones, Day, Reavis & Pogue	US – national	1,565	18
Lovells	UK – international	1,432	55
White & Case	US – international	1,427	60

Source: IFSL, *International Financial Markets in the UK*, May 2004

foreign firms are from the United States, the others being mostly from Europe, Australia and Canada.

Six of the world's largest law firms by head count are UK-based, a global league table performance way ahead of banks, investment banks, asset managers or insurance companies (see Table 8.1). There are also some significant smaller domestic City law firms, including the formidable Slaughter & May. In many of the leading international law firms, at least half of their staff are located outside their home country.

The number and size of London's international law firms ensure that specialist legal expertise is available across the whole range of the City's needs: banking, corporate finance, corporate and financial law, project finance, the international capital markets, insurance, shipping, tax, regulation and dispute resolution. It is common for English law to be adopted by overseas parties to govern their relations to gain the advantages of a mature body of commercial law, the services of City law firms, a trusted and politically independent judicial system and access to a variety of dispute resolution services.

Some 5,000 international arbitrations and mediations take place each year. These are generally a less costly and acrimonious alternative to the law courts. Around 50 organisations provide dispute resolution services in London, including trade associations, professional institutes and derivatives exchanges, which endeavour to resolve disputes arising under their contracts. The leading specialist organisations are as follows:

- ◪ London Court of International Arbitration (LCIA), at the forefront of the development of arbitration services with an international operation and outlook.
- ◪ Centre for Dispute Resolution (CEDR), specialising in the resolution of international commercial disputes through mediation; it is one of the principal providers of alternative dispute resolution services in the world.
- ◪ Chartered Institute of Arbitrators, the world's leading professional body for the training of arbitrators.
- ◪ International Chamber of Commerce (ICC), the global leader in international arbitration with a rapidly expanding presence in London.

Accounting services

Three of the global Big Four accountancy firms – PricewaterhouseCoopers (PWC), KPMG (Klynveld Peat Marwick Goerdeler) and Deloitte Touche Tohmatsu – have City roots and each includes the names of at least two City forerunner firms in their current names. The other, Ernst & Young, is in origin an American firm but had City associates from the 1920s. Today all the Big Four are thoroughly international with huge staffs around the world. For example, PWC, the largest, has 123,000 employees and 768 offices in 139 countries, and Deloitte Touche Tohmatsu has 120,000 employees and 656 offices in 144 countries.

The Big Four undertake the lion's share of City accounting work. Each has an important high-level presence: PWC has 6,000 City staff; Deloitte Touche Tohmatsu 5,000; KPMG 5,000; and Ernst & Young 3,000. Their City clients are financial firms and major corporations to which they provide a range of services, including audit, tax, insolvency, corporate finance and consultancy (see Table 8.2). Much of the work of the City operations of the Big Four is cross-border in nature and many of their clients are overseas companies. The scale of these activities has increased substantially over the last decade, an expansion reflected in the sevenfold increase in UK exports of accounting services since the early 1990s to £701m in 2002. Net UK export earnings were £461m, a ninefold increase compared with the early 1990s.

Audit and tax are the main sources of income, and the Big Four undertake virtually all the auditing of large companies in the UK and

Table 8.2 **Accountancy firms' sources of revenue in the UK, 2003**

	% of fee income
Audit	37
Tax	29
Insolvency and business recovery	10
Consultancy	9
Corporate finance	8
Other	7

Source: IFSL, *International Financial Markets in the UK*, May 2004

around the world (see Table 8.3). In the 1990s, consulting grew rapidly and became second to audit as a source of revenue for the Big Four. Potential conflicts of interest between the audit and consulting functions led PWC, KPMG and Ernst & Young to divest their consulting practices. So did Andersen, the fifth global accounting firm, though not before its audit work for Enron and Worldcom had been compromised leading to the spectacular demise of the accountancy firm in 2002. More recently, the Big Four have been rebuilding their consulting practices to be able to offer clients either audit or consulting services, but not both.

The drive to create a single European market in financial services led to the adoption in 2002 of an EU regulation requiring all listed European companies to prepare their accounts in accordance with International Financial Reporting Standards (IFRS) from 2005. Moreover, the profession has set its sights on the establishment of common global accounting rules that would permit companies to list on any exchange in the world, helping to lower the cost of capital to companies.

Traditionally, accountancy firms were partnerships. In 2001 a new form of partnership, the limited liability partnership (LLP), was introduced in the UK. The LLP preserves the flexibility and tax status of a partnership but provides the protection of limited liability for partners. The UK operations of the Big Four immediately adopted LLP status, as have some smaller firms.

Management consultants

The financial-services industry is the largest consumer of management consultancy services in the UK. Its expenditure of £1.1 billion in 2002 was almost one-quarter of total fee income, with banks spending £357m,

Table 8.3 **Leading UK management consultancies, 2002**

	Revenue (£m)
IBM/PwC	1,377
Accenture	1,140
LogicaCMG	1,086
Deloitte Touche Tohmatsu	845
Cap Gemini Ernst & Young	524
McKinsey	518
EDS	383
CSC	360
Fujitsu	330
BDO Stoy Hayward	306

Source: IFSL, *International Financial Markets in the UK*, May 2004

insurance companies £337m and other sectors together £381m. Out-sourcing and IT services generate more than half of the revenues of management consultancy firms in the UK. Outsourcing has boomed in recent years as many firms have sought to focus on their core business. It has grown in tandem with the increasing importance of IT, which has boosted demand for out-of-house expertise. Human resources is another growth area, driven by firms' need to cut costs, acquire specialist knowledge and outsource some routine tasks. But revenues from the traditional strategic advisory function have stagnated and now comprise only 7% of the total.

In the 1990s the leading firms in the industry, and the principal ones supplying services to the City, were the consultancy offshoots of the Big Five accountancy firms. In the early 2000s these either became independent entities or were sold to new owners. This avoided possible conflicts of interest between the audit and advisory arms of the global accountancy firms. It also permitted the consultancy businesses to gain access to outside capital to fund expansion. Thus, for example, in 2001 Andersen Consulting split off from its sibling accounting firm, Arthur Andersen, to become Accenture, an independent firm with 75,000 staff operating in 47 countries. By contrast, PWC's consulting business was acquired by IBM in 2002 and its 30,000 staff and offices in 52 countries were combined with IBM's existing capabilities to form Business Consulting Services, the world's largest consulting services organisation (see Table 8.3).

Most of the 30 largest management consultants operating in the UK are either firms based in the United States that provide a range of services or IT specialists. They are the UK arms of international businesses, accounting, on average, for around 10% of the parent's total revenues. Their own operations are thoroughly international, generating gross exports of management consultancy services of £2.6 billion in 2002 and net exports of £1.3 billion.

As well as the IT services provided by the major consultancy firms, there is also a thriving undergrowth of specialist independent IT consultants providing services such as writing software on demand, website design and maintenance, and dealing with all kinds of electronic emergencies. Many of these small businesses are located in the so-called "City Fringe", the crescent of former light-industrial areas immediately to the north and east of the Square Mile. Most banks also have their own in-house IT staff who develop new systems and sort out operational problems.

Financial information, publishing and press

Information is the life-blood of the financial-services industry. London is the home base of three of the world's leading financial publishing and financial information providers: The Economist Group, the Financial Times Group and Euromoney Institutional Investor. The European edition of the *Wall Street Journal* is edited and produced in Brussels.

Publications

The Economist Group publishes *The Economist*. Founded in 1843, it now has a global circulation of 880,000, making it the world's fourth best-selling newspaper. The Economist brand family of businesses comprises the newspaper, the Economist Intelligence Unit, a consultancy and research entity, a conference organising arm and a variety of other publications and branded businesses. It has a worldwide staff of around 1,000.

The distinctively coloured salmon pink *Financial Times* (FT) has a daily circulation of 470,000 and an estimated readership of 1.6m. First published in the City in 1888, it has a London staff of around 1,000 and local editions in 20 cities across the globe. Research reveals that typical FT readers earn over £100,000 and are involved in the international activities of their business. The Financial Times Group also owns the leading business newspapers in France and Spain, *Les Echos* and *Expansión*, and a variety of other titles including *The Banker* and *Investors*

199

Chronicle. Many of its publications have a linked internet information service, notably FT.com. There are also other business information and analysis services, including a joint venture with the London Stock Exchange that produces the widely used FTSE 100 stock exchange index.

Euromoney Institutional Investor is a City-based international publishing and events business. Its best known titles are *Euromoney*, which began publication in London in 1969 to serve the burgeoning Euromarket, and *Institutional Investor*, which commenced publication in New York in 1967 to meet the needs of the growing ranks of professional money managers. But it also publishes a huge array of niche business magazines and newsletters, many with financial services titles. The other side of its business is organising conferences, conventions and seminars in the major business centres around the world, many of them annual events.

Financial News, which began publication in 1996, is a weekly newspaper covering the European investment banking, securities and asset management industries. It was founded to fill a perceived gap in the market between the general business press, the *Financial Times* and the *Wall Street Journal*, and specialist publications focused on a particular market, such as *IFR* or *Institutional Investor*. Plainly it met a need and reports a readership of around 90,000.

Electronic media

Electronic financial information is provided by Reuters, Bloomberg and Thomson Financial. Reuters was founded in the City in 1851. Although best known as the world's largest international news agency, 90% of the firm's revenues are generated by its financial services business. The Reuters Group, with 15,500 staff (including 2,400 editorial staff) in 92 countries, had revenues of £3.2 billion in 2003. The information, analysis, trading and messaging capabilities conferred by its platforms (screens) are used by 427,000 workers in financial markets around the world.

Bloomberg was established in 1981 by Michael R. Bloomberg, a Wall Street trader and former partner at Salomon Brothers. In 2001 he was elected mayor of New York. There are two sides of the New York-based company, which has a total staff of 8,000. Bloomberg Media, with 1,600 editorial staff in 94 locations, provides a global news service delivered by television, radio, the internet and publications. Bloomberg Professional provides a combination of financial and other data, news and analysis, e-mail, and electronic trading and processing tools on its platforms. It has 260,000 financial-services industry users.

Thomson Financial is a division of Thomson Corporation, which has its headquarters in Toronto. The New York-based Thomson Financial has 7,700 staff, operates in 22 countries and had revenues of $1.5 billion in 2003. It provides a huge array of financial and economic databases, including the well-known Datastream. It provides software and advisory services to clients, enabling them to take full advantage of its financial intelligence facilities to make "smarter decisions, attain higher productivity, and ultimately achieve superior results". It also publishes a variety of specialist financial titles, including *Acquisitions Monthly* and *IFR* (International Financing Review).

Financial public relations

Public relations (PR) firms specialising in the financial services sector, the "lounge lizards of the financial world" as *The Economist* called them (November 15th, 2001), first made an impact in the takeover battles and privatisations of the mid-1980s and have thrived ever since. All major City firms now employ their own in-house corporate communications staff to deal with the press and the public. The Corporate and Financial Group of the Institute of Public Relations has regular speaker meetings, debates and a "full social programme". The Group, which has a strong City element, doubled in size between its creation in 1989 and the early 2000s, from 200 to 400.

The regulatory framework in which City PR firms ply their trade has become tougher and less tolerant of exaggerated claims. Nevertheless, it was a shock when in November 2001 the Financial Services Authority issued a public warning that putting out misleading information could lead to unlimited fines for those working in financial communications, just like other market participants.

Headhunters

Traditionally, City staff spent their whole career with a single employer. This changed in the 1980s as American banks began to set the pace, importing their hire-and-fire approach to growing and shrinking businesses. This in turn sundered the bonds of loyalty on the part of staff. Anthony Hilton, City editor of London's *Evening Standard*, commented: "An entire industry of headhunters has been built on this institutionalised disloyalty and the desire of firms to buy instant success rather than work for it."

Industry insiders estimate that the financial services executive search (headhunter) industry employs around 2,000. It is dominated by half a dozen global firms, which are retained by the leading banks. There are also numerous niche players. In normal times, headhunters smooth and speed up the operation of the City jobs market to the advantage of both employees and employers. But if a City firm gets into trouble its problems may be magnified by predatory headhunting, which can quickly strip a bank of its best people. Occasionally, the mass defection of a whole team or department to a rival firm hits the headlines, accompanied by furious denunciations from the former employer.

The largest American executive search firms – Heidrick & Struggles, Korn/Ferry, Russell Reynolds and Spencer Stuart – are all major players in the City search market, as are Whitehead Mann, a British firm (parent of Baines Gwinner, financial specialist), and Egon Zehnder, a Swiss firm. Several specialist boutique firms are also prominent, including Armstrong International, Blackwood Group, the Rose Partnership, Sainty Hird and the Whitney Group. Michael Page City and Robert Walters are among the oldest and most active firms, both covering a wide spectrum of jobs from middle management to more senior assignments. The *Financial Times* has a jobs supplement on Thursdays and also runs FTCareerPoint, an electronic database of mostly financial services job vacancies, careers development advice and business education information that is available on its website.

Financial education, training and research facilities

Each year in the UK more than 300 students graduate with a degree in financial services and many thousands attend training courses that often lead to a qualification. Two business schools specialise in training for London's financial-services industry: Cass Business School, part of City University, and the ISMA (International Securities Markets Association) Centre at the University of Reading. London Business School and the London School of Economics also have close ties to the industry and City firms.

The Institute of Financial Services (IFS) is the brand name of the Chartered Institute of Bankers (CIB). It acts as an examining and qualifications-awarding body for the banking sector. It runs a variety of courses, seminars and conferences and provides career development support to its members. It also services the financial-services industry more generally, with programmes on financial regulation, risk and insurance management, and, with an eye to the future, financial education for 14–19 year-olds.

The Chartered Insurance Institute organises courses that prepare 100,000 candidates a year for professional examinations in insurance and financial services. The Securities Institute, the training offshoot of the London Stock Exchange, has 52,000 candidates for its various vocational qualifications. It provides courses, seminars, publications and consultancy services for members and students. The British Venture Capital Association and the Futures and Options Association are active in the provision of professional training for their members. There are also half a dozen commercial financial training companies that provide in-service skills development courses and often run City firms' graduate induction courses. The *Financial Times* is an active organiser of short courses and symposia on subjects of topical interest on a commercial basis.

The Financial World Bookshop, part of the IFS, has an extensive stock of financial publications. The IFS library holds over 30,000 books on banking and finance. It is open to members of the CIB and students on IFS courses and the catalogue is available on its website. Non-members can use the collection for a fee. The City Business Library, a research library run by the Corporation of London, is open to the public without charge. It has an extensive collection of financial books and periodicals.

Economic consultants

A handful of boutique consultancies specialise in economic forecasting and undertake commissioned research reports for City firms and institutions such as the Corporation of London. Lombard Street Research, founded by Tim Congdon, a prominent economist, provides forecasts and insights into the economic scene to improve the strategic decisions of investment institutions, banks and corporations. It claims unrivalled accuracy in predicting turning points in the economy, a success based on its "unique understanding of the relationship between the banking sector, the money supply, and the economy".

The Centre for Economic and Business Research (CEBR) is another well-known City-based economic consultancy. Headed by Douglas McWilliams, it is a leading independent commentator on economics and business trends. Capital Economics is run by Roger Bootle, who achieved celebrity for predicting the "death of inflation" as early as 1990. It is a retained adviser to banks, pension funds, insurance companies and other companies and also undertakes commissioned research projects. Smithers & Co was established in 1989 by Andrew Smithers, a former senior investment banker at S.G. Warburg. It has around 100 clients, mainly in London, the United States and Japan, to whom it provides advice on international asset allocation.

The Centre for the Study of Financial Innovation

The Centre for the Study of Financial Innovation (CSFI) is a London-based independent financial think tank. Formed in 1993, its purpose is to stimulate research into the future of the financial-services industry and to provide a neutral forum for people working in the industry to share ideas and explore future trends. Free from political and commercial pressures, the CSFI provides a unique forum for the City and the international financial-services industry to "think the unthinkable".

Much of the CSFI's work centres on round tables where topical issues are debated. These often spawn working groups that monitor developments. It also organises conferences and publishes reports and books. The CSFI's extensive contacts in the media, the financial-services industry, governments, and universities and business schools, in the UK and abroad, ensure a wide dissemination of its work. In 2002 it opened an office in New York. It is a charity funded by sponsorship from banks and other companies and institutions.

City trade associations

There are at least 50 financial-services industry trade associations in the UK (excluding professional bodies) representing the interests of their members to governments, the media, the public and other industries. Some, such as the British Bankers' Association, the London Investment Banking Association and the Association of British Insurers, are broadly based industry associations and others are more specialised. They employ around 1,000 people and their combined revenues total over £125m, of which £55m comes from subscriptions and the rest from member and other services. Many of them are listed in Appendix 1.

Some large banks and insurance companies, which typically belong to 15 of them, say that there are too many financial services trade associations, that they cost too much and that effectiveness in lobbying goes hand-in-hand with size. A CSFI research report, *Who speaks for the City?*, published in 2002, investigated whether the City would be more effectively served by a smaller number of representatives. The authors came to the conclusion that the existing structure worked "rather well". Moreover, industry trends – the proliferation of products and markets, the increasingly detailed nature of regulation and the weakening cohesion of individual financial sectors – made specialist trade associations more, not less, relevant. They concluded that a major contraction in the number of City trade associations was unlikely: "The City is simply too big and too complicated to pack its interests into a few large trade associations."

9 Shipping and commodities

London is the world's premier provider of maritime services and a major centre for trading commodities and commodity derivatives. From the 17th century to the early 20th century, London was the busiest port in the world and the UK had the largest merchant navy. Maritime services, including financing, insurance and ship chartering, developed in the City to cater for the requirements of the fleet. The City was also the world's principal location for buying and selling the cargoes of commodities that entered international trade.

The shipping and commodities sectors cluster at the east end of the Square Mile. The main institutions for the shipping industry are the Baltic Exchange, the market for ship charters and the buying and selling of new and second-hand ships, and Lloyd's of London, for marine insurance. The principal commodity and commodity-based derivatives markets are the London Metal Exchange, the International Petroleum Exchange and Euronext.LIFFE.

Maritime services

Maritime services employ around 14,000 people in the UK, mostly in London. Shipbroking, marine insurance and specialist legal services are the biggest employers, with smaller numbers working as specialist bankers, consultants, journalists, ship classification experts and agents for overseas shipowners. Maritime services generate £1.1 billion in net exports, a remarkable contribution for a relatively small group of people to the UK's balance of payments.

Bank lending is the principal form of ship finance. The London operations of about a dozen commercial banks specialise in shipping finance, providing loans totalling £15–20 billion out of a global total of £100 billion. The London Market is still the world's leading market for marine insurance, although its share of the global market has decreased from 30% in 1990 to 19% (see Table 9.1). Cover is provided by Lloyd's of London, insurance companies and protection and indemnity (P&I) clubs. Half of the marine business is handled by four leading firms of insurance brokers – Aon, JLT Risk Solutions, Marsh, Willis and Heath Lambert – although around two dozen brokers also do some business. Gross premiums from marine business in 2000 were £3.2 billion.

Table 9.1 **Net marine international insurance premium income, 1999**

	% share
London Market	19
Japan	14
United States	13
Germany	12
France	5
Norway	5
Others	32

Source: Lloyd's of London

P&I clubs are a notable feature of the marine side of the London Market. They are associations of shipowners which provide mutual cover for their members against risks not covered by marine policies, principally third-party liability insurance. These clubs are a longstanding feature of the London Market, the earliest being formed in the 18th century. Most of the major clubs, which together provide 90% of this form of insurance, are members of the London-based International Group for reinsurance and other purposes. Nine out of ten ocean-going ships belong to a P&I club.

Baltic Exchange
The Baltic Exchange is the world's oldest shipping market. Like Lloyd's and the Stock Exchange, it traces its origins to a City coffee house where merchants and ship captains gathered to trade cargoes and arrange ship charters. In this case it was the Virginia and Baltic Coffee House, which opened in 1744 and was named after two of the principal trade routes. With a shortened name, the Baltic Exchange became a self-regulated membership club in 1823. It moved to its present location in St Mary Axe in 1903. The current building opened in 1995, its predecessor having been devastated by an IRA bomb in 1992.

A substantial proportion of global ship charters is arranged through the Baltic Exchange: 50% of the tanker market and 30–40% of bulk dry cargoes. It is also the leading market for the sale and purchase of ships. Over half of the turnover in new and second-hand bulk ships, a market worth $34 billion a year, is handled by exchange members. The business is thoroughly international: less than 10% of deals negotiated on the exchange involve a UK shipowner, importer or exporter. Baltic Exchange business generated £320m in overseas earnings from commissions in 2002.

The membership comprises around 500 corporate members, represented by 1,600 individually elected members from 45 different countries. There are three types of member:

- Principals, who trade on their own account. They own or control ships or have cargoes to transport.
- Brokers, who act as intermediaries between shipowners and shippers.
- Non-market members, such as arbitrators, shipping lawyers and maritime financiers, who do not trade themselves but are part of the broadly defined shipping market.

The Baltic Exchange is a limited company whose shareholders are mostly member companies. The board of directors is responsible for running the market and for its regulation. Members are required to abide by the Baltic Code, a regularly updated code of business conduct. Violations may result in discipline or expulsion from the exchange. The exchange's income derives from membership subscriptions, rents of offices, government charters and the sale of market data.

The Baltic Exchange publishes an extensive range of information about the global freight market. This includes six daily indices that provide comprehensive guidance for brokers and also furnish the price data that underly the freight futures derivatives market. Shipbroking houses use freight derivatives to hedge their risks or to speculate on the future movement of freight rates. The freight derivatives market has grown rapidly in recent years, with the value of over-the-counter Forward Freight Agreements rising from £200m in 1995 to £3.5 billion in 2002. These were pioneered in 1992 by Clarkson Securities, part of Clarksons, the world's largest shipbroking company

Legal services

London is the principal centre for the practice of shipping law, with 40 specialist law firms employing 2,200 staff, as well as 200 shipping barristers. English law is commonly used for shipping contracts and cases are adjudicated in the Commercial and Admiralty Courts. Many disputes are resolved by arbitration with the assistance of 100 specialist arbitrators and the London Maritime Arbitrators Association.

Lloyd's Register Group

Founded in 1760, Lloyd's Register Group is the world's oldest ship classification society. It is an independent not-for-profit organisation dedicated to the improvement of safety, quality and other technical standards in marine and other business. It has more than 200 offices and around 5,000 employees worldwide. Its original activity was the examination of merchant ships and their classification according to their condition. *Lloyd's Register of Shipping*, providing underwriters and merchants with information about the condition of ships they insured and chartered, was first published in 1764. Today it classifies 103m gross tons of merchant shipping, which accounts for 18% of the world fleet. It has extended its activities to include management systems, land-based industries, railways, and oil and gas.

Accounting and other services

Several London accounting firms provide specialist services to the shipping industry. One of the leading firms is Moore Stephens, which has specialised in shipping services since the 1930s and provides accounting services to companies owning more than 2,000 vessels. Other specialist services for the marine industry include management consultancy, human resources, surveying, other technical help, telecommunications and software.

Maritime publishing and training

Many leading maritime publications and firms of maritime event organisers operate from London. Several universities run degree courses in maritime engineering or finance, and a wide range of staff training courses is available.

UK agents of overseas shipowners

Many overseas shipowners from Greece, Scandinavia, the Middle East, eastern Europe, Asia and other parts of the world maintain agents in London. The largest group is the Greeks, with 120 agencies employing more than 1,500 people. The Greek Shipping Co-operation Committee, founded in 1935 and based at the Baltic Exchange, represents the interests of the Greek shipping community in London.

Shipping organisations

The General Council of British Shipping is a veteran City institution. Of the international maritime organisations that have their headquarters in

London, the largest is the International Maritime Organisation, a UN body. Most others are private-sector organisations. Several international professional organisations concerned with the shipping industry are based in London, as is the National Union of Marine Aviation and Shipping Transport Officers (NUMAST), the leading maritime trade union.

Commodities markets

The City's commodities markets developed from the 17th century as part of its international shipping and trade activities. Despite the rise of major commodities markets in New York, Chicago and elsewhere, they continue to be important and have produced an array of futures and options contracts.

London Metal Exchange

The London Metal Exchange (LME) is the world's leading metals futures and options exchange, handling 90% of contracts in non-ferrous metals. It has three primary roles: hedging, pricing and physical delivery. The LME allows producers, merchants and users of non-ferrous metals to hedge against risks arising from volatile metals prices. It generates reference prices that are used globally for benchmarking. It also provides storage facilities that enable participants to make or take physical delivery of approved brands of LME traded metals.

The LME trades contracts in eight metals: aluminium, aluminium alloy, copper, lead, nickel, silver, tin and zinc. There is also an index contract, LMEX, which tracks the six primary base metals: aluminium, copper, lead, nickel, tin and zinc. Introduced in 2000, LMEX is designed to provide investors with access to futures and options contracts based on non-ferrous metals without taking physical delivery. Trading on the LME is conducted in three ways: in person through what is called open outcry, by telephone between members or electronically via LME Select. Open outcry trading, still the main method, is conducted in a "ring" with traders, who make bids and offers for contracts, from dealer member firms arranged in a circle. There are 80 member firms and seven categories of membership. The leading members are the 12 dealer members that engage in open outcry trading and the 31 broker members that trade by telephone and LME Select; the other firms trade as principals rather than dealers or brokers.

The LME was founded in 1887 to provide a marketplace for forward metals contracts with regular trading hours and standardised specifications for contracts. Originally mutually owned, it was converted into a limited company in 2000, in line with the trend towards demutualisation among markets. It is a wholly owned subsidiary of LME Holdings, a private company whose shareholders are members of the LME. Turnover has increased substantially over the last decade and a half, rising from 5m contracts in 1987 to 59m in 2002. Turnover by value is £1,000 billion a year. Over 95% of business originates from overseas and the LME generates annual overseas earnings of £250m.

International Petroleum Exchange

The International Petroleum Exchange (IPE) is Europe's leading energy futures and options exchange. It is a market that allows oil companies and others to use futures and options to manage their exposure to fluctuations in energy prices. Its contracts are used as global benchmarks for energy pricing. The IPE lists contracts for four energy products: Brent crude futures and options; gas oil futures and options; natural gas futures; electricity futures.

Trading is conducted on the trading floor using the noisy and colourful open outcry system. Brokers take orders from clients by telephone and transmit them to traders on the floor. Since 1997 trading has also been done on an electronic platform (IPE ETS), which allows extended trading hours. Over £1 billion in underlying value is traded daily on the IPE. In 2002 turnover was 30m contracts.

The IPE was established in 1980 by a group of energy and futures companies in response to the volatile oil prices of the 1970s. Originally a mutually owned not-for-profit society, in 2000 it demutualised and became a public company, IPE Holdings. In 2001 IPE Holdings became a wholly owned subsidiary of IntercontinentalExchange (ICE), an American corporation.

Euronext.LIFFE

Euronext.LIFFE (see Chapter 3) trades a number of commodity contracts as a result of its acquisition of the London Futures and Options Exchange (LFOX) (a newfangled name for the London Commodity Exchange, which had been formed in 1945). The commodities contracts traded on Euronext.LIFFE are futures and traded options contracts in cocoa, coffee, sugar, grain and potatoes.

LCH.Clearnet

The London Clearing House (LCH) has acted for decades as the central counterparty for contracts entered into by London's commodities exchanges. The role of a central counterparty is to stand between contracting parties as a guarantor of contract performance (see Chapter 3). By minimising default risk, the central counterparties increase the efficiency of markets and underpin their integrity. LCH.Clearnet, created through the merger of the British and French central counterparties in 2003, continues to serve the LME, IPE and Euronext.LIFFE, as well as over-the-counter futures and options contracts.

10 Bank of England

The Bank of England is the UK's central bank. It has been the keystone of the British financial system for three centuries and its banknotes form the country's currency. It has close connections with the government, the banking system, the financial markets and the international financial community. A new phase in the Bank's development began in 1997 when it was given responsibility for the conduct of UK monetary policy.

Responsibilities and activities

The Bank defines its goal as the maintenance of a stable and efficient monetary and financial framework to promote a healthy economy. It explains that it endeavours to accomplish this through the pursuit of three "core purposes":

- Maintaining the integrity and value of the currency.
- Maintaining the stability of the financial system, both domestic and international.
- Seeking to ensure the effectiveness of the UK's financial services.

The Bank's organisational structure reflects these objectives (see Figure 10.1 overleaf). At the summit is the governor, Mervyn King, the 110th holder of the office, appointed in 2003, who was formerly the Bank's chief economist and the principal architect of its successful inflation-targeting regime in the 1990s. There are two deputy governors: Rachel Lomax, who is responsible for monetary policy, and Andrew Large, who is responsible for financial stability. To each of them reports a set of division heads, each charged with aspects of monetary analysis and financial stability. The financial services remit is divided between the deputy governors, as is the conduct of administrative and support services such as personnel and IT. The range of the Bank's functions and the relative cost of undertaking them are shown in Table 10.1 on page 215.

Maintaining the integrity and value of the currency

The maintenance of price stability – defined as the government-set inflation target of 2% measured by the Consumer Price Index – is a

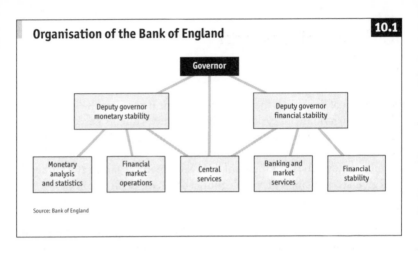

Organisation of the Bank of England `10.1`

Governor

Deputy governor monetary stability

Deputy governor financial stability

Monetary analysis and statistics

Financial market operations

Central services

Banking and market services

Financial stability

Source: Bank of England

precondition for achieving the wider economic goals of growth and employment. High inflation is harmful to the functioning of the economy, whereas low inflation is conducive to long-term expansion and greater prosperity.

Price stability is pursued primarily through the conduct of monetary policy, meaning the interest rate (the price of money). Setting the short-term interest rate is the responsibility of the Monetary Policy Committee (MPC), comprising the governor, the two deputy governors, the Bank's chief economist, the director of financial market operations and four external members appointed by the chancellor.

The MPC meets every month for two days. On the first day it receives briefings on a wide range of domestic and international economic and monetary factors from Bank economists and from its regional agents. On the second day it deliberates and votes, its decision being announced at 12 noon. Minutes of the meeting are published two weeks later and are carefully scrutinised by City economists and commentators hoping to gain insights into the dynamics of its decision-making process. The Bank's assessment of the outlook for inflation is presented in substantial detail in the quarterly *Inflation Report*, which has been published since 1993.

The Bank is able to determine market interest rates because the way the banking system operates ensures that on most days there is a shortage of cash in the market needed for settlement of the day's transactions. As the final provider of cash to the system, the Bank is in a position to choose the rate at which it will provide the required funds.

Table 10.1 **Bank of England, budgeted cost of functions, 2003/04**

	%
Monetary policy	30
Note issue	24
Banking	17
Financial stability	16
Settlement services	7
Services for HM government and government agencies	6

Source: Bank of England Annual Report, 2003

Since the clearing banks immediately adjust their interest rates for borrowers and savers to reflect the rate at which the Bank supplies funds to the banking system, its interest-rate decisions set the basis for the whole structure of interest rates. The price of money (interest rate) also affects the prices of assets (principally securities and property), consumer and business demand, and output and employment.

Maintaining the stability of the financial system, both domestic and international

A sound and stable financial system is a condition for the effective conduct of monetary policy and for economic prosperity. The Bank promotes the stability of the domestic and international financial system in several ways:

- Assisting the development of a robust domestic financial infrastructure, including safe and efficient payment and settlement arrangements, an appropriate legal regime, effective disclosure requirements and sound principles for prudential regulation.
- Monitoring developments in the financial system, at home and abroad, including links among financial market participants and ties between financial markets and the wider economy.
- Contributing to the development of effective means for the prevention and resolution of financial crises, including the debate on the world's "international financial architecture".

The Financial Stability Committee, which meets monthly under the chairmanship of the governor, oversees the Bank's work on monitoring and enhancing financial stability. Research on financial stability issues and an assessment of the current outlook are published in the twice-yearly *Financial Stability Review*.

The Bank's responsibility for financial stability was formally conferred by a Memorandum of Understanding, signed in October 1997, between the Bank, the Treasury and the FSA regarding the allocation of duties for financial regulation and stability in the UK. It states that the Bank is responsible for "the overall stability of the financial system as a whole". The agreement included the establishment of a high-level tripartite standing committee. This meets monthly and provides a forum in which the three institutions can exchange intelligence and develop a co-ordinated response to a crisis.

Internationally, the financial stability remit means that the Bank is a participant in a large number of supervisory committees under the auspices of the Bank for International Settlements (BIS), EU, European System of Central Banks (ESCB), Financial Stability Forum (FSF), G7, G10, G20, IMF, OECD and other bodies.

Despite relinquishing the role of bank supervision to the FSA, the Bank remains the lender of last resort. Should a threat to the stability of the financial system (a systemic threat) arise from the problems of a particular firm or a market downturn, the Bank may intervene to facilitate payments or settlements to protect otherwise sound institutions and avert widespread collateral damage. This safety net exists to protect the stability of the financial system as a whole, not individual institutions or their managers or shareholders. The provision of lender of last resort facilities to a firm in trouble must be justified on grounds of general economic welfare if it requires the commitment of public money. The Bank is also keenly aware of the so-called "moral hazard" problem that may arise from intervention: that it may encourage recklessness on the part of participants in the financial markets who believe that they will be bailed out if they experience difficulties.

In 1890, when Baring Brothers, a leading City firm, was unable to meet its obligations, the Bank organised a rescue fund and itself subscribed the first £1m because of the threat the failure of the firm posed to the City. By contrast, in 1995, when Barings again got into severe difficulties, although the Bank endeavoured to organise a rescue party it refused to commit public funds on the grounds that the failure of a venerable but relatively insignificant firm posed no systemic threat to the City or the UK economy (see Chapter 13).

Seeking to ensure the effectiveness of the UK's financial services
The promotion of the City as an international financial centre is a long-standing Bank endeavour. So is its concern that the financial institutions make effective provision for the requirements of British industry and commerce, particularly small businesses.

In pursuit of these ends, the Bank not only monitors the functioning of the City but also sometimes becomes actively involved in promoting solutions when market forces have proved unable to do so:

- Banking system. The Bank is closely involved in initiatives to improve the security of payment and settlement arrangements. In conjunction with the major clearing banks, it forms part of the UK's money-clearing system in which the final settlement of interbank claims is made. The Bank introduced and operates the sterling and euro Real Time Gross Settlement payments system, which reduces risk and increases efficiency in the UK's domestic large-value payments.
- Stockmarket. After a decade and a half of muddle and failure on the part of the London Stock Exchange to introduce a computerised, paperless equity-settlements system, the Bank designed and implemented the current system known as CREST in 1996.
- Government securities market. The Bank developed the Central Gilts Office service to allow paperless settlement and payment for most gilt-edged transactions.
- Money market. The Bank developed the Central Moneymarkets Office to enhance the security and efficient settlement of money-market operations.
- Futures markets. The Bank has taken a close interest in the development of settlement systems in these markets.
- Foreign-exchange market. The Bank deals in the foreign-exchange market as part of its day-to-day management of the Exchange Equalisation Account, which holds the UK's gold and foreign currency reserves.
- Open-market operations. The Bank implements the official interest rate (the "repo" rate) through open-market operations (buying and selling) in the wholesale sterling money markets.

The financial markets function encompasses banknotes, the Bank's most familiar responsibility as far as the public is concerned. The Bank of England is the sole issuer of notes in England and Wales. Around 1.3 billion notes are produced each year at an average cost of 3 pence each. They are printed by a subsidiary of De La Rue and distributed via the clearing banks.

Scottish and Northern Irish clearing banks continue to issue their own notes, but on condition that they are backed pound for pound by Bank of England notes. The Bank is not responsible for coins: these are issued by the Royal Mint on behalf of the Treasury.

Administration and support services

The head of the Bank of England is the governor, who is appointed for a five-year term by the chancellor. The two deputy governors are also appointed for five years.

The Bank's governing body is the Court of Directors, comprising the three governors and 16 non-executive directors each appointed for three years, which meets once a month. Under the Bank of England Act 1998, the Court's responsibilities are the determination of the Bank's strategy and the oversight of its performance in all matters except monetary policy, which is the responsibility of the MPC (see page 214).

The number of staff employed by the Bank has fallen considerably in recent decades as its functions have become streamlined. The principal reasons have been the end of exchange controls in 1979, the loss of responsibility for banking supervision and debt-management operations in 1997, and the privatisation of the banknote printing works in 2003. From a peak of 7,000 in the mid-1970s, staff numbers fell from 4,500 in the mid-1990s to around 1,700 in the mid-2000s. Recruitment in recent years has focused on securing the services of high-calibre professional economists and the staff today is an intellectually lively, relatively youthful and cosmopolitan group of people.

The Bank's international orientation is reflected in the work of its Centre for Central Banking Studies (CCBS), which provides training and technical assistance for central banks around the world, particularly those of developing countries and countries that emerged from the former Soviet Empire. Its objectives are to foster best practice in central banking throughout the world, promote international financial stability and give Bank staff opportunities to broaden their perspectives and technical skills.

Evolution of the Bank's functions

The Bank was formed in 1694 to act as the government's banker and debt manager, in the sense of providing loans that were required to pay for military operations against Louis XIV of France. Government war finance remained its principal role until Wellington's victory over Napoleon at Waterloo in 1815. The Bank made a vital contribution to Britain's success on the battlefield in most of the many wars in which it was involved in the 18th century by helping to ensure that state finances remained sound, in marked contrast to those of its principal antagonist, France.

For more than a century, in return for acting as the government's banker, the Bank received the monopoly of "joint-stock" (shareholder-owned) banking in England and Wales. All the other banks had to operate as private partnerships with a maximum of six partners. This provided the Bank with a massive head start and a competitive advantage in its commercial banking operations. It was the country's biggest bank and its banknotes, issued originally as evidence of the placement of deposits, were widely accepted.

The century from the battle of Waterloo to the outbreak of the first world war in 1914 was the era of the *Pax Britannica* and of domestic and international economic growth and development. The Bank continued to act as the government's bank, but it developed new functions that contributed to the country's and the City's economic progress. To place the currency on a sounder footing, in 1844 the Bank was given a monopoly over the issue of notes (except in Scotland and Ireland), which in future had to be backed by gold. This laid the foundation for the development of the gold standard as an international monetary system, focused on sterling and run by the Bank through manipulation of the short-term interest rate, in the half century up to 1914. Connected to these developments was the Bank's assumption of the role of policing the London money market, the world's leading money market. Moreover, the Bank assumed the role of lender of last resort to the British banking system – the bankers' bank – in times of financial crisis.

Upon the outbreak of the first world war the Bank reverted to its original role of government fundraiser, organising a series of enormous bond issues and other financial operations on behalf of the state. After the war the Bank promoted an attempt to restore the pre-war gold standard, but it collapsed in 1931, discrediting the Bank's judgement and authority. Thereafter the Treasury assumed control of UK economic policy, with the Bank acting as its agent and adviser in the financial markets. Nationalisation in 1946 formally established the Treasury's authority over the Bank, but in practice this made little difference to the relationship.

The resumption of the use of the interest rate as an instrument of economic management in 1951, after two decades of "cheap money" (low interest rates), intensified the Treasury's interest in the Bank's opinion and its advice was usually heeded. As the City's unwritten but acknowledged leader, the Bank fostered the development of the Euromarkets in London from the late 1950s, a major factor behind the City's boom in the 1960s, and it sorted out the secondary banking crisis of 1973–75. Indeed, the 1960s and 1970s were a heyday for the Bank, with its prestige back at a pre-1931 level and its staff at a record 7,000.

Many of them were engaged in the management of UK exchange controls, which had been introduced in 1939 and were retained after the war to support sterling. With the floating of sterling in 1972, this reason no longer existed; and when exchange controls were abolished in 1979, 750 jobs at the Bank (one-eighth of the total) disappeared overnight, which was a blow to morale. The Bank's standing was also undermined by the "Big Bang" deregulation of the City in the mid-1980s and the influx of foreign players, which eroded its traditional informal authority in the Square Mile. Moreover, a series of episodes attracted unwelcome attention and criticism, notably its bail-out of Johnson Matthey Bankers in 1984, its closing down of the fraudulent BCCI in 1991 and its non-rescue of Barings in 1995 (see Chapter 13). The BCCI affair returned to the public arena in 2004 when the Bank was taken to court by BCCI's liquidator, which claimed that the Bank "knowingly or recklessly" failed to supervise BCCI properly and sought £850m in damages (see Chapter 13).

Sterling's inglorious exit from the Exchange Rate Mechanism in September 1992 thoroughly discredited the Conservative government's economic-cum-monetary policy. Desperate to restore confidence in its economic management, the government decided to give the Bank an enhanced role to bolster credibility. In a series of steps beginning in October 1992, the governor was given greater influence over the setting of UK interest rates. But when he proposed a rate hike in the run-up to the 1997 election, Kenneth Clarke, the chancellor of the exchequer, ignored him.

Five days after winning the May 1997 election, Gordon Brown, the new Labour chancellor, announced that he was transferring full operational responsibility for monetary policy to the Bank. Although the decision was clearly consistent with an international trend towards central bank "independence" and a growing body of evidence that independent status delivered lower inflation and greater economic stability, the announcement took most people by surprise. Control over interest rates was offset by the loss of other responsibilities. Banking supervision was assigned to the Financial Services Authority (FSA – see Chapter 11) and the management of the government debt market was handed over to the Treasury. However, the Bank retained responsibility for the overall stability and health of the UK's financial system and continued to fulfil the role of lender of last resort. The Bank of England Act 1998 is the legal basis of its current activities.

Trends and issues

- **Conduct of monetary policy.** The bestowal of responsibility for the conduct of UK monetary policy to the Bank in 1997 was opposed by some, particularly on the political left, as a transfer of power from elected politicians to remote unelected central bankers. Criticism continued that the Bank was unduly cautious about inflation and was sacrificing growth and jobs in order to be sure of meeting its inflation target; one Labour left-winger accused the governor of being an "inflation-nutter". More soberly, spokespeople for manufacturing industry complained that UK interest rates were supporting sterling at levels that were too high for exporters.

- **The MPC.** The performance of the MPC has silenced most critics, and the skill of its monetary technicians and the transparency of the UK's monetary arrangements are widely regarded as markedly superior to those of the European Central Bank (ECB) in Frankfurt.

- **Membership of the euro.** As a member of the EU, the Bank of England is a member of the ESCB. However, since the UK is not a member of the European single currency the Bank continues to conduct UK monetary policy. Should the UK join the euro zone, it would have the same interest rate as the other members set by the ECB. The Bank's monetary policy functions would disappear and it would be relegated to a local regulatory role. However, the government has undertaken that the UK will not enter the euro unless the decision is ratified by the UK electorate in a referendum, which appears unlikely to be held before 2006, if ever.

- **The Bank, the euro and the City.** The Bank monitors the impact of EU legislation upon the City. It played a major role in the technical preparations for the launch of the euro in 1999 to ensure that London's wholesale financial markets were ready to trade in it. The Bank continues to assess the progress of the euro and publishes a twice-yearly report on developments, *Practical Issues Arising from the Euro.*

11 Regulation

Regulation of the financial services sector exists for three main reasons. First, to safeguard the financial system against the failure of a bank, insurance company, securities firm or asset manager that might trigger the collapse of other institutions. Second, to supervise the integrity of financial firms, protecting customers from malpractice and fraud. Third, to police financial markets, eliminating abuses such as insider dealing and other offences.

A stable financial system promotes economic growth and general prosperity. But financial systems are prone to instability because of the cyclical nature of many markets and managerial shortcomings in financial firms. So fundamental is a healthy banking system that every sophisticated economy imposes prudential standards and regulatory constraints on the conduct of banks for the good of the whole economy as well as the institutions themselves.

It is an inherent trait of financial markets that some participants have greater knowledge than others. Such "asymmetrical information" makes it difficult for buyers to assess the risks and returns from financial products. This is true for both wholesale and retail clients, but particularly for the latter in respect of long-term savings contracts and depository institutions. By safeguarding retail savers, regulation bolsters savings and investment. Hence there is an important role for regulation in promoting the safety of financial assets and the quality of financial advice. Consumer education and greater transparency about charges and other features of financial products promote the interests of consumers and healthy competition in the financial-services industry.

The UK's chief financial regulator is the Financial Services Authority (FSA), an independent body with statutory powers bestowed by the Financial Services and Markets Act 2000. It is run by a chairman, Callum McCarthy, and a chief executive, John Tiner, who are appointed by the Treasury and constitute its governing board. Funding comes from fees paid by those it regulates. The FSA has responsibility for virtually all of the UK's wholesale and retail financial services activity, making it one of the world's most comprehensive financial regulators.

The FSA's staff of 2,300 is responsible for the regulation of around 20,000 financial institutions, including more than 7,500 investment firms and 660 banks, about 70 building societies, 1,000 insurance companies and the Lloyd's insurance market, 700 credit unions, and 9,500 industrial and provident mutual societies. Other business activities under the FSA's remit are mortgage lending, sales and administration, and general insurance advice.

Creation of the Financial Services Authority

The sophisticated and sensitive conduct of the regulation of the wholesale financial-services industry has long been cited as one of the City's principal competitive advantages as a financial centre. Traditionally, this was led by the Bank of England, which had responsibility for the banking sector and whose operations in the financial markets provided it with an early-warning system about rogue firms and market abuses. Some self-regulatory bodies, such as the Stock Exchange and Lloyd's of London, had their own rules which they enforced themselves. Underlying these arrangements was a clubby, gentlemanly ethos – "my word is my bond" is the Stock Exchange's motto – and the notion that those working in the market knew better than rule-based regulators who the "bad apples" were and could apply peer-group pressure to encourage them to mend their ways.

These ad hoc arrangements, which had grown up over centuries, were codified by the Financial Services Act 1986, which came into operation in 1988. The new system attempted to do two things: to take account of the demise of the club-like City caused by the deregulation of the securities industry and the influx of new, and often foreign, market participants; and to resolve the regulatory paradox that aggressive regulation deters market operators, which might undermine the City, whereas weak regulation deters customers. The act was a compromise, providing a statutory regulatory framework while preserving a large element of devolved self-regulation on a sector-by-sector basis. The resulting edifice was immensely complicated (and costly), with an array of Self-Regulatory Organisations (SROs) reporting to a new statutory body, the Securities and Investments Board (SIB). Moreover, it failed to put paid to financial scandals, failures and upsets.

City self-regulation had always been mistrusted by many on the political left, who favoured an American-style statutory system with rules and a tough enforcement agency, or even nationalisation. The pensions mis-selling scandal (see Chapter 13) confirmed their view that the City was perpetrating daylight robbery, and reform of financial services regulation was a pledge in the 1997 Labour Party election manifesto. In May 1997, soon after its election victory, Gordon Brown, the new chancellor of the exchequer, announced the creation of a new single superregulator for both wholesale and retail financial services operating on a statutory basis. This was a truly radical step with no precedent anywhere in the world: so radical that *The Economist* suggested that perhaps an appropriate name for the as yet nameless new institution would be the British Life Assurance and Investments Regulator or BLAIR.

Brown himself pointed out that as financial firms combined, the old distinctions between banks, insurers and securities firms were blurring, as were the boundaries between financial products. Both developments were making sector-based regulation too narrowly based. Another advantage of a single regulator, it was argued, was economies of scale and scope in management and central support costs – and the FSA did prove initially to be less costly than the sum of the entities it supplanted. Further improvements were greater consistency and coherence regarding standard-setting, authorisation, supervision, enforcement, consumer education and the defeat of financial crime.

A single regulator is able to define clear and consistent regulatory objectives and responsibilities, resolving internally any conflicts that may arise between them. It is unequivocally accountable for the fulfilment of its statutory objectives, regulatory failures and the cost of regulation. Moreover, a single regulator permitted the adoption of a sophisticated "risk-based" approach to the supervision of individual firms.

The huge and painstaking task of framing policy, writing new rules (the predecessor bodies had no less than 14 rule books and 13 codes of practice) and turning a staff of more than 2,000 into an effective team took more than four years. An intermediate milestone in the process was the amalgamation in June 1998 of the staff of the SIB (renamed the Financial Services Authority in October 1997) with the banking supervision personnel from the Bank of England and their joint move to new accommodation at Canary Wharf. Eventually, after much debate and redrafting, the Financial Services Markets Act, establishing the new authority and defining its remit, received Royal Assent in June 2000. The act came into force in December 2001.

The FSA took over the powers of 13 predecessor bodies responsible for bank supervision; investment business and exchanges; securities listing; securities and derivatives business; regulation of overseas exchanges; Lloyd's of London; insurance and the analysis of insurance returns; asset management; building societies; friendly societies; and retail investment business.

A new regulator for a new millennium

In January 2000 the FSA published *A New Regulator for a New Millennium*, a paper setting out its objectives and explaining how it proposed to achieve them. It defined its goal as: "to maintain efficient, orderly and clean financial markets and help retail consumers achieve a fair deal". The starting point was the four statutory objectives laid down in the Financial Services and Markets Act 2000:

- **Maintaining market confidence.** Confidence in the integrity of the UK's financial markets and market participants is crucial for parties to be willing to trade. This requires prevention of damage to the soundness of the financial system through failure or abuse by firms or markets or inadequacies in the financial infrastructure. However, in the absence of risk to the system (systemic risk), badly managed firms should be allowed to fail so as not to reward and encourage imprudent conduct (the "moral hazard" problem).
- **Promoting public awareness.** Many consumers do not understand the financial system or financial products and how these relate to their financial needs. The FSA is committed to a major enhancement of public financial literacy and the improvement of information and advice to consumers.
- **Protecting consumers.** The FSA is charged by statute with "providing an appropriate degree of protection for consumers". Its regulatory framework provides consumers with a measure of protection against the risk of loss arising from the incompetent management of financial firms, fraud and the misrepresentation or mis-selling of financial products. But it is not responsible for the protection of consumers from the risk that financial products do not deliver hoped-for returns, which is inherent in investment markets.
- **Reducing financial crime.** Criminal activity undermines confidence in a financial system and consumer protection. The FSA plays a significant role in seeking to prevent money laundering, fraud (including fraudulent marketing of investments) and criminal market misconduct (including insider dealing).

The Financial Services and Markets Act also specified six "principles of good regulation":

- Efficiency and economy. The optimal use of limited resources.
- Role of management. Financial firms' senior management to be held responsible for regulatory compliance.
- Proportionality. The use of a proportional cost/benefit approach to regulatory requirements.
- Innovation. To be encouraged in both products and market participants.
- International character of financial services and markets and the desirability of maintaining the competitive position of the UK. Taking account of the international mobility of much financial business to avoid inflicting damage on the competitive position of the City. This involves co-operating with overseas regulators, both to agree international standards and to monitor global firms and markets effectively.
- Competition. The avoidance of unnecessarily impeding or distorting competition.

It is the FSA's declared aim to be respected for its effectiveness, integrity and expertise as a world-leading regulator both at home and abroad. Such excellence will enable it to fulfil its duty of consumer protection and contribute to the maintenance of London's competitive position. In operational practice, says the FSA, this means:

- Getting a fair deal for consumers by emphasising the importance of disclosure of information by financial firms and others. Transparency of information in the marketplace encourages market discipline, which in turn maintains standards of conduct.
- Improving industry performance by creating incentives for firms themselves to maintain standards and seek improvement in practices, making it possible for the regulator to step back.
- Flexible regulation, focusing resources on the areas of greatest risk to its statutory objectives by drawing on effective intelligence-gathering to identify the most important risks, and using its new operating framework to focus resources to address them.
- Proactive regulation, with a bias towards prevention, seeking to identify and reduce risks before they cause significant damage.

This includes speaking out promptly and publicly on major issues, highlighting both good and bad practice among regulated firms and drawing attention to potential problems for consumers.

◪ Maximising effectiveness by selecting from a full range of regulatory tools. Focusing regulatory activities with targeted inquiries into specific issues rather than open-ended information gathering and routine inspection. Recruiting and retaining high-quality staff. Taking full advantage of technology. Playing an influential role on the world stage.

The FSA's "risk-based" operating framework

The FSA has developed an operating framework that is designed to identify the principal risks to the achievement of its statutory objectives as they arise and to deal with them. The principle behind its new approach is "risk-based" rather than "rule-based" supervision. Regulatory attention is focused on institutions and activities that are likely to pose the greatest risk to consumers and markets. It means using a light touch, agreeing with firms on the risks being run and working with their management, rather than simply prescribing hard-number ratios and requiring boxes to be ticked. The approach recognises the responsibilities of both consumers and management, and the impossibility and undesirability of eliminating all risk and failure from the financial system.

The process proceeds in the six stages shown in Figure 11.1.

Stage 1: identification of risks to the statutory objectives

Inputs include intelligence gathered during the supervision of firms, direct contacts with customers, and economic and market monitoring.

Stage 2: risk assessment and prioritisation

The FSA uses an elaborate risk-assessment process applied consistently across all its activities. It involves scoring risks against a variety of probability and impact factors:

◪ Probability factors relate to the likelihood of an event occurring.
◪ Impact factors indicate the scale and significance of a problem were it to occur. These considerations include the number of retail consumers potentially affected and the systemic threat posed by a problem.

A combination of probability and impact factors provides a score of

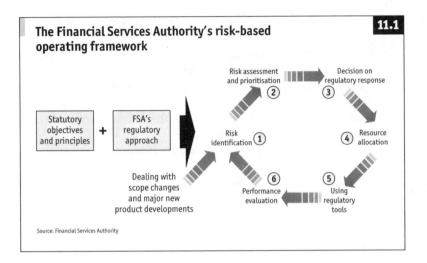

The Financial Services Authority's risk-based operating framework

11.1

Statutory objectives and principles **+** FSA's regulatory approach

1 Risk identification
2 Risk assessment and prioritisation
3 Decision on regulatory response
4 Resource allocation
5 Using regulatory tools
6 Performance evaluation

Dealing with scope changes and major new product developments

Source: Financial Services Authority

the overall risk posed to the FSA's objectives. This is used to prioritise the risk, inform decisions on the regulatory response and, together with an assessment of the costs and benefits of using alternative regulatory instruments, assist with resource allocation.

Stage 3: decision on regulatory response
The FSA decides how to respond to the risks, applying the principles of good regulation to determine the most appropriate regulatory instruments.

Stage 4: resource allocation
Resources are allocated by the board during the FSA's annual planning process.

Stage 5: using regulatory tools
The FSA has a wider range of objectives to meet than previous regulators and thus employs a more diverse array of instruments and initiatives. They may be divided into three categories.

1 Instruments/initiatives intended to influence the behaviour of consumers:

- Disclosure. Providing consumers with better and clearer information on products.

- Consumer education. Creating more knowledgeable consumers ought to reduce the need for firm-specific regulation.
- Complaints handling mechanism and ombudsman service. Enabling consumers to pursue complaints against firms and secure redress.
- Compensation scheme. Providing a safety net for consumers when a firm collapses. Its existence mitigates the impact of failures when they occur and enables the FSA to adopt a proportionate approach to regulation.
- Public statements. Warnings to alert the public and market participants to risks.
- Product approval. Safeguards in respect of the issuance of securities to protect investors.

2 Instruments/initiatives intended to influence the financial-services industry as a whole:

- Training and competence regime. Designed to raise standards and improve compliance in the industry; this has clear benefits for consumers and reduces the need for firm-specific regulatory activity.
- Rule making. Needed to set regulatory standards, but gives rise to compliance costs for firms and monitoring costs for the FSA which need to be weighed against the benefits.
- Market monitoring. Keeping abreast of economic developments at home and abroad that may pose threats to markets, firms, products or consumers.
- Sector-wide risks. Best dealt with through a sector-wide project that co-ordinates a range of regulatory activities designed to investigate, understand and address the risk.
- International activities. Playing an active role in international working groups and liaising with overseas regulators in information sharing, thus increasing understanding and promoting best practice.

3 Instruments/initiatives intended to influence the behaviour of individual institutions – regulated firms, exchanges and clearing houses – and of approved individuals in firms:

- Authorisation of firms and approval of individuals. Vetting at entry to allow only firms and individuals who satisfy standards of honesty, competence and financial soundness to engage in regulated activity.

- Perimeter injunctions and prosecutions. To stop unauthorised activity or secure restitution for losses.
- Supervision of individual firms. Includes desk-based reviews and on-site visits to deal with firm-specific risks and provide insight into industry developments. The FSA envisages a net reduction in overall routine supervisory activity at the firm level, but a significant increase in the extent of "thematic" regulation, dealing with identified risks across categories of firms through targeted supervisory efforts.
- Investigation. To develop a more detailed understanding of risks or problems at particular firms.
- Intervention. To be used when risks are immediate and a firm fails to take appropriate remedial action.
- Discipline. The FSA has a range of disciplinary powers enabling it to respond to events in differentiated and targeted ways, including private warning, public censure and financial penalties.
- Restitution of loss. When failure to comply with regulatory requirements results in losses for consumers (or improper profits for a firm), the FSA may apply to a court for restitution.

Stage 6: performance evaluation

Performance is monitored and evaluated in an annual review, which compares achievements with goals set. Account is also taken of progress in meeting the FSA's overall objectives.

The FSA at work

The FSA has four operating divisions, as shown in Figure 11.2 overleaf:

- Consumer, Investment and Insurance Division, responsible for insurance firms, the pensions industry, investment firms, consumer education and industry training.
- Regulatory Processes and Risk Division, responsible for authorisation of firms and individuals and enforcement, as well as identifying the risks and opportunities that the FSA faces in meeting its objectives.
- Deposit Takers and Markets Division, responsible for prudential standards of financial soundness, deposit takers, markets and exchanges, major financial groups and listing.

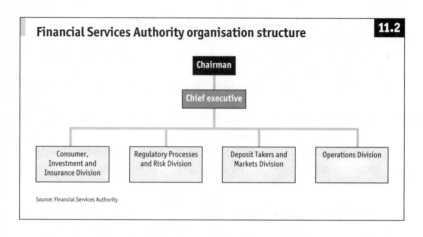

Financial Services Authority organisation structure — 11.2

Chairman

Chief executive

Consumer, Investment and Insurance Division | Regulatory Processes and Risk Division | Deposit Takers and Markets Division | Operations Division

Source: Financial Services Authority

◪ Operations Division, responsible for providing essential services, notably human resources, information systems, premises, finance and business planning, to ensure the FSA's efficiency and effectiveness in meeting its objectives.

The FSA is funded by fees charged to authorised firms and other bodies, such as exchanges, engaged in the activities regulated by the FSA. It is an independent body and receives no government funding. Firms pay three types of fee:

◪ Application fees, which cover part of the cost of processing applications.
◪ Periodic fees, annual charges which provide most of the FSA's funding.
◪ Special project fees, where the FSA undertakes regulatory activity at the request of fee-payers.

The cost of funding the FSA in 2002/03 was £250m (although Anthony Hilton, City editor of London's *Evening Standard*, estimates the total cost of regulation to UK financial services firms at £1 billion). A comparative table published by the FSA relating the cost of regulation to the scale of regulated financial assets demonstrates that the UK's regulatory regime is considerably cheaper than those of various other developed countries, including the United States, Hong Kong and France.

The FSA works with other financial institutions and government departments with regulatory responsibilities. A joint Memorandum of

Understanding with the Bank of England and the Treasury defines the basis upon which they work together to achieve the goal of financial stability. These arrangements include a tripartite standing committee that meets monthly to discuss developments relevant to financial stability. Institutions the FSA has dealings with include:

- the Department of Trade and Industry, which has responsibility for company law and insolvency;
- the Department for Work and Pensions, which is responsible for pensions policy and the regulation of occupational pension schemes;
- the Occupational Pensions Regulatory Authority (OPRA), the independent regulator set up under the Pensions Act 1995 to regulate the operation of occupational schemes in the UK;
- the Office of Fair Trading, which covers consumer credit, consumer protection and competition issues;
- the Serious Fraud Office, which handles the investigation and prosecution of serious and complex fraud cases;
- the National Criminal Intelligence Service, which provides leadership in criminal intelligence to combat serious and organised crime.

Takeover Panel

One aspect of City regulation that remains independent of the FSA is the supervision of corporate control, which is conducted by the Panel on Takeovers and Mergers. The Takeover Panel was established in 1968 at the joint instigation of the Bank of England and the Stock Exchange in response to concerns about the equal treatment of shareholders in takeover bids. It draws its members from the major financial and business institutions, making the panel an effective enforcer of its published code governing the conduct of UK mergers and acquisitions. Since 1968 it has handled more than 7,000 announced offers.

Performance and issues

While the FSA was being put together, concerns were expressed in the City that a body combining the regulation of wholesale market activities and the protection of retail investors would inevitably prioritise the safeguarding of retail savers because of their significance as voters. It was also feared that the FSA would be legalistic and rigid and would stifle innovation, undermining London's traditional regulatory advantage.

Table 11.1 **Perceptions of financial centre regulatory environment, 2003**

How do the regulatory environments of the major financial centres compare?
Average score 1 = less, 5 = very attractive

1	London	4.18
2	New York	3.84
3	Frankfurt	2.98
4	Paris	2.96

Source: Lascelles, D., *Sizing Up the City – London's Ranking as a Financial Centre*, CSFI, 2003

A survey of City practitioners and observers carried out in mid-2003 by the Centre for the Study of Financial Innovation, 18 months after the FSA assumed its full powers, found that such worries had so far proved unfounded. *Sizing Up the City – London's Ranking as a Financial Centre* reported that respondents took a positive view of both the value of a single integrated regulator and the FSA's competence as a regulator. There was widespread agreement that the FSA took a "reasonably sophisticated" view of the regulation of the wholesale markets, was transparent in its processes and was accessible.

Invited to rank the regulatory environment in London, New York, Frankfurt and Paris, respondents placed London top of the list by a substantial margin (see Table 11.1). New York, following the passage of the Sarbanes-Oxley Act in response to the investment banking scandals of the early 2000s, was perceived as an increasingly inhospitable environment. Frankfurt and Paris suffered from a reputation for inflexibility.

Although London and the FSA scored favourably relative to other centres and other regulators, many respondents were uneasy about the mounting regulatory burden almost everywhere. Frustration was expressed about the growth of regulatory interference, mounting paperwork and the apparent mindlessness of much of regulatory activity. But matters were even worse elsewhere: "There is not less regulation here," remarked a London-based American investment banker, "only better."

A common complaint among those working in the City was excessive regulatory zeal on the part of the EU in pursuit of single-market convergence, exacerbated by overzealous implementation of directives from Brussels by the British authorities. The creation of a European single market in financial services is a long-cherished ambition of the

EU, but it has proceeded slowly because national governments have been reluctant to agree or adopt directives that they believe may disadvantage their financial sectors. Part of the problem is the patchwork of regulatory authorities, reckoned to number 40 in the 15 EU states in 2001.

The UK's example of the creation of a single national regulator inspired others – led by Sweden and Denmark, followed by Germany and Austria – to do the same. It may also have inspired an audacious suggestion by the French finance minister in 2000 that a single pan-European super-regulator should be established with headquarters (naturally) in Paris. The UK staunchly opposed this, but it was unable to prevent the setting up of a study group of "wise men" under Alexandre Lamfalussy, an eminent Belgian ex-central banker. Its report backed the establishment of a single regulatory authority in each member state, though not a Europe-wide super-regulator. It also proposed that the national regulators should be complemented by a set of committees and consultation processes to accelerate the development and enforcement of common financial legislation.

The introduction of the euro in 1999 was another source of impetus to European regulatory reform. The European Commission's Financial Services Action Plan (FSAP), a blueprint for integrated capital and financial services markets across the EU, was endorsed at the Lisbon summit in 2000. The FSAP recommended 42 measures to streamline the regulation of retail and wholesale financial markets, with a deadline of 2005.

The idea of a pan-European regulator was taken up by the Economic and Monetary Affairs Committee of the European Parliament. In November 2002 it adopted a resolution in favour of a treaty amendment that could give the European Central Bank (ECB) powers of financial supervision or create a single European regulator. Support for a more centralised system of financial supervision has also been expressed by Eurofi 2000, a mainly French financial-industrial leaders' forum, which advocates three pan-European super-regulators for securities, insurance and banking.

Currently, it is the decentralised Lamfalussy approach that is being pursued. But if that is judged to have failed, the calls for the creation of a European super-regulator may be heeded. However, the practical difficulties are formidable. Pan-European banking supervision would appear to necessitate a Europe-wide lender of last resort, which is not part of the ECB's remit. Changing the ECB's status to meet this responsibility would have broad constitutional and fiscal implications. Moreover, doubts have been expressed about the ability of a single organisation to protect investors, police financial institutions and watch markets in 25 different jurisdictions. Opponents point out that a single supervisor would need cross-border enforcement powers, which would be problematic without harmonised civil and criminal law.

The increasing influence of the EU on the financial-services industry, and the need for regulatory reforms to be proportionate and not to impede competition, is one of the risks identified in the FSA's *Financial Risk Outlook*. This publication, which appears at the beginning of every year, identifies what the FSA believes to be the principal issues, both short-term and long-term, facing it and the industry to highlight its priorities and provide a context for its actions. Current risks include the financial weakness of the insurance industry, the problem of consumer financial ignorance, mounting indebtedness in a low-inflation environment and the ageing of the population. It is a tribute to the big-picture approach of the FSA that it should dwell on such broad social and economic issues, but its ability to do much about them is distinctly limited.

12 Financial centre league tables

London, New York and Tokyo, the three global financial centres, form the apex of a world hierarchy of financial centres. They provide a comprehensive array of wholesale financial services that are used by major corporations, governments and international institutions. Each is the largest financial centre in its time zone.

New York and London have similarly sized wholesale financial services industries and rank roughly as equals, though with different emphases. London's business orientation is primarily international, whereas New York services both its huge domestic economy and an international clientele. But activity in both centres is dominated by the same set of leading firms and in many senses their operations are complementary. Tokyo's standing has diminished in recent years because of the decline of the stockmarket since 1990, the lack of capital of its domestic banking system and the absence of a large, skilled, English-speaking workforce, which is essential for a thriving international financial centre today.

There are also other important financial centres that deal with an international but more regionally focused clientele. In Europe, the main ones are Frankfurt, Paris and Zurich, and to a lesser extent Amsterdam, Geneva, Madrid and Milan. In Asia, they are Hong Kong and Singapore but also Seoul, Sydney, Taipei and, increasingly, Shanghai. In North America they are Chicago (especially for derivatives), Boston (especially for asset management), San Francisco, Los Angeles, Philadelphia and Toronto. Dubai, Johannesburg and Rio are significant financial centres in their respective regions.

The web of international financial centres also features a number of "offshore" financial centres. These are financial flags of convenience where transactions are booked largely for tax reasons, although in reality much of the banking or investment work is done in one of the "onshore" international financial centres already mentioned. Offshore centres include the Cayman Islands, the Bahamas, Bermuda, the Netherlands Antilles, Luxembourg, the Channel Islands and the Isle of Man.

Lastly, forming the base of the hierarchy are domestic financial centres that serve the financial needs of their locality. They have links both to a local retail clientele, comprising individual savers and small

Table 12.1 **Foreign-exchange trading, 2001**

	Daily average ($bn)	% share
UK	504	31
United States	254	16
Japan	147	9
Singapore	101	6
Germany	88	5
Switzerland	71	4
Hong Kong	67	4
France	48	3
Others	338	21
Total	1,618	100

Source: Bank for International Settlements, triennial census of foreign-exchange and derivatives trading

businesses, and to providers of financial services located in regional and international, and perhaps global, financial centres in their country or time zone.

A number of yardsticks are available to indicate the relative standing of London and other financial centres. Much of the data are available only on a country basis, but the discrepancy between countries and their major financial centres is mostly minor.

Foreign exchange

London is the leading centre by far for foreign-exchange trading. According to the triennial survey of foreign-exchange and derivatives trading conducted by the Bank for International Settlements (BIS), the average daily turnover in 2001 was $504 billion, nearly one-third of the global total (see Table 12.1). This was about the same as the volume of activity in the United States, Singapore and Japan combined, and much more than in any European centre. London's pre-eminence is a reflection of the international nature of the City's business and the presence of more foreign banks than anywhere else. The combination of location and time zone makes the City a convenient centre for foreign-exchange trading with banks in Europe, Asia and the United States.

International bonds

International bonds (Eurobonds) are interest-bearing securities issued

Table 12.2 **Domestic equity markets, end-2002**

	Market capitalisation ($bn)	% of world market value	Domestic turnover ($bn)	Value as % GDP
New York	9,015	40	9,410	136[a]
Tokyo	2,095	9	1,551	53
NASDAQ	1,994	9	7,000	–
London	1,801	8	1,881	115
Euronext	1,539	7	1,956	74
Deutsche Börse	686	3	1,110	35
Toronto	570	3	397	80
Switzerland	547	3	584	227
Others	3,623	18	–	–
Total	22,810	100	–	–

a New York and NASDAQ combined.
Source: IFSL, *Securities Dealing*, 2003

across national borders, often in a currency other that that of the borrower's home country. London-based bookrunners (see Chapter 4) account for 60% of primary issuance of international bonds and 70% of secondary market trading. London is also the leading European location for bond trading overall (domestic plus international bonds), with 42% of transactions being conducted there. The next largest volumes of business are conducted, perhaps surprisingly, in Copenhagen (19%) and Stockholm (17%).

Equities

The largest stock exchanges in the world, measured by domestic equities market capitalisation, are the New York and Tokyo stock exchanges and NASDAQ, reflecting the size of their domestic economies. The London Stock Exchange ranks fourth in the world, with a market capitalisation only slightly smaller than Tokyo (see Table 12.2). The importance of equity capital for business funding in the UK is reflected in the ratio of market capitalisation to GDP, which at 115% is not far behind the ratio of 136% in the United States. It is much higher than in Germany, the Euronext member countries (Belgium, France, the Netherlands and Portugal) and other European countries (except Switzerland). Trading turnover of domestic equities in London falls a long way short of the American exchanges and is also less than the combined Euronext

Table 12.3 **Markets for international equities, 2003**

	Turnover ($bn)	% of world turnover
London	1,470	45
New York	728	22
Bermuda	365	11
NASDAQ	360	11
Germany	99	3
Switzerland	46	1
Others	157	5
Total	3,292	100

Source: IFSL, *International Financial Markets in the UK*, May 2004

exchanges (Amsterdam, Brussels, Paris and Lisbon), although it is greater than in Tokyo.

The London Stock Exchange is the leading market for trading international equities (equities whose primary listing is on a foreign exchange). In 2003 turnover was $1,470 billion, double that of the New York Stock Exchange and far greater than that of any other financial centre. In early 2004, 373 foreign companies were listed in London to gain access to international funds.

International banking

There are more foreign banks in the City – 287 foreign bank branches and subsidiaries, or 550 including representative offices – than any other

Table 12.4 **Largest banking centres**

	Cross-border lending 2003 (% share)	Foreign banks[a] 2003 (number)	Bank deposits 2002 ($trn)
UK	19	287	3.0
Germany	11	129	2.5
United States	9	246	4.5
Japan	9	84	4.4
France	6	179	1.0

a Branches and subsidiaries of foreign banks in New York, Tokyo, London, Frankfurt and Paris, March 2003.
Source: IFSL, *International Financial Markets in the UK*, May 2004

Table 12.5 **Over-the-counter derivatives turnover, 2001**[a]

	Turnover ($bn)	% share
UK	275	36
United States	135	18
Germany	97	13
France	67	9
Japan	22	3
Switzerland	15	2
Others	153	20
Total	764	100

a Average daily turnover in April 2001 census.
Source: Bank for International Settlements, triennial census of foreign exchange and derivatives trading

financial centre (see Table 12.4). This explains why more cross-border banking – 19% of the world total – is conducted in the UK than in any other centre. With deposits of $3 trillion, the UK is the third largest banking centre in the world after the United States and Japan. It is the largest in Europe, even bigger than Germany, because of the high level of overseas deposits.

Derivatives

The UK is the leading centre for trading over-the-counter derivatives, with turnover averaging $275 billion a day in April 2001, according to the BIS's triennial census (see Table 12.5). This was a 36% share of world turnover (compared with 27% in 1995) and greater than the combined total of other European centres.

On a value basis, the largest derivatives exchanges are the Chicago Mercantile Exchange, the merged Euronext.LIFFE (of which 97% of

Table 12.6 **Largest derivatives exchanges by daily turnover, 2003**

	$bn
Chicago Mercantile Exchange	1,324
Euronext.LIFFE	884
Eurex	354

Source: IFSL, *International Financial Markets in the UK*, May 2004

Table 12.7 **Insurance markets, 2002**

	Gross premiums ($ bn)	% share
United States	1,000	38
Japan	446	17
UK	237	9
Germany	136	5
France	125	5
Italy	84	3
South Korea	55	2
Others	544	21
World total	2,627	100

Source: IFSL, *International Financial Markets in the UK*, May 2004

business takes place on LIFFE, the London International Financial Futures and Options Exchange) and Eurex (see Table 12.6 on the previous page). A high proportion of business undertaken in London is for international customers.

Insurance

The UK is the third largest insurance market in the world, behind the United States and Japan, with 9% of global premium income (see Table 12.7). Both the life and the non-life markets are the largest in Europe, and UK insurance companies' assets of $1,400 billion are almost double those of any other European country. Premiums per head are the third highest in the world, being exceeded only by the prudent, risk-averse inhabitants of Switzerland and Japan.

Asset management

The United States is much the largest source of assets under management, with more than half of the global total (see Table 12.8). The UK ranks third, accounting for 9% of the global total. It is much the largest European source of assets under management because of its substantial life insurance industry and funded pensions.

The UK has the third largest volume of global pension assets after the United States and Japan, and much more than any other European country (see Table 12.9)

Table 12.8 **Assets under management, 2001**

	Assets ($bn)	% share
United States	17,927	52
Japan	3,336	10
UK	2,991	9
France	1,553	4
Germany	1,174	3
Netherlands	698	2
Italy	669	2
Switzerland	596	2
Others	5,772	16
Total	34,716	100

Source: IFSL, *International Financial Markets in the UK*, May 2004

This measure understates the UK's significance as a location for asset management because it does not take account of the management of funds on behalf of overseas clients. London's leading role as a centre for asset management was identified by a survey conducted by Thomson Financial in 2000 which ranked cities by the management of equities owned by institutional investors (see Table 12.10 overleaf). London, New York, Tokyo and Boston constitute a top tier of centres for the

Table 12.9 **Global pension assets, 2001**

	Assets ($bn)	% share
United States	7,010	61
Japan	1,235	11
UK	1,200	10
Netherlands	384	3
Germany	316	3
Other Europe	400	3
Canada	297	3
Others	642	6
Total	11,484	100

Source: IFSL, *International Financial Markets in the UK*, May 2004

Table 12.10 **Asset management, leading locations, 1999**

City	Country	Assets*a* ($bn)
London	UK	2,461
New York	United States	2,363
Tokyo	Japan	2,058
Boston	United States	1,871
San Francisco	United States	726
Los Angeles	United States	569
Paris	France	458
Philadelphia	United States	419
Zurich	Switzerland	414
Denver	United States	340

a Assets under management are by institutional equity holdings.
Source: Thomson Financial, *Target Cities Report 2000* (latest available report)

management of assets owned by institutional investors. Six of the leading locations for asset management are American cities, reflecting the predominance of the United States as a source of assets under management. Paris (seventh) and Zurich (eighth) are the other leading European locations for asset management, although both handle less than one-fifth of the volume of funds managed in London.

Table 12.11 **Management of offshore private assets, 1999**

	% share
Switzerland	33
UK	15
United States	12
Caribbean	12
Channel Islands	6
Luxembourg	6
Hong Kong	5
Others	11

Sources: IFSL, *International Private Wealth Management*, 2002

Table 12.12 **Mergers and acquisitions, 2001[a]**

	% share
United States	60
UK	11
Japan	10
Germany	3
France	2
Others	14

a Estimates derived from total value of mergers and acquisitions contracts.
Source: Corporation of London, *The City's Importance to the EU Economy 2004*, 2004

Private wealth management

Private wealth management services are provided in both onshore and offshore centres. London is one of the main centres for onshore private wealth management, along with New York, Tokyo, Singapore and Hong Kong. It is also the second largest offshore centre after Switzerland (see Table 12.11).

Mergers and acquisitions

The UK is probably the world's second largest centre for corporate mergers and acquisitions activity after the United States and considerably ahead of other European countries (see Table 12.12).

Financial-services industry of the EU

Estimates of the output of wholesale financial services in the EU countries have been made by the Centre for Economic and Business Research, a City-based consultancy, for the Corporation of London. These indicate that London is much the largest financial centre in the European time zone (see Table 12.13 overleaf). The value of the UK's (mostly London's) output exceeds that of the rest of the EU combined.

Financial centre employment

Employment in financial services in financial centres ought to provide a simple measure of relative overall size (see Table 12.14). However, comparisons are not easy to make because of limited availability of data and factors such as inconsistent job classifications and city boundaries. Only for London are there estimates confined to those employed

Table 12.13 **Output of wholesale financial services in the EU, 2003**

	€bn
UK (mostly London)	68.3
Germany (mostly Frankfurt)	19.7
France (mostly Paris)	14.3
Italy	10.1
Netherlands	4.0
Spain	3.2
Belgium	2.4
Rest of EU	4.6
Total	126.6

Source: Corporation of London, *The City's Importance to the EU Economy 2004*, 2004

in the provision of wholesale financial services (although they include professional support services). The statistics for New York City, Hong Kong and Frankfurt contain some element of retail activity, although it can be assumed that a high proportion is wholesale activity. However, the New York City statistics do not include those located in New Jersey, New York state or Connecticut, of which some certainly are involved in wholesale activities. The figure for Tokyo includes a substantial proportion of retail jobs. Moreover, there has been a major contraction of

Table 12.14 **Estimates of employment in financial services in leading financial centres**

	Workforce ('000)
New York City (2004)	314
London (2004)	311
Tokyo (1997)	522
Frankfurt (2003)	90
Paris (2003)	65
Rest of EU (2003)	110
Hong Kong (1996)	158

Sources: London, Paris, Frankfurt, EU: Corporation of London, *The City's Importance to the EU Economy 2004*, 2004; New York: New York State Department of Labor; Tokyo, Hong Kong: author's estimates

financial activity in Tokyo since the beginning of the 1990s, with the number of employees in the securities industry falling by two-fifths.

London and New York City both have financial services sectors with workforces of around 310,000–315,000. Both workforces were smaller in 2004 than in 2001 (368,000 and 326,000 respectively) because of the market downturn and in New York's case the devastation and dislocation wrought by the September 11th terrorist attack on the World Trade Centre. New York City experienced a 15% fall whereas in London the drop was only 3%. Discounting the Tokyo statistics by two-thirds (an arbitrary and perhaps insufficient amount) gives an adjusted workforce figure of 172,000. These numbers suggest that total employment in wholesale financial services in the three global centres is around 800,000.

The combined wholesale financial-services sector workforces of Frankfurt, Paris and other EU countries number perhaps 265,000 (estimates based on Table 12.13 pro-rata to London workforce). The number for Hong Kong includes some retail employment and thus needs downward adjustment, say by half, which reduces it to about 80,000. Thus the combined wholesale financial services workforce of the EU and Hong Kong is perhaps around 350,000. Workforce data are not readily available for the rest of the world's international financial centres – Switzerland, Luxembourg, Singapore, Shanghai, Sydney, Seoul, Chicago, Boston, Toronto and other places, both onshore and offshore – so a guess must suffice: say, a further 350,000. These speculative guesstimates suggest that the workforce of the global wholesale financial-services industry is probably in the region of 1.5m.

Perceptions of London's ranking as a financial centre

Research undertaken in 2003 for the Corporation of London by the Centre for the Study of Financial Innovation (CSFI), a London-based think-tank, explored perceptions of London's competitiveness as a financial centre compared with New York, Paris and Frankfurt. It was based on input from 350 City banks, brokers, fund managers, insurers, technology suppliers, lawyers, accountants, consultants, trade associations and public officials. More than half of the respondent firms were under non-UK ownership.

New York was ranked the top financial centre by an index of overall competitiveness, with London a close second (see Table 12.15 overleaf). Both were significantly ahead of Paris and Frankfurt. The index was based on survey responses on a variety of key attributes: regulation, labour market, tax, government responsiveness, and the living and working environment.

Table 12.15 **Financial centre index of competitiveness, 2003**

1=least competitive 5=most competitive	
New York	3.75
London	3.71
Paris	2.99
Frankfurt	2.81

Source: Lascelles, D., *Sizing Up the City – London's Ranking as a Financial Centre*, CFSI, 2003

New York scored highest for its pool of skilled labour, its personal and corporate tax regime, and the responsiveness of government. London was ranked top for regulation (see Chapter 11). Paris came first for its living and working environment.

The City scored well as regards the following:

- Regulation. The competence of the Financial Services Authority was highly regarded. However, respondents were concerned that ill-judged measures taken by the British government, particularly those emanating from Brussels, could lead to the deterioration of the City's regulatory environment. Respondents reported that if their firms quit London they were more likely to relocate to New York than to another European centre.
- Labour. The abundance of skilled labour and the flexibility of working practices were highly rated, although the latter are being increasingly eroded by EU directives.
- Tax. The UK's lower tax rates were an advantage over the other European centres and almost on a par with New York. But new taxes on foreign banks and possibly resident foreign nationals were perceived as discriminatory and potentially damaging.
- Access to markets. The City scored highly on this important factor. Confirming other research findings, many foreign banks considered that a presence in London conferred the status of an international bank and that this helped to justify the high cost of their London operations.
- Financial innovation. The City's creative culture is a crucial attribute that places it at the forefront of the industry along with New York.

But the City was poorly rated in respect of the following:

- Government responsiveness. Respondents were not impressed by the support that the City receives from the government, with two-thirds believing that other governments were more supportive of their wholesale financial services sectors. Some complained of neglect or confusion, and others even detected hostility. Many felt that the British administration was not adept at protecting City interests at the European Commission in Brussels.
- Living and working environment. London was rated bottom of the four centres for internal public transport, housing and medical facilities. However, there were some positive comments on its openness and lively ambience.

Quality-of-life criticisms of London emerged even more strongly in an annual survey by Cushman & Wakefield Healey & Baker, a property services company, based on interviews with senior executives of 501 of Europe's leading companies and published in summer 2003. The company's *European Cities Monitor 2003* revealed that London had slipped from third out of 30 cities in 1999 to 16th in 2003 as regards "best in terms of quality of life for employees". However, it still ranked top for the important business priorities: easy access to markets, qualified staff, external transport links, quality of telecommunications and languages spoken. Thus overall, London remained the "best city to locate a business", scoring substantially higher than Paris and more than twice as high as Frankfurt in the *European Cities Monitor 2003* league table (see Table 12.16).

Table 12.16 **The best European cities to locate a business, 2003**

	Weighted score
London	0.91
Paris	0.64
Frankfurt	0.39
Brussels	0.29
Amsterdam	0.28

Source: Cushman & Wakefield Healey & Baker, *European Cities Monitor 2003*, 2003

The City versus Paris and Frankfurt

In the 1990s both Paris and Frankfurt mounted a challenge to London to win a greater share of Europe's wholesale international financial business. In Paris, a high-powered promotional body, Paris Europlace, was formed in 1993 to promote the city as a financial centre. It was backed by the Banque de France, Paris city council, the bourse, the major banks and more than 100 financial institutions, French and foreign, and the government. The purpose of the new body was to persuade foreign corporations, especially American banks, to locate in the French capital and to win business for the Paris markets.

The formation in 2000 of Euronext, a merger of the Amsterdam, Brussels, Paris and Lisbon stock exchanges, led by the Paris bourse, was evidence that things were stirring in the French capital. It became the leading exchange in Europe for trading domestic equities by value (though second to London by market capitalisation). Rather more alarming from the City's point of view was Euronext's £555m takeover of LIFFE in 2001, despite counter-offers from the London Stock Exchange and the Deutsche Börse's Eurex derivatives division. This made Euronext the second largest derivatives exchange (by value) in the world after the Chicago Mercantile Exchange, although a substantial part of its business was now conducted in London.

Despite this coup, the estimated value of wholesale financial services transacted in Paris is one-fifth of that undertaken in London (see Table 12.13 on page 246). Moreover, despite top marks for its appealing quality of life, respondents to the CSFI poll rated it poorly on commercial criteria. Paris came bottom of the class relative to London, New York and Frankfurt as regards the quantity and quality of regulation and the availability of skilled labour (a "patchy" talent pool) and second from bottom for tax and government responsiveness. In reality, it is not London but Frankfurt that Paris is in competition with for the role of leading continental European regional financial centre.

The choice of Frankfurt as the location of the headquarters of the new European Central Bank in 1994 spurred its aspirations to challenge London's pre-eminence as the leading financial centre in the European time zone. It was argued that proximity to the institution that would in future set European interest rates would give banks a competitive advantage, making Frankfurt a magnet for financial firms. To help things along, in 1996 Frankfurt set up a promotional organisation, Finanzplatz Deutscheland, backed by the three large German banks, the Deutsche Börse and the local government authority. Its mission was to promote Frankfurt as an international financial centre by identifying and remedying structural weaknesses and pushing its case at all levels of government.

The following year, Eurex, Frankfurt's derivatives exchange, mounted a bid to topple LIFFE from its position as the leading market for trading German government ten-year bond (bund) derivatives contracts, then Europe's biggest derivatives product. The struggle revolved around the respective merits of the trading systems used by LIFFE, the larger and longer-established exchange, and Eurex. At LIFFE the contracts were traded on the floor of the exchange by the traditional method of open outcry, but at Eurex dealing was screen-based. Eurex was able to demonstrate that electronic trading was cheaper and more efficient than open outcry, with devastating results for LIFFE's contract as traders deserted to Eurex en masse in autumn 1997.

Eurex's victory in the "battle of the bund" was hailed as a turning-point for Frankfurt and an ominous omen for the City. The 1998 edition of the *European Cities Monitor* survey of senior executives of leading European companies reported that, for the first time, more of them (45%) expected Frankfurt to be Europe's leading financial centre in five years' time than London (40%). The conviction that "Mainhattan" or "Bankfurt" was about to overtake London was boosted by the imminent introduction of the euro without the UK's participation. This, it was argued, would lead to the emergence of a euro-denominated European capital market based in Frankfurt, leaving the City out in the cold.

The euro duly arrived in 1999, but the City hardly shivered. Soon it was being pointed out that the location of the board of the Federal Reserve in Washington DC had done little to promote that city as a financial centre to rival New York. Nor did it matter much in the electronic age where an exchange was located; the important factor was where its clients operated from, and that continued to be London. But even worse than these disappointments was the conduct of the big three Frankfurt banks, which, at the same time as they were helping to bankroll the Finanzplatz initiative, were shifting their securities, foreign-exchange and derivatives trading to London. Deutsche Bank, the leading German bank, made major acquisitions in the City and on Wall Street, and by 2002 more than half of its employees lived and worked outside Germany. There were repeated rumours that it intended to move its headquarters to London, where it had no less than 11,000 staff, all on the wholesale side of the business. Meanwhile, the other two big Frankfurt banks, Dresdner and Commerz, passed into the control of Munich-based proprietors who were more concerned about the bottom line than the promotion of Frankfurt.

Then in 2002 came the shock of the collapse of the Neuer Markt, the Deutsche Börse's five-year-old "new economy" stockmarket, as well as a blight of empty office space as the German economy slowed to a snail's pace. The leaked revelation that a report for the Deutsche Börse written by McKinsey & Co, a management consulting firm, had come to the conclusion that Finanzplatz Frankfurt was "falling apart" caused consternation in the city. These developments were reflected in the shift in the answers given to the *European Cities Monitor* survey in 2003, which reported a fall in those expecting Frankfurt to be Europe's leading financial centre in five years' time to a mere 20% of respondents.

Stanislas Yassukovich, a veteran international investment banker, comments: "The expatriate community that populates an international financial centre has cultural and lifestyle expectations which Frankfurt cannot meet. Germany has moved its international financial business to London for the simple reason that London is where the people to operate it can be found. Frankfurt's main handicap is, quite simply, Frankfurt."

So London continues to be the leading financial centre in the European time zone by a substantial margin. Indeed, such is its lead that perhaps the greatest threat to its supremacy is complacency, which heads Yassukovich's list of the City's shortcomings. In a similar vein, the CSFI report concludes: "The fact that there are no ready alternatives to London in the European time zone is comforting, but worrying too. It provides at best a negative reason for being in London – one that could quickly disappear if conditions changed."

13 City scandals and calamities

Financial scandals are as old as financial markets. The most famous early City scandal, although not the first, was the South Sea Bubble of 1719–20. It involved speculation in the shares of the South Sea Company, whose business, despite the name, comprised the ownership and management of a substantial part of the national debt. The company was closely connected with the crown and ministers, and it was in the government's and everyone else's interests that the share price should rise. Moreover, as has happened many times since – most recently in the dotcom boom of the late 1990s – when prices soared speculators suspended their critical judgment. When the bubble burst in August 1720, the insiders, including the royal family and the chancellor of the exchequer, got out first, leaving the mass of speculators nursing large losses.

Britain was almost continuously at war during the 18th century, necessitating large-scale government borrowing. There were many financial scandals involving the issuance of government bonds, which were used by successive administrations as a form of patronage to buy political support. Supporters were awarded allocations at a discount to the issue price, enabling them to make large profits. In a particularly notorious episode in 1767, the chancellor of the exchequer himself purchased a large part of an issue at a discount and pocketed the profits.

Bond market speculation

Fluctuations in the market price of government bonds (gilts), which comprised almost the whole market in quoted securities at the time, provided ample scope for speculation. The most notorious episode occurred in 1814, when a cabal of speculators led by Lord Cochrane, a naval war hero, rigged the gilts market by spreading false information to boost bond prices. They arranged for an open carriage with passengers dressed in French royalist officers' uniforms to parade around the City crying "Vive le roi", suggesting an Allied victory over Napoleon. This led to a rally in British government bonds from which the conspirators benefited by selling the substantial holdings they had bought at depressed prices in previous weeks. They were quickly identified from the registers at the Bank of England and apprehended. After a spell in jail, Cochrane continued his activities as an adventurer in

South America, where he became a hero in the liberation struggles against Spain.

The battle of Waterloo in 1815 brought an end to the wars against France. This led to a big reduction in British government borrowing and scandal shifted to other sectors of the market. In the 1820s there was a borrowing spree by foreign governments in the London securities market, notably some thoroughly non-creditworthy, recently independent South American republics offering extravagant yields. The scramble for the bonds created a new speculative bubble, which collapsed in 1825 when many defaulted on their bonds.

For a generation investors were wary of foreign government bonds, but by the 1850s the losses of the 1820s had been long forgotten and the world had moved into the era of the steamship and the electric telegraph. In the 1860s and early 1870s, less and less creditworthy borrowers were gaining access to the international capital market, although they had to offer fancy yields to do so – the junk bonds of the day. Again it was too good to be true, and in the mid-1870s there was an avalanche of defaults on the part of Latin American and other exotic borrowers. Overlending to Latin America was the underlying cause of the Baring Brothers' crisis of 1890, when one of the City's leading merchant banks was rescued by a lifeboat of other City bankers orchestrated by the Bank of England.

Company promotion frauds

Much of the action in the 19th century stockmarket focused on the securities of railway companies, the technology stocks of their day. In the mid-1830s and again the mid-1840s there were railway "manias", with speculators pushing the securities to absurd heights only for them to come crashing down. The arch manipulator was George Hudson, the so-called "railway king" and a member of Parliament, but he too fell to earth. He was prosecuted for paying dividends out of capital and for misuse of shareholders' funds and went to jail. In subsequent decades, speculators shifted their focus to even more casino-like "chips", such as the shares of overseas mining companies and later oil, rubber and nitrates companies.

Scandals based on hyped and sometimes fraudulent initial public offerings (IPOs) of domestic manufacturing companies began in the 1890s, a development associated with Ernest Hooley, a company promoter who went spectacularly bankrupt in 1898. In the 1920s there were many more hyped IPOs, especially of companies involved in the new technologies of radio, electricity and automobiles, and although some important new enterprises emerged there were also many flops. Clarence Hatry, the leading company promoter of the decade, suffered a sensational fall from grace in September 1929 when he admitted fraud and was sentenced to seven years in jail. It has been argued that the Hatry scandal was a contributory factor in the Wall Street crash of October 1929. Another major scandal – the accusation that the directors of the Royal Mail Shipping Company, a leading shipping company, had issued a fraudulent prospectus – resulted in a trial in September 1931. It was a fraught moment in the City, with sterling's exchange rate against gold under threat from the banking crisis that had engulfed central Europe. The almost simultaneous rout of sterling and imprisonment of some Royal Mail directors helped further to undermine confidence in the City and the financial markets for more than a generation.

In the 1930s and 1940s, decades dominated by economic depression and war, the subdued markets presented unpromising opportunities for speculation and there were only minor financial scandals, most colourfully the pepper market corner of 1935. The 1950s saw the arrival of the hostile takeover bid, a highly controversial development. Takeovers were often followed by the break-up and sell-off of assets of the acquired company, a process that came to be known by the pejorative term "asset-stripping". Public outrage at such financially driven rationalisations was given voice by Edward Heath, the Conservative prime minister who in 1973 called the activities of the ruthless and unscrupulous Tiny Rowland the "unpleasant and unacceptable face of capitalism", a phrase that immediately became associated with the business buccaneers of the era.

Bank failures

In the 18th and 19th centuries there were numerous bank failures, resulting in losses of savings by depositors. Among City-based banking scandals, the failure in 1866 of Overend, Gurney, a specialist dealer in the money market which was brought down by a combination of fraud and incompetence, ruined many other City firms. It was the City's worst systemic bank failure and the severity of the losses led the Bank of England to develop the role of lender of last resort to the banking system, which it successfully applied at the time of the Barings crisis of 1890.

The failure of the City of Glasgow Savings Bank in 1878, which has been described as "Scotland's Wall Street Crash", was not strictly a City calamity, but the scale of the losses sustained by small savers cast a

Table 13.1 **Recent City scandals and calamities**

Institution	Year
Midland Bank and Crocker Bank	1984
Johnson Matthey Bankers	1984
Guinness	1986
Blue Arrow	1987
Barlow Clowes	1988
Hammersmith & Fulham swaps	1989
British & Commonwealth Holdings	1990
Bank of Credit and Commerce International (BCCI)	1991
Robert Maxwell	1991
European Bank for Reconstruction and Development (EBRD)	1993
Pensions mis-selling	1994
Barings	1995
Lloyd's of London	1996
Morgan Grenfell Asset Management	1996
Flaming Ferraris	1999
Equitable Life	1999
NatWest Capital Markets	2000
Marconi	2001
Split capital investment trusts	2002
Investment products mis-selling	2003

shadow over all deposit-taking institutions for a generation. The last major British banking scandal involving substantial losses by retail investors was the failure of Farrow's Bank in 1920.

In the early 1970s there was a new crisis among a group of City financial institutions (see Chapter 2), the so-called "secondary banking crisis" of 1973–75. Serious damage to the overall financial system was avoided by the organisation of a "lifeboat" by the Bank of England, whereby the stricken secondary banks, which had got into trouble by overlending to the property market, were bailed out by the major clearing banks and either recapitalised or closed down.

Recenty City scandals and calamities

The principal City scandals and calamities of the last two decades are listed in Table 13.1 and sketched in this chapter. These episodes attracted sensational and often unfavourable publicity for the City, but they are a pale shadow of the scandals that beset Wall Street in the same period.

Midland Bank and Crocker Bank

In July 1980, Midland Bank announced that it had agreed to buy Crocker National Bank of San Francisco, a substantial west-coast commercial bank. The acquisition was the outcome of a strategic decision to enter the North American market, pursuing its rivals Barclays and NatWest, but the timing and target were driven by the threat of imminent restrictions on foreign acquisitions of American banks. Midland paid $597m for 51% of Crocker, and committed a further $225m to increase its holding, ownership being eventually transferred in October 1981. In the meantime, while the lawyers steered the deal through American banking regulatory procedures, Crocker's managers took advantage of the almost complete autonomy bestowed by the terms of the deal. Harbouring the ambition of turning Crocker into the "Citicorp of the west coast", and relieved of the burden of moral hazard by virtue of Midland's resources, they leveraged the forthcoming capital injection from Midland and went on a lending spree, much of it to Latin American borrowers and the Californian real-estate market.

The announcement by Mexico in August 1982 that it was unable to service its foreign debt is generally regarded as the beginning of the 1980s less-developed country (LDC) debt crisis. Crocker's loans to Latin America resulted in Midland being twice as exposed to Latin American non-performing debt as UK clearing banks were on average. And for good measure, the Californian real-estate market collapsed too.

Midland's problems with Crocker's loan book began to become public knowledge in 1984 when it was obliged to make a £75m bad-debt provision for 1983, wiping out much of that year's profits. In May 1984, the American government was obliged to engineer a rescue of Continental Illinois, Chicago's biggest bank and the eighth largest in the United States, which had got into trouble as a result of real-estate, energy and LDC loan losses. Heightened anxiety about the systemic threats to the banking system led American regulators to adopt a stringent attitude to Crocker's non-performing loans. Midland was informed that it would have to make an additional £200m bad-debt provision and inject a further £165m into Crocker, with £80m more on standby.

Eventually, in February 1986, under Sir Kit McMahon, its new chairman and chief executive hired from and effectively installed by the Bank of England, Midland managed to extricate itself from Crocker by selling it to Wells Fargo Bank. Overall, its disastrous North American expansion cost Midland at least £1 billion, and for a while it was probably technically insolvent. The episode was a cautionary tale of the pitfalls of expansion overseas through acquisition, exemplifying problems of controls over local management and the potential cultural divide in operating standards and attitudes.

Midland's reputation and balance sheet were so battered that in summer 1987 Saatchi & Saatchi, a voguish advertising agency, enquired about acquiring it, but the cheeky approach got short shrift from the bank and the authorities. In June 1992 Midland was acquired by the Hongkong and Shanghai Banking Corporation (HSBC), which moved its headquarters from Hong Kong to London around the same time.

Johnson Matthey Bankers

In 1984 Johnson Matthey, a precious metal company formed in 1817, employed 6,000 people in the UK and a further 4,000 abroad. The bulk of its business was as a refiner of precious metals and a manufacturer of the products that use them, such as jewellery and industrial equipment. In the City it was best known as a bullion dealer, one of the five members of the London Gold Fixing, a group that meets twice a day to set a world price for gold. But it also conducted wholesale banking activities through Johnson Matthey Bankers (JMB), a subsidiary established in 1965.

In the early 1980s JMB adopted a bolder credit policy in an attempt to increase earnings on that side of the business, boosting its loan book ninefold between 1980 and 1984. By summer 1984 many of these loans, including two huge ones equivalent to 76% and 34% of its capital base of £170m, had become non-performing. This flagrant breach of sound banking practice had not been picked up by the bank's auditors, and it was only in September 1984 that the Bank of England became aware that JMB was insolvent because of its non-performing loans. Consultations with the City led the Bank to the conclusion that JMB's problems could drag down its parent company and have serious consequences for the bullion market and the City as an international financial centre. Moreover, it was judged that there was a significant risk of the infection spreading to the banking system itself, posing a threat to the economy. Midland's parlous state as a result of its massive losses from Crocker National Bank gave particular cause for concern about a loss of confidence in the banking system.

Initially, the Bank tried to arrange for JMB to be acquired by the Bank of Nova Scotia, but the Canadians passed. So the Bank decided to mount a rescue, along the lines of the lifeboat it had organised in 1973 to bail out the banks caught up in the secondary banking crisis. On Sunday September 30th 1984, some 200 City bankers were summoned to an urgent meeting at the Bank to work out a way in which they could save JMB. But the clearing banks refused to help, in part because the Bank had not supported them in 1979 when the government had imposed a much resented windfall-profits tax. Their insouciance, inconceivable a decade earlier, was indicative of the diminished authority of the Bank over the City, as its business became increasingly dominated by large and foreign banks. Fearful of a City crisis, the Bank itself purchased JMB for £1, having secured undertakings from members of the London Gold Fixing group and the clearing banks that they would contribute to an indemnity fund and thus cover part of any eventual losses.

The Bank established that JMB had lent a total of £450m, of which more than half was non-performing and might never be collected. The staggering level of incompetence led the Bank to sue JMB's accountants for negligence. In the end, the Bank's share of the final indemnity fund was £21m, much less than initially feared.

The Bank of England's acquisition of JMB was challenged by the Conservative government's political opponents. They contrasted the administration's willingness to commit public money to rescue a bank while refusing to subsidise unprofitable coalmines and industrial companies. They challenged the contention that the failure of JMB would have constituted a risk to the financial system and portrayed it as pandering to friends in the City. It was also argued that the Bank had been negligent in its bank supervisory role in not acting more promptly to pre-empt the failure of JMB. In December 1984, Nigel Lawson, the chancellor, seeking to take the heat out of these attacks – in one bad-tempered exchange a Labour member of Parliament had called him a "snivelling little git" – announced the establishment of an inquiry into the system of bank supervision.

Controversially, the inquiry's report, published in June 1985, proposed a streamlining of the structure of bank supervision that extended the Bank's authority over all the UK's deposit-taking institutions and extended its scope. To fulfil this enhanced responsibility it was recommended that the banking-supervision staff should be increased in number and given commercial banking experience. The Bank's supervisory responsibility for the whole of the British banking system and significant increases in its supervisory powers, including a limit on exposure to a single customer of 25% of capital, were enacted by the Banking Act of 1987. However, the legislation also provided for the establishment of a new Board of Banking Supervision, outside the Bank's control and backed by statute, to advise the Bank. This marked the beginning of the end of the Bank's supervision of the banking system, although it took several more scandals before that came about.

Guinness

The Guinness scandal was about illegal share purchases undertaken for the purpose of supporting the price of Guinness shares during a bitter and highly publicised takeover battle for Distillers, a whiskymaker, in 1985–86. It was an episode that revealed a cavalier disregard for the law, let alone low ethical standards, on the part of some prominent City players and was highly damaging to the City's reputation.

Ernest Saunders, appointed managing director of Guinness in 1982, had ambitious plans to turn the drowsy brewing group into a major player in the international drinks industry. Assisted by strategic consultants Bain & Co, he devised a plan to expand and reposition Guinness through a series of acquisitions. The takeover spree began modestly in June 1984. A year later, Guinness launched a hostile bid for Arthur Bell, a Scottish whisky producer, which it won for the price of £370m. Then came the big one: Distillers.

Distillers was the largest independent Scottish whiskymaker and owned many famous brands. Its directors had a proud sense of the firm's history and of its product's iconic national significance. With 90% of sales going abroad, it was also arguably Scotland's foremost ambassador. In early December 1985, the directors received and rejected an unwelcome bid from Argyll Group, a UK retail group, worth £1.9 billion. Advised that independence was no longer a feasible option, the board gave its support to a counter-bid in January 1986 by Guinness, advised by merchant banker Morgan Grenfell, which valued the firm at £2.2 billion. The struggle for Distillers quickly developed into acrimony, with both sides making unprecedented use of the press to belittle each other. Doubtless another factor stimulating greater than usual public interest in a City contest was familiarity with Distillers' product: Scotch whisky. When Argyll upped its bid to £2.3 billion, Guinness responded with £2.35 billion.

The Guinness offer to Distillers' shareholders comprised part cash, part Guinness shares. The higher the price of Guinness shares, the more attractive its offer became. Correspondingly, any decline in the Guinness share price made its offer less attractive. Thus a "concert party" of friendly financiers was organised to sustain the Guinness share price by purchases in the stockmarket, the participants being indemnified against losses by undertakings from Guinness. This was illegal, but allegedly was a common behind-the-scenes practice in the City in the mid-1980s takeover boom. It was also effective: on April 18th 1986 Ernest Saunders announced ecstatically that the firm had control of 50.7% of Distillers' shares. With the assistance of £258m in improper share purchases, Guinness had won the City's most savage takeover battle.

The euphoria did not last long. In July an ugly row erupted in public when Saunders reneged on an undertaking given to win the support of the Distillers board. This was that Sir Thomas Risk, an eminent Scottish banker, should become chairman of the combined company to safeguard the mega-firm's Scottish heritage. But Saunders, who was riding high, having in five years increased the value of Guinness by 35 times and turned a family firm into a world-class player in the global drinks industry, bagged the job for himself, combining the roles of chairman and chief executive. As things turned out, it was a classic instance of pride coming before the fall.

One of the members of the "concert party" that conducted the illegal share price support operation for Guinness during its bid for Distillers in early 1986 was Ivan Boesky, a Wall Street arbitrageur. When Boesky was arrested in the United States later in the year on charges of insider dealing on a colossal scale, he negotiated a plea bargain: a reduced sentence in exchange for singing like a proverbial canary. Boesky's revelations about the Distillers takeover were passed on by America's Securities and Exchange Commission to the UK's DTI, which in December 1986 began to look into the bid.

Before the year was out Roger Seelig, Morgan Grenfell's star investment banker who had orchestrated the Guinness bid, had been forced to resign. But Margaret Thatcher, the prime minister, and Robin Leigh Pemberton, the governor of the Bank of England, were so enraged by Morgan Grenfell's conduct that they insisted that the chief executive and the head of corporate finance should walk the plank as well. So too should Patrick Spens, head of corporate finance at Henry Ansbacher, a minor merchant bank, which had also been involved in the share-price ramping shenanigans. Saunders was sacked in January 1987 and placed under arrest in May 1987.

In August 1990, after a trial lasting 107 days, Saunders and three co-defendants were found guilty on 28 charges of conspiracy, theft and false accounting. They went to jail. A second Guinness trial of Seelig and Spens got under way in April 1991, but it collapsed because of the defendants' ill-health. A third trial of Seelig and David Mayhew of Cazenove was planned, but it was abandoned.

Blue Arrow

The Blue Arrow scandal, like the Guinness scandal, was about an illegal share-price support operation. It was perpetrated by Blue Arrow's City advisers, investment bank County NatWest and brokers Phillips & Drew, in September 1987 in support of a massive £837m rights issue to finance a bid for employment agency Manpower, Blue Arrow's much larger American rival. Investigative probing by *The Economist* in subsequent months led to revelations that the professional advisers to the deal had themselves secretly purchased 13% of the offering to support the price.

County NatWest's two leading executives resigned in February 1988, and the publication of a DTI report on the affair in July 1989 led to resignations at the top of National Westminster, the parent commercial bank. In February 1992, following a year-long trial, four of Blue Arrow's City advisers were found guilty of conspiracy to defraud. They received suspended sentences, but the convictions were overturned on appeal.

In the league table of great City scandals the Blue Arrow affair ranks pretty low, but it inflicted significant damage to the reputations of the firms of advisers and it was yet another blow to the standing of the City at a difficult time.

Barlow Clowes

The Barlow Clowes scandal, which broke in May 1988 when the firm collapsed, was about the theft of £150m from 15,000 mostly elderly investors by executives of the Barlow Clowes group of investment management firms. Investors' funds were supposedly risk free because they were fully invested in British government bonds. Yet miraculously, and suspiciously, Barlow Clowes promised a guaranteed higher rate of income than that generated by the gilt-edged securities themselves. This combination of high income and the security of risk-free, familiar investments – an investor's holy grail – was successfully marketed to thousands of retired pensioners in the early and mid-1980s.

Barlow Clowes was unable to generate the necessary returns from gilts and soon diversified into higher-yielding, higher-risk assets. Moreover, senior managers diverted investors' funds to finance a lavish lifestyle comprising fast cars, luxury homes, a Bordeaux chateau, a Lear-jet and a £1.3m yacht; investigators later quipped that Barlow Clowes's only gilt-edged assets were the vessel's gold-plated taps.

With allegations of fraud flying around, the firm was wound up by compulsory order in July 1988 and liquidators were appointed. Many pensioners lost their life savings and it was reported that 16 suicides resulted. The public outcry led to two official inquiries, which castigated the DTI for maladministration regarding the licensing and regulation of Barlow Clowes. In response, the government announced an unprece-dented payment of £150m in compensation to the victims. Liquidators eventually recovered £76m, cutting the cost to taxpayers to £74m.

The principal villain, Peter Clowes, received a ten-year prison sen-tence in 1992. Released early with sentence remission, in March 1999 he was back in court charged with a "sophisticated and deliberate" welfare fraud for which he was jailed for four months.

Hammersmith & Fulham swaps

In February 1989, local taxpayers and the City were astonished to learn that Hammersmith & Fulham, a local government authority in west London, had sustained losses from swap transactions of perhaps as much as £500m. It transpired that 78 local authorities were using swaps in the ordinary course of business as a means of hedging interest-rate risk on their borrowings.

An independent inquiry published in April 1991 revealed that Ham-mersmith & Fulham had entered into swap transactions on a scale 20 times greater than that of any other local authority, and that it had been using the market not just for hedging purposes but also to try to make money. It had been doing business with no less than 110 counterparties covering the whole spectrum of market participants: mostly banks, but also pension funds, corporations and 19 other local authorities. In the first seven months of 1988, Hammersmith & Fulham had entered into 365 swap transactions and its risk exposure at the end of the period was £3.3 billion.

In January 1991 the House of Lords ruled that all local authority inter-est-rate swaps were *ultra vires* (meaning beyond the powers delegated by Parliament to local authorities) and thus illegal. This meant that any losses (or profits) generated by the transactions would have to be borne by the banks that were counterparties to them. More than 1,000 swap agreements involving 130 authorities were annulled by the decision, causing losses at 78 UK and foreign banks amounting to an estimated

£750m. A survey by the International Swap Dealers Association in 1992 found that British local authorities were the source of almost half of the cumulative losses suffered by dealers since they began swaps trading.

The episode demonstrated the hazards of dabbling in complex financial markets by people who thought they knew more than they did and of over-reliance on the advice of brokers, whose principal interest is to generate trading revenue, not to safeguard the interests of customers. They were lessons that could have been learned to advantage by the treasurer of Orange County, California, which in December 1994 stunned the markets with the announcement of a loss of $1.6 billion from derivatives trades. This was the largest loss recorded by a local government authority and led to the bankruptcy of the county.

British & Commonwealth Holdings

In the late 1980s British & Commonwealth Holdings (B&CH) was a thrusting financial services group whose principal activities were money broking, fund management and investment. It expanded rapidly, a major step being the acquisition in 1987 of Mercantile House, a money-broking conglomerate, for £500m. The following year it paid £407m for Atlantic Computers, a computer-leasing company. At the time Atlantic Computers appeared to be earning healthy profits, but it was later revealed that there were irregularities in its accounting practices and a basic flaw in the leasing options given to customers. By 1990 accumulated losses on the computer-leasing business amounted to £550m.

In June 1990 B&CH collapsed, brought down by the losses at Atlantic Computers. A DTI investigation into the collapse criticised BZW, an investment bank which had advised B&CH on the acquisition, for adopting an "insufficiently robust approach" to its investigation of Atlantic Computers and failing to spot the serious flaw in the leasing agreements, work for which BZW was paid £1m. In January 1999 an agreement was reached between Barclays Bank, BZW's parent, and B&CH's administrators. This cost the bank £116m in compensation for the inadequate due diligence work undertaken by its subsidiary which had allowed the disastrous acquisition to proceed.

Bank of Credit and Commerce International

The Bank of Credit and Commerce International (BCCI) – "Bank of Crooks and Corruption International" – scandal was the biggest bank fraud in history. When it was closed down in July 1991, by a concerted international central bank operation led by the Bank of England, a "black hole" of $18 billion was discovered at the centre of its complex labyrinth of accounts.

BCCI was founded in 1972 by Agha Hassan Abedi, a charismatic Pakistani businessman, and Suraleh Naquvi, an associate, as an international bank focusing on serving Muslim and developing-country clients who felt neglected by western banks. Abedi's backers were mostly fellow Muslims, including the sheikh of Abu Dhabi, but they also included the giant Bank of America, which took a 30% shareholding as part of an ill-judged overseas expansion drive. Abedi's management culture was a novel cocktail of Muslim mysticism, posturing developing-country idealism and cynical materialism. Senior managers seemed more interested in soul searching than sound business practice; on one occasion Abedi startled a meeting of executives by explaining: "The reason I was late is that I met God in the corridor and I had to talk to him. I had to bring his feelings to you." Staff meetings resembled revivalist gatherings, with ordinary members of the "BCCI family", many of them deferential fellow Shia Muslims, voicing tearful adulation of "Agha Sahib". But the boss was no ascetic, revelling in his private jet, fleet of luxury cars and retail therapy expeditions. BCCI was more like a cult than a bank, and prayers proved a poor substitute for credit controls.

BCCI expanded rapidly. Between 1972 and 1991 its capital base grew from $2.3 billion to $23 billion. By then it had 420 offices around the world and a presence in 70 countries. The UK was an important location for its operations, a British banking licence being obtained in 1973, and by 1978 there were 45 UK branches. Although it was registered in Luxembourg, London was BCCI's international operating headquarters.

Abedi was eager to establish a presence in the United States, but this was impossible under American banking legislation because of Bank of America's shareholding. So BCCI entered the American market illegally through frontmen, who first acquired control of the National Bank of Georgia and then in the late 1970s of the larger First America Bank. With a sigh of relief, Bank of America sold its BCCI stake in 1980.

A driving force behind the rapid growth of BCCI's balance sheet was the quadrupling of oil prices in 1973-74, providing Arab oil producers with unprecedented amounts of money to put on deposit. On the lending side, the expansion was achieved with little regard to the quality of business. BCCI had dangerously large exposures to favoured companies and individuals, violating prudent banking practices. An inquiry in 1978 revealed that loans to the Gulf Group, a Pakistani shipping company, totalled $185m, three times the bank's then capital and 30 times the prudent maximum exposure to a single client. Although BCCI's published results showed ever-increasing profits, by the late 1970s the bank was suffering from an alarming level of bad debts.

Reality was not reflected in BCCI's accounts because the losses were concealed in a Cayman Islands subsidiary, a bank within a bank known internally as "the dustbin", safe from regulatory scrutiny. From the outset BCCI's complex structure – registered in Luxembourg, headquarters in London and operating across the world with numerous tax-haven offshoots – was designed to prevent outsiders from gaining an accurate view of what was going on at the bank. Two prestigious firms of auditors were used, but neither of them had access to the whole picture. As the losses mounted, the accounts became more and more phoney, and Abedi was obliged to resort to increasingly reckless ways of keeping the bank afloat.

Big and bold "proprietary trading" – trading using the bank's own capital geared up with borrowings, in other words large-scale gambling – was Abedi's answer. But BCCI's traders lost money by the bucketful – $849m between 1982 and 1986 – and the situation shifted from debacle to disaster. The bank was kept afloat only by creative accounting and massive misappropriations of depositors' funds. Abedi desperately needed new sources of deposits and revenue. So he became banker to Latin America's drug barons, who were happy to pay handsomely for international money-laundering services.

Following the death of its president in an air crash in 1981, Panama fell under the sway of General Manuel Noriega. In 1982 Noriega opened an account with BCCI's Panama City branch into which went the pay-offs from the Colombian cocaine cartels for allowing them to use Panama as a transit point. Soon the drug barons themselves were using BCCI's services to launder their proceeds. BCCI provided similar services for other drug dealers in Hong Kong and Abu Dhabi. Investigations after the bank's collapse revealed a rogues' gallery of shadowy clients, not only narcotics dealers but also black-market foreign-exchange operators, arms traders, intelligence agencies (including the CIA) and assorted terrorists. One deal, bizarrely, even financed the purchase by Arab terrorists of Israeli-built weapons.

In 1987 the head of BCCI's Miami branch made the mistake of offering the bank's money-laundering facilities to an undercover American customs agent. The customs service "sting" operation resulted in a fine of $14.8m and jail for four employees in 1989. When subsequent American and British investigations revealed the bank's criminal culture and found "evidence of massive and widespread fraud", the authorities stepped in.

The closure of BCCI left 150,000 depositors around the world scrambling to recover lost money. The biggest loser of all was the sheikh of Abu Dhabi. By May 2003 small depositors had recovered 75% of their claims, a great deal more than the 5–10% predicted at the time of BCCI's demise, leaving a final loss to depositors of around $2 billion. The cost of the liquidation was a record $1.2 billion. Even towards the end of the process, there were 100 lawyers and accountants working on it housed in their own building in London. By then they had amassed 88,000 boxes of documents, storage charges for which constituted a substantial part of the liquidation operation's $70m premises costs.

Abedi and Naquvi were indicted by the American authorities but could not be extradited. Abedi's death in 1995 put him beyond the law; 13 BCCI executives were convicted of fraud in Abu Dhabi.

Recriminations abounded about negligence on the part of the various regulatory authorities and the bank's accountants, and whether the way in which the bank had been shut down had exacerbated depositors' losses. The liquidator decided to take the Bank of England to court, claiming that it "knowingly or recklessly" failed to supervise BCCI properly and seeking £850m in damages on behalf of 6,500 British depositors. The case opened in January 2004 and was expected to last until 2006 at an estimated cost of £200m, a record for a British trial.

The BCCI scandal demonstrated how criminally minded international bankers could outwit regulators and accountants with national remits. BCCI with its Luxembourg registration, London headquarters, Middle-Eastern shareholders and global operations was regulated by everyone and no one. The need for closer international co-operation was a lesson taken to heart by the leading central banks.

Robert Maxwell

In November 1991 Robert Maxwell, a 68-year-old publishing tycoon, was found drowned near the Canary Islands where he had been cruising in his luxury yacht. Investigations revealed not only that Maxwell's publishing and newspaper empire was bust, owing a bevy of banks £2.8 billion, but that he had stolen an estimated £526m from the pension funds of his 16,000 employees.

Maxwell had had a colourful and controversial business and City career. Born in Czechoslovakia, he fought with distinction in the British army in the second world war and changed his name twice (initially styling himself du Maurier after a brand of luxury cigarette). In 1951 he acquired Pergamon Press, a publisher of textbooks and scientific journals, which he built into a hugely profitable public company, conducting business on a large scale with Comecon countries. Turning his hand to politics, from 1964 to 1970 he represented Buckinghamshire as a Labour MP. In 1969 he agreed to sell Pergamon to Leasco, an American finance group. A row erupted when Leasco challenged the veracity of Pergamon's profits and Maxwell lost control. A DTI inquiry found that the firm's profits did indeed depend on transactions with Maxwell family private companies, and it concluded that Maxwell was "not a person who can be relied on to exercise proper stewardship of a publicly quoted company".

However, Pergamon languished without Maxwell and in 1974 he was able to re-acquire control with borrowed funds. In 1980 he bought the troubled British Printing Corporation, which he turned round and grandly renamed Maxwell Communications Corporation. His ambition to own a national newspaper was realised in 1984 when he acquired the Labour-supporting *Daily Mirror*, which henceforth dutifully publicised its proprietor's every move. The purchase in 1988 of Macmillan, an American book publisher, was yet another major step, but it necessitated taking on yet more debt.

By the end of the 1980s the Maxwell empire, which comprised more than 400 companies, was experiencing acute financial difficulties and was kept going by shifting funds around the labyrinth of interlocking private companies, by misappropriating pensioners' funds and by deal-making. No one could quite keep up with Maxwell, but his voracious appetite for deals kept his City advisers, the beneficiaries of all the investment banking fees, onside as cheerleaders. Desperate for money, Maxwell sold Pergamon and floated Mirror Group Newspapers as a public company. But it was too late; his financial position worsened and he must have known he would be found out. Rather than face the humiliation, it is generally believed he committed suicide. But there is no shortage of other theories, with his death being attributed to the Israeli secret services, the Mob, the Russians and sundry other parties.

The revelations of Maxwell's crimes led to the commissioning of a report by DTI inspectors. At a cost of £8m, it was finally published ten years later in April 2001. The inspectors identified successive layers of guilt, beginning with the fraudster himself, chronicling how he bullied and bribed his way to the top, taking in gullible or cowed financial journalists, brokers and bankers. They found that Maxwell's sons also bore considerable responsibility, along with several members of the Mirror board, as did his auditors and investment bank advisers, notably Goldman Sachs, whose vision may have been clouded by Maxwell's fat fees. In 1999 PricewaterhouseCoopers, his accountants, agreed an out-of-court settlement of £67m with the liquidators for auditing failures and were fined a further £3.4m by the industry's disciplinary body for having "lost the plot" in the auditing of the failed publishing empire.

In 1995, after the most expensive trial in British history, Maxwell's sons were acquitted of wrongdoing. Subsequently the fees – in excess of £30m – charged by the professional advisers handling the receivership of Maxwell's companies became yet another scandal. The high court judge handling the matter made a public pronouncement calling the fees "profoundly shocking" and declaring "I find it shameful that a court receivership should produce this result".

European Bank for Reconstruction and Development

The London-based European Bank for Reconstruction and Development (EBRD) was set up in 1990 to provide financial assistance to the countries of central and eastern Europe for the transition from communism to a market economy. It was funded by more than 40 developed countries, with most of its funds being subscribed by the United States and the EU.

Three years later in April 1993, it was revealed that the EBRD had spent more than £200m on overheads, more than double the amount it had disbursed as loans. The fitting out of its palatial headquarters had cost £66m alone, its Carrara marble fascia earning it the nickname of "the glistening bank". Jacques Attali, its flamboyant first president, resigned unrepentant a few months later. He was succeeded by Jacques de Larosière, a distinguished career central banker, who was installed, as an insider put it, "to clean out the Augean stables". Thereafter the EBRD focused on its mission and there was no more scandal.

Pensions mis-selling

In 1988 the British government introduced new pensions rules designed to encourage people to make private provision for their old age in addition to the state pension through the purchase of personal pension plans. The generous commission levels offered by the life insurance companies encouraged their sales staff to sell the new personal pension plans not only to the target market of those without pension cover, but also to people who were covered by pension schemes provided by their employers. Between April 1988 and June 1994, 2m personal pension plans were sold to such people.

Mis-selling occurred when fast-talking salespeople advised people who would have been financially better off at retirement in their employer's pension scheme to leave the scheme or not to join it, or persuaded them to transfer pension benefits from a previous employer's scheme and take out a personal pension plan instead.

As the huge extent of the mis-selling became apparent, in 1994 the financial services regulator instructed the industry to stop such practices and to review all personal pension plan sales to ascertain whether mis-selling had occurred, as a preliminary step towards compensating the victims. A two-phase case review schedule was established: Phase One would cover the 655,000 most urgent cases comprising people in or close to retirement and was to be completed by the end of 1998; Phase Two would cover an estimated 1.8m younger customers, typically in their 30s and 40s, and was to be finished by June 2002.

The industry dragged its feet and initially little progress was made in reviewing cases. In 1996 44 firms were fined for delays in case reviews. Despite the penalties, by mid-1997 only 5% of cases had been cleared up, prompting the newly elected Labour government to announce its intention to "name and shame" the laggards. As the UK's largest life insurance and pensions company, Prudential was on the receiving end of probably more than its fair share of abuse. In July 1998 Sir Peter Davis, the chief executive, was subjected to a grilling by the Treasury Select Committee of the House of Commons which led to angry exchanges, although he did apologise for Prudential's part in the scandal and "the suffering and loss" that people had suffered.

The cost of the pensions mis-selling debacle to Prudential was estimated at a record £1.1 billion. But Royal & Sun Alliance set another record: a fine of £1.35m in August 2002, the largest penalty under the pensions review, which dwarfed the Prudential's £650,000 fine. The penalty was imposed because of the firm's tardy and ramshackle handling of the process of case review. During the pensions mis-selling review, disciplinary action was taken against 349 firms resulting in fines totalling £11m. The Financial Services Authority estimates that the final outcome of the pensions mis-selling scandal will be 1.6m cases reviewed and nearly £12 billion paid in compensation to policyholders.

Barings

The collapse of Barings, a venerable and prestigious London merchant bank, in February 1995 was the most sensational failure of a City firm for more than a century. The day after the news broke, William Rees-Mogg wrote in *The Times*: "For those of us who can remember the second world war, the loss of Barings has something of the same impact as the sinking of the Hood. At one moment in time it is unthinkable; at the next it has happened."

Baring Brothers, established in 1762, was the UK's oldest merchant bank and a highly esteemed firm: Queen Elizabeth II was a client. Like other merchant banks, Barings developed securities and derivatives trading in the 1980s and 1990s, following the example set by the American investment banks. Such trading could be highly profitable, but it also brought risks of big losses. Barings was brought down by massive losses incurred by Nick Leeson, a "rogue trader", in the bank's Singapore office.

Leeson had left school at 18 with A levels in English and history but having failed mathematics. He worked for a couple of banks in junior clerical jobs, joining Barings in 1989 as a book-keeper. In April 1992, aged 25, Leeson was posted to Singapore to run Barings new futures office. Travelling with his new wife, Lisa, he left behind £3,000-worth of unpaid county court judgments, tokens of a cavalier attitude to other people's money. As well as running the back office that handled the accounts and the settlement of deals, Leeson was allowed to trade on behalf of clients. This combination of responsibilities was contrary to good practice, but was apparently excused by the smallness of the Singapore operation.

Leeson had long wanted to become a trader, but unfortunately his ability did not match his ambition. Another Singapore trader recollected: "We admired Nick because he had almost no fear. It was like watching someone juggling hand grenades, but we always thought if he dropped one he would blow just himself up."

Almost from the start Leeson made losses – by October 1992 they amounted to £4.5m – but he hid his humiliating performance in a secret account, "error account 88888", opened in July 1992, hoping to win back the money. By summer 1993, benefiting from a rising market, he was almost back in the black, but then he hit another bad patch and by the end of the year he was nursing secret losses of £25m and sleeping badly. To keep his bosses in London happy and off his back, Leeson reported fictional profits and soon came to be regarded as one of the firm's "star performers". Between January and July 1994, his trading activities supposedly generated profits of £30m, but in reality the losses mounted to

£100m. Nevertheless, he was earning £200,000 plus bonus and drove a Porsche and a Mercedes.

Back in London, Leeson's bosses believed the story he told them: that his trading profits were principally generated by inter-exchange arbitrage activities, involving "switching" between the Singapore International Monetary Exchange (SIMEX) and Japanese exchanges. Leeson reported that futures based on the Nikkei 225 index, Japan's leading share index, on the Osaka stock exchange traded at a premium to identical contracts on SIMEX. By capturing the difference – in effect buying contracts in Singapore and selling them in Osaka – there was money to be made. The profit on each trade was minute, but if conducted on a large scale the operation could be very lucrative. He was also convinced that the Nikkei would rise, generating a capital gain on top of the arbitrage profit. To insure Barings against the possibility that prices would move against him, Leeson claimed to be hedging his positions with fully matched countertrades, but these assurances turned out to be, as a colleague put it, "a stream of unadulterated falsehoods". Moreover, far from restricting himself to trading on behalf of clients and inter-exchange arbitrage, relatively risk-free activities if properly conducted, Leeson was persistently trading as principal and transgressing the trading limits set by the firm.

Leeson used a range of devices to conceal his unauthorised activities, including suppression of the existence of account 88888, the submission of falsified accounts, the misrepresentation of profits, the invention of non-existent clients, and the creation of false trading transactions and accounting entries. Neither Barings' management nor its auditors in London and Singapore noticed anything amiss over two and a half years. Moreover, such was the prestige of the firm that even the Bank of England was content not to challenge its version of its performance, with the head of banking supervision simply noting that the recovery in the profitability of the firm's securities operations had been "amazing".

Amazing was an apt word for something else: the £208m in secret losses that Leeson had accumulated by the end of 1994. So deep was the hole in the books that the only way out was a really, really big play. In early January 1995, still convinced that Japanese shares were undervalued, he built up a large and uncovered position in Nikkei 225 futures contracts. Then the Kobe earthquake on January 17th sent Japanese share prices tumbling, generating a further loss of £144m, although he reported a profit of £10m. This drove Leeson to a final, deranged, devil-may-care throw of the dice: in the days after the earthquake he doubled his exposure to $7 billion, betting the bank on the upturn.

The scale of Leeson's commitments required huge margin payments – deposits against potential losses required by financial exchanges – to SIMEX. To make these payments, some £500m – more than half the bank's capital – was forwarded by London in early 1995. But at last senior managers were beginning to ask what their man in Singapore was up to. In mid-February, an audit of his operations was undertaken and it soon became clear that Barings was facing huge losses. The Bank of England was informed and Eddie George, the governor, was whisked back from a skiing holiday without even setting his skis on a piste.

Over the weekend of February 27th–28th 1995 the Bank and leading City firms endeavoured to put together a rescue package to recapitalise Barings and keep it going. Their task was bedevilled by the nature of the commitments Leeson had entered into – open-ended futures contracts – which meant that the extent of the eventual losses depended on the level of the Nikkei 225 on settlement day, March 10th 1995. Not even the world's richest man, the Sultan of Brunei, was prepared to assume this open-ended risk.

George took the view that the failure of Barings, a prestigious but now relatively minor player, would not pose a threat to the banking system as a whole. Mindful, no doubt, of the flak that the Bank had run into over its bail-out of Johnson Matthey Bankers in 1984, he argued that as there was no systemic threat there was no justification for the expenditure of public money on a rescue of the firm. Moreover, the repeated rescue of British banks that got into trouble would smack of favouritism on the part of the authorities, which would be damaging to London's reputation as an international financial centre. It would also undermine the discipline of "moral hazard" – the threat that a badly managed business will not care about going bust if it thinks the Bank will step in and pick up the pieces. Nonetheless, as an American regulator remarked at the time: "Thank heavens it was only a small bank."

After the failure of the City's rescue attempt (in contrast to the previous Baring crisis in 1890 when the City had clubbed together to salvage Barings and maintain its independence), administrators were appointed to oversee the stricken bank's affairs. They quickly came to terms with ING, a Dutch bank, which acquired Barings and its liabilities for a nominal £1. As David Kynaston in his book *The City of London* (Chatto & Windus, 2001, p. 763) puts it: "Such a resonant name, such a sudden demise – it was perhaps the most memorable, sad, blood-quickening moment in the City's peacetime history."

When Leeson realised the game was up he disappeared with his wife, leaving a two-word farewell note to colleagues on his desk saying "I'm sorry". "Where's Leeson?" ran the joke in City wine bars. "Wandering about in the jungle having lost his bearings." After a couple of nights in resort hotels, Leeson boarded a flight to Frankfurt where he was arrested. Extradited to Singapore, he found himself in court and sentenced to six and a half years in jail for securities violations.

Leeson's antics received worldwide media attention and he became a celebrity. The rights to his autobiography, *Rogue Trader*, were reportedly sold for £500,000 and a film of the same name, in which he was played by Ewan McGregor, was released in 1999. It flopped. Upon Leeson's release from jail, he found himself in demand as a public speaker and his wife divorced him.

The senior managers of Barings emerged from the episode looking absurdly amateurish and complacent and were lambasted by the chancellor of the exchequer for "the total collapse of management control". They were greedy, too: as the ship went down many of them seemed more concerned about getting their hands on promised bonuses than about the plight of the firm, not to mention the losses suffered by hapless Barings bondholders. These investors, many of them pensioners, had subscribed for a perpetual loan of £100m issued by the firm in late 1994 to fund the margin calls required by the firm's star trader. Several of Barings' senior managers lost their jobs and some were barred from working in the financial-services industry.

Barings' auditors were also put through the wringer – claims of negligence against them on behalf of Barings amounted to over £1.3 billion. By the time the case came to trial in May 2002, Barings had settled with the two Coopers & Lybrand firms (one in London and one in Singapore) for £65m. Deloitte & Touche, however, contested the claims and was almost entirely vindicated and paid no damages at all.

The Bank of England was criticised for "lack of vigour" in its supervision of Barings, prompting the riposte that there was no way that closer oversight would have prevented the failure of Barings given Leeson's devious deceptions and the lax management controls over a far-flung office. Nevertheless, the episode further tarnished the Bank's reputation for banking supervision and contributed to the transfer of this responsibility to a new regulatory body, the Financial Services Authority, in 1997.

Overall, the incident highlighted the hazard posed by a rogue trader in modern markets and highlighted the need for stringent controls over trading, especially of derivatives. It was not the first such incident, nor will it be the last. Other firms have been hit by rogue trader scandals in the past two decades: Kidder Peabody, an American investment bank, lost $350m in 1994; Daiwa Bank lost $1.1 billion in 1995; Sumitomo Corporation lost a record $3 billion in 1996; NatWest Capital markets lost £90m in 2000; and Allied Irish Banks found itself short of $750m in 2002. But none of these was as sensational or historic as the fall of the house of Barings.

Lloyd's of London

August 1996 saw a settlement of a long-running dispute between Lloyd's of London, the insurance exchange, and thousands of Lloyd's "Names", the individuals who provided the funds that backed Lloyd's policies. The Names were non-professional members of Lloyd's syndicates (outsiders) who effectively lent their backing to the professional underwriters (insiders) who decided which risks to accept and what the premiums would be. To become a Lloyd's Name it was necessary to have realisable assets of £100,000 – a huge sum in the 1970s, whereas today it would not be enough to buy a one-bedroom apartment in an unfashionable part of London. However, liability for losses was as an individual and unlimited.

From the late 1970s to the mid-1990s Lloyd's was beset by scandal. The sorry saga began in 1978, when a syndicate led by Tim Sasse, an underwriter, made a loss of £20m on marginal American and Canadian property business, computer leasing and other poor-quality risks underwritten in the mid-1970s. But the syndicate's Names, who were facing huge losses, asserted that the underwriting had been conducted in breach of the exchange's rules, which had been inadequately policed by Lloyd's management. They refused to pay and resorted to legal action. Eventually a compromise was reached in 1980, whereby the Names stumped up £6m and Lloyd's contributed £14m.

The Sasse affair prompted the Committee of Lloyd's, the market's ruling body drawn from members, to initiate reforms before they were imposed by the government. The Bank of England was also pushing for change, even though it had no formal jurisdiction over Lloyd's. The outcome was a set of reforms that were enshrined in the Lloyd's Act of July 1982, which established the Lloyd's Council, a new body with tougher regulatory powers than the old committee, although its members were still mostly chosen by and from Lloyd's insiders. The management was also strengthened by the appointment of Ian Hay Davidson, the market's first permanent chief executive, who took up office in February 1983.

The ink of the Queen's signature on the act had hardly had time to dry before two more Lloyd's scandals broke. The first, in September 1982, concerned Alexander Howden Group, a brokerage firm that had recently been acquired by Alexander & Alexander, a broker based in the United States. Upon closer inspection of the books, Alexander & Alexander claimed that $55m had been improperly diverted from the firm and its underwriting subsidiaries to some of the directors. One of those named was Ian Posgate, the most successful underwriter of the day. His acquittal of serious malpractice by an internal disciplinary committee raised again the issue of self-regulation. The second scandal, which broke in December 1982, concerned PCW Underwriting Agencies (a subsidiary of broker Minet Holdings) and involved the misuse of reinsurance premiums. In this case it was claimed that the Names involved in the syndicate had suffered not only the misappropriation of their funds but also a trading loss of more than £130m.

Hay Davidson, an accountant by profession, was horrified by the cavalier exploitation of the conflicts of interest intrinsic in the way Lloyd's operated. One of the most outrageous practices, which he tried to stamp out, was that the insiders who ran the underwriting syndicates backed by the Names also ran parallel so-called "baby syndicates", to which they and a few favoured friends belonged. Much of the most attractive business that came to a syndicate was diverted to these baby syndicates, effectively diverting profits from the outsiders (the Names) to the insiders. He observed: "This was clearly improper. I would have said that every single member of the Committee of Lloyd's was a member of a baby syndicate." One estimate in 1990 was that such practices diverted £100m from outsiders to insiders. An old hand described it as "the rape of the greedy by the very greedy".

During the 1970s the number of Lloyd's Names tripled and the increase continued in the 1980s, despite the scandals, rising to a peak of 32,433 in 1988, making combined private assets of £11 billion available for Lloyd's underwriting. In the 1980s, much of the new capacity went into reinsurance business, which generated higher premiums than plain vanilla insurance underwriting. Initially, the focus was on the reinsurance of outstanding American general liability risks as older syndicates were happy to pay the reinsurance premiums to pass on part of the risks outstanding on these policies, especially potential asbestos claims. Subsequently, the upsurge in capacity was channelled into the reinsurance of catastrophe cover.

A report by Sir Patrick Neill, a senior lawyer, on the protection of Lloyd's Names was published in February 1987. It spelt out the institution's endemic conflicts of interest, including the baby syndicate abuse, and proposed that henceforth the Council should have a majority of outside members. But the losses that the Names had sustained over the previous decade were as nothing compared with what was about to hit them.

In the late 1980s and early 1990s, Lloyd's suffered losses totalling more than £8 billion. The main causes were catastrophes – notably the Piper Alpha oil-rig disaster in 1988 and Hurricane Hugo in 1999 – soaring American liabilities, particularly in relation to asbestos, and the incompetence and indifference of the market's so-called professionals. The Names revolted, and 20,000 of them combined to sue their underwriting agents for negligence. Particularly aggrieved were the new Names, many of them American and Canadian, who had signed up in the 1980s recruitment drive and now accused Lloyd's insiders of cynically passing on massive pending asbestos and pollution claims to them through reinsurance policies. It was claimed that as many as 30 Names committed suicide because of the stress.

In April 1993, in the midst of the litigation, a new management team produced Lloyd's first business plan, which imposed much more direct and centralised management on the market. It also introduced corporate Names with limited liability, beginning the process by which corporate funds replaced the unlimited liability of individuals as the market's capital base. By 2000, corporate members accounted for more than four-fifths of Lloyd's capacity, and the number of individual Names had dwindled to 5,000.

Lloyd's returned to profit in 1993, which helped the management negotiate a deal with the aggrieved individual Names. Eventually, in August 1996, a £3.2 billion settlement – the UK's largest out-of-court settlement – was agreed between Lloyd's and the Names.

Morgan Grenfell Asset Management

This scandal, which broke in autumn 1996, concerned allegations of an elaborate unit trust scam on the part of Peter Young, a Morgan Grenfell Asset Management (MGAM) fund manager, and some accomplices. It cost Deutsche Bank, MGAM's parent company, £600m: £400m in compensation to investors and £200m to keep MGAM afloat.

Young, aged 38, an Oxford mathematics graduate who specialised in

European equities and high-tech investments, was one of the City's most highly rated investment managers and had just been voted "Fund Manager of the Year" by *Investment Week*. The unit trusts he managed were top performers.

It turned out that Young had been making unauthorised investments in the shares of unquoted or obscure high-tech Scandinavian companies, which he had revalued himself on behalf of MGAM's European Growth Fund, thus helping it to outperform the market. Most of the shares turned out to be worthless. Young obscured these misapplications of funds by routing the transactions through Luxembourg holding companies. But the stress of the deceptions began to take a heavy psychological toll and his behaviour became strange; he spent a lot of time in dark rooms muttering to himself and on one shopping trip he bought 30 jars of pickled gherkins.

When the "irregularities" came to light in September 1996, Young was suspended and he and others were later fired. The Serious Fraud Office (SFO) charged Young with conspiracy to defraud and breaches of the Financial Services Act, charges that potentially carried a seven-year jail sentence. For his appearance at the magistrates hearing in April 1999, Young dressed as a woman, wearing a scarlet blouse and matching tight skirt, black stockings and high-heeled shoes, with a neatly bobbed hairstyle and immaculately applied make-up. Nonetheless, he was committed for trial at the Old Bailey.

Young's transvestite attire led to speculation that he was imitating Corporal Klinger, a character in *M*A*S*H*, a TV comedy series set in the Korean war, who dressed as a woman to prove that he was mad in order to win a discharge from the military. However, when Young's case finally came to trial in 2001 his lawyers presented lurid medical evidence of schizophrenia. It was related that he had told psychiatrists that he heard voices urging him to change sex, which had led him to repeated attempts to castrate himself using a craft knife, fishing line and scissors, resulting in horrific injuries and the loss of a testicle. The jury unanimously found him unfit to stand trial because of insanity.

The criminal cases brought by the SFO against three of Young's alleged accomplices also collapsed or failed for other reasons. The series of trials in this bizarre episode was estimated to have cost British taxpayers £10m. MGAM was fined £2m by the industry regulator in April 1997.

Flaming Ferraris

The Flaming Ferraris, a group of five traders at Credit Suisse First Boston

(CSFB), came to public attention in December 1998 when photographs of them arriving at the firm's Christmas party in a stretch limousine appeared in newspapers. The accompanying text described them as the world's most successful equity traders, betting, so it was claimed, up to £3 billion a time on a deal and allegedly expecting to share a £5m bonus. Another point of media interest was that one of them, James Archer, was the 24-year-old Eton- and Oxford-educated son of Jeffrey Archer, a best-selling novelist and Tory politician. A few years earlier, Archer senior had been caught up in allegations of insider dealing.

It soon became clear that the claims about the scale, audacity and success of the group's trading were absurdly extravagant. They specialised in index arbitrage, which involves betting on anomalies between index prices and futures contracts, one of the least risky forms of proprietary trading if done properly; in fact, most of the opportunities are spotted by computers. It transpired that the spate of publicity was a stunt arranged by a financial PR man, who came up with the Flaming Ferrari name – derived from a rum and Grand Marnier cocktail – for the group. Money and fame were the objects of the exercise, assisting the Famous Five to claim bigger bonuses.

James Archer had to go one better. He took positions that would make money if the OMX, the main Swedish share index, fell. He attempted to make this happen during the low-volume trading period between Christmas and New Year by selling thousands of shares of Stora, a pulp company, at a ridiculously low price to himself. To evade CSFB's compliance safeguards and the regulators, the trades were not made from his desk but from a mobile phone. But Archer's amateurish bear scam was immediately spotted by the Swedish exchange. In May 1999 CSFB was fined SKr2m (£150,000) by the Stockholm exchange.

Challenged by CSFB, which was distinctly unamused by his antics, Archer attempted to lie his way out of trouble, and his two bosses, both fellow Ferraris, tried to cover up for him and for their own inadequate supervision of his activities. After an internal investigation, all three were fired in March 1999. Two years later, following an investigation by the Securities and Futures Authority, they were struck off the register of City professionals, which meant they were banned from working in the Square Mile.

Coincidentally, Jeffrey Archer was back in the headlines just a week before the ban was imposed, when he was jailed for four years for perjury and perverting the course of justice. Michael Crick, Archer's biographer, commented: "It's like father, like grandfather, like grandson.

Jeffrey Archer was jailed for perjury, his father William was accused of fraud and jailed for embezzlement, and now James has been shown to be dishonest."

Equitable Life

Founded in 1762, Equitable Life is the UK's oldest mutual life insurance company. For decades it had an impeccable reputation for integrity and competence, attracting a clientele of professional people and high earners. It was also a leading provider of corporate pension schemes, servicing more than half the UK's 500 largest companies, and was second only to the Prudential in the scale of its UK life insurance business. In 1999 it was named "Pension Provider of the Year" by the pension industry magazine.

In the high-inflation and high-interest-rate 1970s, Equitable sold policies that paid a guaranteed annuity rate (GAR) each year, typically around £12,000 on £100,000 invested, plus a bonus when the policy matured. With the decline in interest rates in the late 1990s and longer life expectancy, Equitable found that it could no longer afford to honour its undertakings to its 90,000 GAR policyholders.

In January 1999 Equitable launched court proceedings to gain approval to impose a cut in guaranteed payouts in order to maintain payments to the majority of its 1m customers who did not have guaranteed policies. But the GAR policyholders responded by taking legal action for breach of contract. Equitable won the first round of the battle when the court ruled that it acted lawfully in cutting the guaranteed payments. But the GAR policyholders appealed and the Court of Appeal reversed the decision, ruling that Equitable had to honour its commitments. This judgment was upheld by the House of Lords in July 2000.

Unable to meet the £1.5 billion liability to the GAR policyholders, Equitable closed its doors to new business, increased penalties for withdrawals of funds and put itself up for sale. In February 2001 Halifax offered to buy Equitable's salesforce and non-profits policies for £1 billion. The bid was accepted, allowing the firm some room for financial manoeuvre. Further negotiations with the various groups of policyholders ensued, and the eventual outcome was the formulation of a rescue package aimed at salvaging the company's finances and meeting its liabilities. In January 2002 Equitable announced that the package had been overwhelmingly approved by policyholders.

The pared-down Equitable Life had won a reprieve, but its future remained clouded. Many with-profits policyholders, who had lost out, were expected to take their savings elsewhere as soon as possible. Although Equitable was at last able to begin winning new business, it remained to be seen whether there were any life insurance customers out there who wanted to entrust their savings to a firm with such a tarnished reputation.

NatWest Capital Markets

In May 2000 the Securities and Futures Authority (SFA) announced that NatWest Bank and NatWest Capital Markets, its former investment banking arm, were being fined £320,000 plus £100,000 costs. The penalty was imposed because trading losses totalling £90.5m incurred in 1995 had not been spotted by NatWest until 1997. This was despite repeated notifications about inadequate controls by internal and external auditors and the chilling example of what inadequate controls had permitted Nick Leeson to get up to at Barings.

The trading losses had been incurred by a pair of derivatives traders who had covered them up by overvaluing options positions held on their books. After an internal inquiry, the firm concluded that a set of over-the-counter options had been deliberately mismarked, resulting in the large write-down. Both the traders were fined by the SFA and one of them was banned from working in the City. Even though no one had gained personally from the cover-up and there was no loss to any third party, some senior executives lost their jobs for the control failure. Senior dealers were obliged to sacrifice bonuses worth £8m to make good some of the loss.

For NatWest, which was still recovering from the bruising it had sustained in the Blue Arrow scandal, the 1997 options mispricing scandal was a public relations disaster and a demoralising blow for management. Instead of implementing plans to expand its investment banking activities, which were within weeks of being activated, the board beat a hasty retreat and decided to sell the business to avoid further debacles. But its reputation as a competent custodian of shareholders' interests had been further undermined and in September 1999 Bank of Scotland, one of the UK's smaller clearing banks, launched a £21 billion hostile takeover bid. Eventually, a higher bid from Royal Bank of Scotland won the prize in February 2000.

Marconi

In early 2000 Marconi, a UK electronics business, was valued at £35 billion; a year and a half later its value was around £1 billion. The company's shares had not been so much in the news since an earlier Marconi scandal on the eve of the first world war, when there were rumours about ministers having bought shares ahead of the announcement of a big government contract. What had happened this time?

The Marconi debacle of 2001 had its origins in an exercise in corporate restructuring undertaken in the late 1990s to transform the stodgy but steady General Electric Company (GEC) into a zingy high-tech growth company. GEC had been put together in the late 1960s by Arnold Weinstock, who remained chairman for 33 years. He forged an engineering giant that dominated the UK's defence, power and electronics industries. But Weinstock was risk-averse and conservative in his business approach: he preferred reliable government contracts and cash in the bank to risky investments in new technologies, and for that he was much criticised by City analysts and media commentators.

Weinstock retired in 1996, handing over control of GEC to George Simpson, a Scottish accountant, who had spent most of his working life at carmaker British Leyland and then British Aerospace. Simpson promptly moved GEC out of its drab premises to a swanky office off Bond Street in fashionable Mayfair. He then sold GEC's defence business to his old friends at British Aerospace, netting GEC £6 billion from the deal, which when added to the £2 billion cash pile inherited from Weinstock made an £8 billion war chest.

Simpson and his deputy, John Mayo, a former whizz-kid investment banker, then went on an ill-judged and egregiously ill-timed acquisitions binge with the object of turning the firm into a major player in the telecoms business. Their spending spree soon turned the cash mountain into a £4.4 billion debt burden. Purchases included two American telecoms equipment companies for which they paid $6.6 billion in 1999, just nine months before the peak of the technology bubble. The following year GEC was rebranded Marconi (taking the name of an historic subsidiary company) and the headquarters of the communications business was moved from London to Pennsylvania.

When the technology bubble burst in 2000 Marconi shares, which had been listed in the United States on the NASDAQ market only a few months earlier, plunged along with other telecoms, media and technology shares. A botched profit warning in July 2001 infuriated investors, who dumped the shares, sending the price to new depths and triggering Mayo's departure. By September 2001, when the share price had dropped by 80%, shareholders had had enough and Simpson and his close associates were kicked out. Under a new chief executive, Marconi opened negotiations with its bankers and its bondholders. The eventual outcome 18 months later, in May 2003, was a major capital restructuring, involving a dilution of shareholders' interests that caused them further losses.

Weinstock looked on appalled as Marconi's shares melted down, destroying the company he had created and wiping out much of his family's fortune. He died on July 23rd 2002, aged 77. That day the shares of the company he created, which had been worth £12.50 at their peak, slipped to a new low of 4 pence. The cause of death, ventured his friend Lord Hanson, was probably a broken heart.

Split capital investment trusts

The downturn in share prices that began in spring 2000 dismayed all shareholders, but it led to a crisis at some split capital investment trusts (split-caps). Split-caps are a type of investment trust: companies that are listed on the London Stock Exchange whose business is investing in other companies. They have a set wind-up date, which is often around ten years. Generally, investors in investment trusts benefit from both dividend income and capital growth. Split-caps separate dividend income and capital growth between two classes of shareholders with different investment requirements:

◪ Income shareholders receive dividends and expect their capital to be returned when the trust is wound up. The income offered by many split-caps was typically around twice what was on offer from a portfolio of blue-chip shares.
◪ Growth shareholders are promised a share in the capital growth of the fund, but they do not receive dividend payments. Annual capital growth of 20% was not unusual in bull markets.

Although split-caps had been around since the 1960s, they had constituted a minor part of the market and had been used mainly by asset managers. During the bull market of the late 1990s, split-caps were heavily marketed to retail investors. Income shares were sold to pensioners looking for extra income, and growth shares were targeted at parents planning for school fees or investors saving for a lump sum. Investment managers at the asset management firms that promoted the split-cap boom profited handsomely, earning huge bonuses.

A "contagious cocktail" comprising a slump in share values, cross-shareholdings and high levels of gearing (bank borrowings in addition to investors' funds to finance share purchases) left some split-caps unable to meet expected payments. In October 2002 it was estimated that about 40 of the 120 split-caps had run into difficulties and around 20 had gone into receivership. As many as 50,000 investors were said to have lost money in these supposedly low-risk funds, with individual losses ranging from £6,000 to £5m. It was believed that in total investors were out of pocket to the tune of £6 billion.

Several months earlier, the Financial Services Authority (FSA) had begun an inquiry into split-caps. Of particular interest was the alleged operation of a "magic circle" of split-cap managers who had agreed to invest in each other's funds to sustain share prices. Research by the FSA revealed that on average 17% of the gross assets of split-caps comprised the shares of other split-caps. Although the majority of trusts in the £13 billion sector had invested less than 2% in other split-caps, one-fifth of them held more than 40% and one-tenth in excess of 60%, which looked distinctly questionable. By summer 2003 the split-cap scandal had become the biggest investigation ever carried out by the FSA, which declared that it was "determined to secure justice" for those who had lost out. More than 60 FSA staff had been assigned to the investigation and were reported to be sifting through documents that would fill 700 lever-arch files.

In the eye of the storm was Aberdeen Asset Management, the biggest player in the sector. Several of its energetically marketed split-caps had collapsed and the company found itself under attack from politicians and in the media. It agreed to compensate investors in one of its split-cap funds and faced legal action over its management of others, although it declared its determination to fight the claims. Its prospects of success were perhaps not improved by the public pronouncements of Martin Gilbert, its chief executive, who stated that problems in the market were "everyone's fault to some extent" and that with hindsight it was "blindingly obvious" that many split-caps were overgeared.

Investment products mis-selling

In September 2003 Lloyds TSB was fined a record £1.9m by the FSA for the mis-selling of an investment product to retail consumers. It also incurred a £98m bill to compensate 22,500 customers who bought its Extra Income and Growth Bond. These bonds promised a high income of around 10%, but the return of investors' capital was linked to stock-market performance. The formula had led to them being nicknamed "precipice bonds", because investors' capital returns "fall off a cliff" if markets fall below set trigger points. The mis-selling occurred because many purchasers were inexperienced investors who were exposed to inappropriate risk of substantial loss.

The Lloyds TSB fine was also a warning by the regulator that it intended to clear up the mis-selling of financial products once and forever. Following the pensions mis-selling scandal of the mid-1990s, there had been another furore about mortgage endowment mis-selling. In the early 2000s, 24 companies had been required to pay out £700m in compensation to investors to whom they had mis-sold endowment mortgages and some had been fined substantial amounts. In his first address as FSA chief executive, on the eve of the announcement of the fines being imposed for the mis-selling of precipice bonds, John Tiner gave notice to a City audience that the FSA was determined to stamp out the "persistent malfunctioning of the market – pensions mis-selling, mortgage endowments, precipice bonds". But even if it succeeds in this admirable ambition, the City has certainly not seen its last financial scandal or calamity.

14 Challenges and outlook

What is the outlook for the City as an international financial centre? In the short term, the signs are that recovery from the downturn of the early 2000s, when employment in wholesale financial services dipped to just below 300,000 in mid-2002, is well under way. The Centre for Economic and Business Research (CEBR), a City-based consultancy, estimates that the number of City jobs will rise to 320,000 by 2005 and 330,000 by 2007.

Focusing on the long-term fundamentals, in forthcoming decades demand for international financial services is likely to expand along with world output – but faster – perpetuating the experience of the past half-century (see Chapter 1). Hence the underlying driver of demand for the services provided by the City is likely to continue to grow substantially, although there will be ups and downs. Of course, this rather optimistic scenario of the future depends on an absence of major wars and an open international economy, the conditions that have broadly prevailed since 1945. Should the governments of the major economies adopt inward-looking protectionism, international finance and the City would be casualties.

But how certain is it that London will be the beneficiary of the optimistic scenario? What are the challenges that confront the City's traditional competitive advantages? Could Frankfurt or Paris knock London off its pedestal? Or New York? Or smaller centres? In the era of the internet and global telecommunications, are financial centre clusters an outmoded phenomenon?

Regulation

Harmonisation of the EU's financial-services industry presents several challenges. Probably the most important is to the City's distinct regulatory regime, a key competitive strength (see Chapter 11). The prospect of a pan-European super-regulator located in Paris fills people in the City and at the Financial Securities Authority (FSA) with alarm. But even if that never comes to pass, there is a growing divergence between the regulatory requirements of the international wholesale businesses conducted in London and the largely consumer-driven markets elsewhere in Europe, which are the focus of the European Commission's interest.

Collateral damage to London's competitiveness from consumer-oriented directives is of little concern to Brussels, and the British government has been less than adept in defending the City's interests there.

Government support and City stewardship

Respondents in a poll on financial centre competitiveness, conducted by the Centre for the Study of Financial Innovation (CSFI) in 2003, were distinctly underwhelmed in their estimation of the British government's responsiveness to the requirements and interests of the City. Labour politicians, particularly the House of Commons Select Committee on the Treasury, have discovered that denouncing the shortcomings of the financial-services industry is an easy way of getting media coverage. Although the industry has deserved much of the flak, regular bouts of City bashing diminish public support and are a perverse way of promoting a key pillar of the UK economy. Moreover, crowd-pleasing cries for more controls and stiffer punishments push the FSA in the direction of greater intrusion and inflexibility. Thus the job of providing intelligent and appropriate regulation becomes more difficult, again threatening London's lead in regulatory sophistication.

The City's chief spokesman used to be the Bank of England, but its stewardship role was curtailed when it lost its powers to regulate banks in 1997. Although the Corporation of London and International Financial Services London have strengthened their promotional activities, there is a widespread feeling that the City lacks a powerful sponsor to represent it both at home and abroad.

Tax

Tax is another cause for concern. The UK tax on share trading (stamp duty) is a long-standing grievance since it increases transaction costs and decreases market liquidity. It is also increasingly self-defeating, driving wholesale business to the products offered by the untaxed derivatives markets. The shock imposition of a new tax on foreign bank branches in the UK in 2002 caused dismay and anger in the banking sector. Threatened changes in the treatment of the personal taxation of the foreign earnings of non-domiciled residents may lead to the relocation of some market participants, notably shipowners, to the benefit of neither the tax authorities nor the City. Both these measures have been perceived as contrary to the City's tradition of providing open access to its markets. Moreover, corporate and personal taxation have been mounting through the imposition of small but numerous "stealth taxes", which are cumulatively eroding the UK's position as a low-tax location.

European tax harmonisation is also perceived as a menace. In 1999 there was a major row over a European Commission draft directive to impose an EU-wide withholding tax on interest paid to residents. Late in the day, the British government woke up to warnings that a possible outcome would be that the international bond market would move offshore and vetoed the move. The withholding tax was part of a bigger EU tax harmonisation agenda intended to end what the European Commission perceives as "harmful tax competition" among EU members, which in practice means the levelling-up of tax rates and the erosion of this competitive advantage.

Transport and cost of living

The squabbling between the government and the elected mayor of London over the control and funding of London's underground mass transit system, while the system degenerates even further, has been a demoralising spectacle as well as a scandalous squandering of time and resources. The flow of surface transport has improved since the introduction of the daily £5 congestion charge in 2003, a tax that highly paid City staff are happier to pay than other Londoners. A report by Oxford Economic Forecasting in summer 2003 estimated the cost of transport delays to the City at £230m a year, equivalent to £750 for each Square Mile worker. These costs exacerbate the generally high cost of living in London for individuals and of operating there for firms. The high cost base makes the City vulnerable to loss of competitiveness through the erosion of the productivity of City staff.

Labour market flexibility

The ability to shed staff quickly and reasonably cheaply in a downturn has been an attractive feature of operating in the City for American banks. The same is true for European banks, which face much higher redundancy costs at home (some up to eight times as much). This has been a major reason for the migration of jobs to London from other European centres. The UK's adoption of the EU Social Chapter and other labour market directives from Brussels has decreased the capacity of City firms to hire and fire. This, like other EU harmonisation measures, puts London in the same position as Frankfurt and Paris, although London retains a competitive edge deriving from the critical mass of skilled personnel and economies of scale and scope. But competitiveness is eroded relative to New York.

The euro

The UK's non-participation in the European single currency was widely regarded as placing the City at a disadvantage at the time of the launch of the euro in 1999. A report published by the London Investment Banking Association, the industry's trade association, took a pessimistic view, as did the City's own Lord Mayor. Three-quarters of respondents in the *European Cities Monitor* 2000 survey of leading European business managers predicted a significantly negative effect.

Yet a study conducted by the Anglo-German Foundation in 2001 found no harmful effects to City activities from the UK's non-adoption of the euro, a verdict echoed by other research and the Bank of England. By 2003 a majority of respondents in the annual *European Cities Monitor* survey had come round to the view that staying out of the euro had not had an adverse effect on London's position as a financial centre. However, most believed that the City's leading position would be undermined over the medium term if the UK continued to remain aloof.

Proponents of the UK joining the euro argue that only full membership of the EU's economic institutions will secure the City's position as Europe's pre-eminent financial centre in the long term. Membership will enable the UK to have greater influence over monetary and financial decision-making and allow the City to have full access to expanding EU markets, especially for savings and pensions. Opponents assert the superiority of the UK's independent monetary arrangements and the risk of greater interference by the European Commission and the European Central Bank if the UK became part of the euro zone. Moreover, the bulk of new euro-denominated wholesale financial business – international bond issues, foreign exchange and corporate fundraising – is conducted in London. For decades the City successfully conducted most of its business in dollars, D-marks and yen, so what is different about the euro?

"Wimbledonisation"

Today most large international financial firms in London are foreign-owned and more than half of the City's employees work for overseas employers. The foreign ownership of much of the City has given rise to comparisons with the Wimbledon Tennis Championship, a tournament hosted by the UK but dominated by foreign players. Some, including the Bank of England, take the view that ownership is not important and that liberalised markets maximise economic efficiency and wealth creation. After all, the UK gets the benefits of hosting the event: the jobs, the taxes, the indirect employment and the contribution to the balance of payments. And what is the alternative? Intervention to support British players, whatever that might mean, would alienate foreign firms and undermine the City's openness and attraction as a level playing field for all participants. In any case, as globalisation proceeds international banks are shedding their national identities as they embrace staff, clients and shareholders from around the world.

Others are uneasy, arguing that in hard times overseas outposts are more vulnerable to cuts than head office. One proposition is that American firms' dominance in the international investment banking industry casts New York in the role of the industry's global head office, with all other locations as subordinate satellites. What is emerging, the argument goes, is a "hub and spoke" model run from New York with an array of subsidiary centres, including London, around the world. The downturn of the early 2000s certainly saw retrenchment in London, but the cuts in New York appear to have been proportionately greater (although the terrorist attack on the World Trade Centre in September 2001 makes the data difficult to interpret). Research has found little evidence of the relocation of activity from London to New York or elsewhere in the recent downturn. The CSFI survey reported that the City would emerge as a beneficiary from the downturn, which was leading banks to concentrate their activities there and to close down operations in smaller European centres.

Frankfurt and Paris?

The City has a massive head start over Frankfurt and Paris, in terms of both size and competitiveness. The output of UK (mostly London) wholesale financial services in 2003 was an estimated €68.3 billion, three and a half times as large as Germany (mostly Frankfurt) at €19.7 billion and almost five times greater than France (mostly Paris) at €14.3 billion. Moreover, London's lead over other European centres appears to be increasing. Centralisation of European wholesale financial services activity in the City is under way, making it even more a focus of high-paid and high-powered decision-makers, deal-makers, financial engineers, fund managers, analysts and traders. This is happening through both the penetration of the European market by City-based firms, notably American investment banks, and the consolidation of wholesale financial operations in London by European banks.

The City is also a particularly efficient producer of wholesale financial services. A quantitative study of the competitiveness of international financial centres by the CEBR in 1999 found that London had the greatest economies of scale and was second only to New York for economies of scope. Overall, London is 40–60% more competitive than Frankfurt, Paris and Tokyo and around 15% more competitive than New York. Although trailing Paris in the quality of the living and working environment, London outclasses other European centres in all commercial considerations according to the CSFI's 2003 study of financial centre competitiveness. This is confirmed by the *European Cities Monitor* surveys and other evidence (see Chapter 12).

In current conditions, these challenges are almost certainly insufficient, even in total, to outweigh the competitive advantages London enjoys relative to other European time-zone financial centres by virtue of its superior economies of scale and its critical mass of financial skills. But perhaps in conjunction with a major shock they might be sufficient to drive away sufficient international business and skilled labour to undermine London's position. Such a shock might take the form of a severe crisis in global finance or the global economy; possible sources include a collapse of the dollar or the destabilisation of Saudi Arabia, the world's largest oil exporter. With more at stake, London has more to lose, but other European financial centres would not be immune to such crises either.

New York?

Does New York pose a threat to London? Many respondents in the CSFI's study identified New York as London's main competitor and the most likely location from which they would operate if they quit London (although since they are probably American this may be less telling than it appears). Theoretically, the powerful economies of scale and scope that are a feature of financial centres militate in favour of the emergence of a single pre-eminent global financial centre. That means New York: the principal financial centre of the world's largest economy, and home to the world's biggest capital market and many leading financial firms.

A reconfiguration of the hierarchy of international financial centres with New York in a class of its own at the top, and other international centres, including London, as second- or third-order locations, would be a reversion to the natural order of things. Before the first world war London was the lone hegemonic international financial centre, as was New York in the decades from the end of the second world war to the mid-1960s. But following the American government's imposition of a tax on foreign borrowings in the capital market, the international bond market shifted to London, which from the 1960s re-emerged as a peer through hosting the Euromarkets and becoming a second home to Wall Street's leading players.

This episode demonstrated the sensitivity of the international bond market to changes in tax and regulatory arrangements. New EU tax and regulatory developments potentially pose an analogous threat to London's position, which could lead to the business shifting to New York. Other activities, such as foreign exchange, derivatives and insurance, appear to be less vulnerable, although as they are conducted by the same global investment banks they might relocate along with international capital market operations.

London and New York scored almost evenly in the CSFI study of financial centre competitiveness, with New York ahead by a whisker (see Table 12.14 on page 246). They currently have similar-sized financial-services industry workforces of 310,000–315,000. However, New York's pre-eminence relative to other American financial centres has been slowly diminishing in recent decades. In the mid-1980s New York had 35–37% of securities industry jobs, but during the 1990s the proportion fell steadily, reaching 20% in 2003. Although partly explained by the displacement of back-office staff to cheaper locations, it appears that the number of front-office jobs in other American financial centres is growing faster than in New York. Despite the decline in the share of the head count, the absolute number of securities industry jobs on Wall Street rose in the 1990s, but since 2000 the number has fallen each year. It may be a temporary phenomenon – the terrorist attacks of September 11th are an obvious factor – or it may mark an acceleration of the longer-term trend. If it is the latter, the City may overtake Wall Street for the first time since 1945.

Smaller centres?

Do smaller or aspiring centres present a threat? Switzerland, the domicile of two of the nine global investment banks, is a potential beneficiary of tax or regulatory developments, such as the proposed EU withholding tax on international bonds that would make London and other EU financial centres relatively unattractive places to conduct business. Yet New York is a more plausible home for the international capital market than Zurich or Geneva, although they might pick up some European time-zone business.

Some envisage a growing challenge from smaller financial centres beyond the main industrial countries. Their competitive advantages are

that they have low (or even no) tax regimes and regulatory arrangements deliberately designed to win business from the existing financial
centres. Hong Kong and Singapore, already important and sophisticated
Asian financial centres, may attract more global business. Dubai,
Bermuda and Caribbean centres are other candidates. Dubai, located
about halfway between London and Tokyo and adjacent to the markets
of the Middle East and the Indian subcontinent, has deliberately targeted the expansion of international financial services as a development
strategy. Between 1990 and 2000 the sector grew at more than 12% a
year. The Dubai International Financial Centre has a modern infrastructure and offers a zero tax regime for foreign banks. It is envisaged that
the centre will propel financial services to account for 20% of Dubai's
GDP in future years, a higher proportion than in London (though tiny in
absolute terms). Much of the growth will come from the region, but if
tax and regulatory environments deteriorate in the global financial centres there could be a significant migration of business.

An outmoded phenomenon?

The leading financial centres, their streets lined with brash, iconic tem-
ples of capitalism, make tempting targets for terrorists. The City was one
of the IRA's favourite targets; many attacks were foiled, although not
those on the Baltic Exchange in 1992 and Bishopsgate in 1993. But the
attack on the World Trade Centre in September 2001 was murder of
apocalyptic proportions. The spectre of terrorism prompts the question:
is there a future for high-profile international financial centres?

For at least a decade communications technology has permitted
financial firms to operate almost anywhere. Location is no longer an
issue as regards access to financial information or to participation in
most markets. Yet the major firms have continued to site their headquarters in the leading financial centres, which have become even
greater concentrations of front-office staff as back-office colleagues
have been relocated to less costly places. This is because clustering confers advantages both to individual workers and to financial firms. There
is the stimulus of being surrounded by like-minded colleagues and competitors, enhancing performance and driving innovation. For individuals, there is the opportunity to get a new job in an uncertain and rapidly
changing industry; for firms, there is access to a pool of highly skilled,
specialist staff.

The transformation of many leading firms in the international financial-services industry into giant global financial conglomerates has led to

an increasing proportion of business being conducted within firms, making face-to-face contact with outsiders less important. Co-location of staff in huge headquarters buildings provides the benefits of human clustering in-house. In theory, this diminishes the importance of being in a financial centre, allowing firms to locate somewhere cheaper, and perhaps safer. But so far, where it has taken place, relocation has been within the major financial centres – to Canary Wharf and the West End in London and to up-town in New York – not to provincial cities or greenfield sites.

The reason is another labour market feature: the people who work in the international wholesale financial-services industry demand the lifestyle amenities of metropolitan life. London and New York are the world's biggest, brightest and most cosmopolitan metropolises. As such, their joint status as the world's leading international financial centres seems likely to continue for the foreseeable future.

Appendix 1
City institutions and organisations

Bank of England

The Bank of England, formed in 1694 (see Chapter 10), occupies a 3.5-acre site in Threadneedle Street in the heart of the City, where it has been since 1734. It is encircled by a high, windowless, fortress-like curtain wall erected in 1828, its form being partly inspired by an episode in which it was attacked by a rioting mob. The threat led the government to provide an overnight military guard, which every day from 1780 to 1973 marched to and from the Bank from its barracks near Buckingham Palace, causing havoc with London's traffic. The Bank within the curtain wall was extensively rebuilt in the 1920s and 1930s, with the new building extending seven storeys above ground and three below. This is the building visible today from the outside, but inside an extensive refurbishment programme has brought office accommodation up to modern standards. There is an on-site museum open to the public that tells the story of the Bank and its banknotes.

The City Club

The City Club in Old Broad Street is a St James's-style gentlemen's club in the Square Mile. The oldest club in the City, it was founded in 1832 by a group of prominent merchants, bankers and shipowners led by a City member of Parliament. The founder members included the Duke of Wellington, Sir Robert Peel (at that time prime minister), and members of the Rothschild family. The imposing cream stucco building in the Regency Palladian style was completed in 1834.

The club has 1,200 members, with new members being proposed by existing members. However, non-members may hire rooms for meetings, conferences, private dining, cocktail parties and even wedding receptions.

Corporation of London

The Corporation of London is the oldest local government authority in the UK, tracing its origins to before the Norman Conquest of 1066. Regular meetings of the Court of Common Council, the Corporation's assembly of elected representatives, have been held since 1376. The area is divided into 25 wards with an electorate comprising businesses physically occupying premises within the City and local residents. There are about 26,000 potential business voters and 6,000 residents. The Court of Common Council operates through committees, like any other local authority, but it is unique in being non-party political. There is also the Court of Aldermen, one from each ward, which constitutes a sort of senate.

The Corporation provides local government services for the Square Mile, such as policing, education, refuse collection, housing and social services. It also has a mixed bag of other responsibilities acquired over its long history: the Central Criminal Court (the Old Bailey); five Thames bridges; the quarantine station at Heathrow Airport; the Thames estuary Port Authority; and three wholesale food markets – Billingsgate (fish), Smithfield (meat) and Spitalfields (fruit, vegetables and flowers). (Billingsgate moved from Lower Thames Street to the Isle of Dogs in 1982 and Spitalfields ceased to be a wholesale market in 1991; it is now famous for its food court, where most world cuisines are represented.) It owns and manages various historic monuments, notably John Keats's house in Hampstead, Queen Elizabeth I's Hunting Lodge in Epping Forest and the Monument, a 222-foot column built to commemorate the Square Mile's Great Fire of 1666. It also administers over 10,000 acres of open spaces in and around London which provide public recreation facilities, including Hampstead Heath, Epping Forest, Burnham Beeches, Ashtead Common and Highgate Wood and an abundance of gardens within the City itself.

The gothic Guildhall, construction of which began in 1411, houses the Corporation of London's offices and a substantial public library. The imposing medieval Great Hall is the meeting place of the Court of Common Council and was once the setting for state trials, including that of the ill-fated Lady Jane Grey in 1553. Today it serves as a venue for state and civic banquets.

The Lord Mayor of London is head of the Corporation of London and presides over its governing bodies: the Court of Common Council and the Court of Aldermen. The first Lord Mayor was appointed in 1189 and to date about 700 men and one woman have held the position. It is an annual appointment, with an election every September. The most famous incumbent is Dick Whittington, who held office three times in 1397, 1406 and 1419, and according to legend made his fortune by lending his black cat to the king of the Barbary Coast to rid his kingdom of a plague of rats. In fact, like virtually all his successors, he was a successful City businessman.

The Lord Mayor's official residence for the duration of his term of office is the Mansion House. This grand Georgian town palace, built between 1739 and 1752, has sumptuously decorated interiors featuring elaborate plasterwork and carved timber ornamentation. The substantial dining room, known as the Egyptian Hall, is the venue for dinners for visiting heads of state and other dignitaries. The annual Bankers and Merchants Dinner, at which the chancellor of the exchequer addresses the Lord Mayor and an audience of people who work in the City, is held there in June. The Lord Mayor is also patron of the annual Lord Mayor's Show, a pageant dating from 1189 and held in early November, which takes the form of a procession around the City with the Lord Mayor in a ceremonial gold coach followed by a succession of colourful floats.

Lord Mayors are now active ambassadors for the City at home and abroad, personifying the Corporation of London's commitment to the maintenance and enhancement of the City's status as the world's leading international financial centre. During their term they travel extensively abroad, working with the Foreign and Commonwealth Office, to promote British trade and the services of the City. They also make numerous visits around the UK, fostering ties between the regions and the City.

Livery companies

Another historical legacy is the City's 103 livery companies, most of which are descended from the medieval guilds that controlled various crafts and trades, such as brewers, fishmongers, grocers, goldsmiths and haberdashers. Some retain a connection with their original activity but most have lost all ties and are a mixture of private dining club and charitable foundation. Their charitable activities are particularly associated with education, many having traditional links with schools, and with assistance to the elderly. There are around 30 Livery Halls dotted around the City, often dating back centuries. Besides hosting dinners and events for members, many can be hired and provide a colourful and historic venue for meetings or receptions.

Royal Exchange

The Royal Exchange was the City's first marketplace, inaugurated by Queen Elizabeth I in 1571 on the same site as the Victorian building (opened in 1844), which still stands today. For centuries it was the commercial hub of the City, being complemented by the subsequent location of the Bank of England, which moved to its present adjacent site in

1724, the Mansion House, erected opposite in 1752, and the Stock Exchange, built nearby in 1802. This cluster of institutions formed the core of the traditional financial district.

For several centuries the Royal Exchange was the City's most important commercial building, a place where merchants met to buy and sell shipments as well as a fashionable shopping precinct and promenade. As the City became more focused on finance so did the activities conducted at the Royal Exchange, which served at different times as home to the money market, Lloyd's of London, the foreign-exchange market, the Guardian insurance group and the London International Financial Futures and Options Exchange (LIFFE). When LIFFE moved to new premises in 1991, the Royal Exchange building was converted into an upmarket shopping mall with a set of high-end retailers rivalling Bond Street's to meet the shopping demands of the City's cash-rich but time-poor workforce.

Useful addresses

Asset management
Alternative Investment Management Association (AIMA)
10 Stanhope Gate
London W1K 1AL
Tel: +44 20 7659 9920
E-mail: info@aima.org
Website: www.aima.org

Association of Investment Trust Companies (AITC)
8–13 Chiswell Street
London EC1Y 4YY
Tel: +44 20 7282 5555
E-mail: info@aitc.co.uk
Website: www.aitc.co.uk

Association of Private Client Investment Managers and Stockbrokers (APCIMS)
112 Middlesex Street
London E1 7HY
Tel: +44 20 7247 7080
E-mail: info@acpcims.co.uk
Website: www.apcims.co.uk

Investment Management Association (IMA)
65 Kingsway
London EC2B 6TD
Tel: +44 20 7831 0898
E-mail: info@investmentuk.org
Website: www.investmentuk.org

National Association of Pension Funds (NAPF)
6 Victoria Street
London SW1H ONX
Tel: +44 20 7808 1300
E-mail: info@napf.co.uk
Website: www.napfco.uk

Banking
Association of Foreign Banks (AFB)
1 Bengal Court
London EC3V 9DD
Tel: +44 20 7283 8300
E-mail: secretariat@fbsa.org.uk
Website: www.fbsa.org.uk

Bank of England, The
Threadneedle Street
London EC2R 8AH
Tel: +44 20 7601 4444
E-mail: enquiries@bankofengland.co.uk
Website: www.bankofengland.co.uk/

British Bankers' Association (BBA)
Pinners Hall
105–108 Old Broad Street
London EC2N 1EX
Tel: +44 20 7216 8800
E-mail: info@bba.org.uk
Website: www.bba.org.uk

Council of Mortgage Lenders (CML)
3 Savile Row
London W1S 3PB
Tel: +44 20 7437 0075
E-mail: info@cml.org.uk
Website: www.cml.org.uk

International Project Finance Association (IPFA)
70 Wheelhouse
Burrells Wharf
Westferry Road
London E14 3TA
Tel: +44 20 7358 9891
E-mail: info@ipfa.org
Website: www.ipfa.org

Capital markets and securities
Bond Market Association (BMA)
Tel: +44 20 7743 9300
Website: www.bondmarkets.com

London Investment Banking Association (LIBA)
6 Frederick's Place
London EC2R 8BT
Tel: +44 20 7796 3606
E-mail: liba@liba.org.uk
Website: www.liba.org.uk

London Stock Exchange (LSE)
Old Broad Street
London EC2N 1HP
Tel: +44 20 7797 1000
Website: www.londonstockexchange.com

British Venture Capital Association (BVCA)
Tower 3, 3 Clements Inn
London WC2A 2AZ
Tel: +44 20 7025 2950
E-mail: bvca@bvca.co.uk
Website: www.bvca.co.uk

Gilt-edged Market Makers Association (GEMMA)
C/o Barclays Capital
5 The North Colonnade, London E14 4BB
Tel: +44 20 020 7773 9608

International Securities Lenders Association (ISLA)
Rigistrasse 60
PO Box
8033 Zurich, Switzerland
Tel: +41 1 363 4222
E-mail: info@isma.org
Website: www.isma.org

International Securities Markets Association (ISMA)
Rigistrasse 60
PO Box
8033 Zurich, Switzerland
Tel: +41 1 363 4222
E-mail: info@isma.org
Website: www.isma.org

London Money Market Association (LMMA)
C/o Investec Bank (UK) Ltd
2 Gresham Street, London EC2V 7QP
Tel: +44 20 7597 4485
E-mail: Rvardy@investec.co.uk

National Association of Securities Dealers (NASD)
No. 1 Poultry
London EC2R 8JR
Tel: +44 20 7623 2799

Commodities and derivatives
Futures and Options Association (FOA)
One America Square
17 Crosswall
London EC3N 2PP
Tel: +44 20 7426 7250
E-mail: info@foa.co.uk
Website: www.foa.co.uk

International Petroleum Exchange (IPE)
International House
1 St Katharine's Way, London E1W 1UY
Tel: +44 20 7481 0643
E-mail: info@ipe.uk.com
Website: www.ipe.uk.com

International Swaps and Derivatives Association Inc (ISDA)
One New Change, London EC4M 9QQ
Tel: +44 20 7330 3550
E-mail: isda@isda-eur.org
Website: www.isda.org

London Bullion Market Association (LBMA)
6 Frederick's Place, London EC2R 8BT
Tel: +44 20 7796 3067
E-mail: mail@lbma.org.uk
Website: www.lbma.org.uk

London International Financial Futures and Options Exchange (LIFFE)
Cannon Bridge House
1 Cousin Lane
London EC4R 3XX
Tel: +44 20 7623 0444
E-mail: exchange@liffe.com
Website: www.liffe.com

London Metal Exchange Limited (LME)
56 Leadenhall Street
London EC3A 2DX
Tel: +44 20 7264 5555
E-mail: info@lme.co.uk
Website: www.lme.com

OM London Exchange
131 Finsbury Pavement
London EC2A 1NT
Tel: +44 20 7065 8000
E-mail: info@om.com
Website: www.omgroup.com

Financial services
Institute of Financial Services
E-mail: customerservices@ifslearning.com
Website: www.ifslearning.com

London office (bookshop, library, information centre, advertising)
90 Bishopsgate
London EC2N 4DQ
Tel: +44 20 7444 7111

Canterbury office (qualifications, examinations, training, publishing,
administration, customer services, marketing, sales)
IFS House
4–9 Burgate Lane
Canterbury
Kent CT1 2XJ
Tel: +44 1227 762 600

ACI UK – The Financial Markets Association
PO Box 28952
London SW14 8WQ
Tel: +44 20 8876 6697
E-mail: sec@aci-uk.com
Website: www.aci-uk.com

Insurance
Association of British Insurers (ABI)
51 Gresham Street
London EC2V 7HQ
Tel: +44 20 7600 3333
E-mail: info@abi.org.uk
Website: www.abi.org.uk

British Insurance Brokers Association (BIBA)
BIBA House
14 Bevis Marks
London EC3A 7NT
Tel: +44 20 7397 0201
E-mail: williamsm@biba.org.uk
Website: www.biba.org.uk

Chartered Insurance Institute (CII)
20 Aldermanbury
London EC2V 7HY
Tel: +44 20 8989 8464
E-mail: info@cii.co.uk
Website: www.cii.co.uk

International Underwriting Association of London (IUA)
London Underwriting Centre
3 Minster Court
Mincing Lane
London EC3R 7DD
Tel: +44 20 7617 4444
E-mail: info@iua.co.uk
Website: www.iua.co.uk

Lloyd's of London
One Lime Street
London EC3M 7HA
Tel: +44 207 327 1000
Website: www.lloyds.com

Lloyd's Market Association (LMA)
Suite 1085
One Lime Street
London EC3M 7DQ
Tel: +44 20 7327 3333
Website: www.the-lma.com

London Market Insurance Brokers' Committee (LMBC)
BIBA House
14 Bevis Marks
London EC3A 7NT
Tel: +44 20 7397 0213
E-mail: enquiries@lmbc.co.uk
Website: www.lmbc.co.uk

Press and media
Bloomberg
Website: www.bloomberg.co.uk

The Economist
25 St James's Street
London SW1 1HG
Tel: +44 20 7830 7000
Website: www.economist.com

Euromoney Institutional Investor
Nestor House
Playhouse Yard
London EC4V 5EX
Website: www.euromoneyplc.com

Financial News
Stapleton House
29–33 Scrutton Street
London EC2A 4HU
Website: www.efinancialnews.com

Financial Times
Number One
Southwark Bridge Road
London SE1 9HL
Tel: +44 20 7873 3000
Website: www.ft.com

Reuters
Website: www.reuters.co.uk

Promotional bodies
International Financial Services London (IFSL)
1–2 Bank Building
Princes Street
London EC2R 8EU
Tel: +44 20 713 9100
E-mail: enquiries@ifsl.org.uk
Website: www.ifsl.org.uk

London First
1 Hobhouse Court
Suffolk Street
London SW1Y 4HH
Tel: +44 20 7665 1500
E-mail: staff@london-first.co.uk
Website: www.london-first.co.uk

ProShare (UK)
Centurion House
24 Monument Street
London EC3R 8AQ
Tel: +44 20 7220 1730
E-mail: info@proshare.org
Website: www.proshare.org

Regulators
Financial Services Authority (FSA)
25 The North Colonnade
Canary Wharf
London E14 5HS
Tel: +44 20 7676 1000
Website: www.fsa.gov.uk

Takeover Panel (Panel on Takeovers and Mergers)
PO Box 226
The Stock Exchange Building
London EC2P 2JX
Tel: +44 20 7382 9026
Website: www.thetakeoverpanel.org.uk

Settlement and clearing
Association for Payment Clearing Services (APACS)
Mercury House
Triton Court
14 Finsbury Square
London EC2A 1LQ
Tel: +44 20 7711 6200
E-mail: corpcomms@apacs.org.uk
Website: www.apacs.org.uk

CHAPS Clearing Company Limited
Mercury House
Triton Court
14 Finsbury Square
London EC2A 1LQ
Tel: +44 20 7711 6227
E-mail: chaps@apacs.org.uk
Website: www.apacs.org.uk

Cheque and Credit Clearing Company Limited
Mercury House
Triton Court
14 Finsbury Square
London EC2A 1LQ
Tel: +44 20 7711 6371
E-mail: corpcomms@apacs.org.uk
Website: www.apacs.org.uk

CRESTCo Ltd
33 Cannon Street
London EC4M 5SB
Tel: +44 20 7849 0000
E-mail: info@crestco.co.uk
Website: www.crestco.co.uk

London Clearing House Limited (LCH)
Aldgate House
33 Aldgate High Street
London EC3N 1EA
Tel: +44 20 7426 7000
E-mail: corporatecommunications@lch.co.uk
Website: www.lch.com

Shipping
Baltic Exchange (The Baltic)
38 St Mary Axe
London EC3A 8BH
Tel: +44 20 7623 5501
E-mail: enquiries@balticexchange.com
Website: www.balticexchange.com

Chamber of Shipping
Carthusian Court
12 Carthusian Street
London EC1M 6EZ
Tel: +44 20 7417 2800
Website: www.british-shipping.org

Lloyd's Register of Shipping (LR)
71 Fenchurch Street
London EC3M 4BS
Tel: +44 20 7709 9166
E-mail: lloydsreg@lr.org
Website: www.lr.org

Other organisations
Association of Independent Financial Advisers
Austin Friars House
2–6 Austin Friars
London EC2N 2HD
Tel: +44 20 7628 1287
E-mail: info@aifa.net
Website: www.aifa.net

City Club
19 Old Broad Street
London EC2N 1DS
Tel: +44 20 7588 8558
Website: www.cityclub.uk.com

City Disputes Panel (CDP)
70 Fleet Street
London EC4Y 1EU
Tel: +44 20 7936 7060
E-mail: info@citydisputespanel.org
Website: www.citydisputespanel.org

Corporation of London
PO Box 270
Guildhall
London EC2P 2EJ
Tel: +44 20 7606 3030
Website: www.cityoflondon.gov.uk

City Business Library
1 Brewers Hall Garden
London EC2V 5BX
Tel: +44 20 7332 1812
Website: www.cityoflondon.gov.uk

London Chamber of Commerce and Industry (LCCI)
33 Queen Street
London EC4R 1AP
Tel: +44 20 7248 4444
E-mail: lc@londonchamber.co.uk
Website: www.londonchamber.co.uk

Serious Fraud Office (SFO)
Elm House, 10–16 Elm Street
London WC1X 0BJ
Tel: +44 20 7239 7272
E-mail: public.enquiries@sfo.gsi.gov.uk
Website: www.sfo.gov.uk

Appendix 2
Principal players

All data on assets and principal activities are 2003 or the latest available from the company. Terminology follows company usage.

Aviva
UK-based insurance group

St Helen's,
1 Undershaft
London EC3P 3PQ
Website: www.aviva.com

Principal activities	% of premium income
Life assurance, investment sales, including share of associates	68
General insurance	29
Health	3

Total assets	£208 billion
Equity shareholders' funds	£6.3 billion
Employees	61,000 worldwide; 37,000 in the UK

Barclays
Major UK bank group

54 Lombard Street
London EC3P 3AH
Website: www.barclays.com

Principal activities	% share of pre-tax profits
Business banking	34
Personal financial services	21
Barclays Capital	20
Barclaycard	18
Private clients	6
Barclays Global Investors	5
Barclays Africa	3
Head office functions and other operations	−7

Total assets	£443 billion
Equity shareholders' funds	£16 billion
Employees	74,800

Cazenove
UK-based independent securities and investment banking firm

20 Moorgate
London
EC2R 6DA
Website: www.cazenove.com

Total assets	£1.3 billion
Equity shareholders' funds	£256m
Employees	1,300

Citigroup
US-based financial services conglomerate

Citigroup Centre
33 Canada Square
Canary Wharf
London E14 5LB
Website: www.citigroup.com

Principal activities	% share of net income
Global consumer group	55
Global corporate and investment banking group	31
Global investment management	10
Smith Barney (private client services)	4

Total assets	$1,264 billion
Shareholders' equity	$104 billion
Employees	275,000

Credit Suisse Group
Swiss-based universal bank

Credit Suisse First Boston
One Cabot Square
London E14 4QJ
Website: www.creditsuisse.com

Principal activities	% share of operating profit
Credit Suisse Financial Services	
Private banking	45
Insurance	30
Corporate and retail banking	14
Life and pensions	11
Credit Suisse First Boston	
Institutional securities	87
CSFB financial services	13

Total assets	Swfr962 billion
Shareholders' equity	Swfr34.6 billion
Employees	61,000

Deutsche Bank

German-based universal bank

For addresses see website: www.db.com

Principal activities	% share of pre-tax profit
Corporate and investment banking	77
Private clients and asset management	29
Corporate investment	−6

Total assets	€803 billion
Total shareholders' equity	€28 billion
Employees	68,000

Dresdner Bank

German-based universal bank

Dresdner Kleinwort Wasserstein
PO Box 560
20 Fenchurch Street
London EC3P 3DB
Website: www.dresdner-bank.com

Principal activities	% share of operating income
Private and business clients	45
Corporate banking	16
Dresdner Kleinwort Wasserstein	33
Institutional restructuring unit	8
Corporate investments	−1
Corporate items	−1

Total assets	€477 billion
Shareholders' equity	€11.5 billion
Employees	42,000

Goldman Sachs
US-based investment bank

Peterborough Court
133 Fleet Street
London EC4A 2BB
Website: www.goldmansachs.com

Principal activities	% share of net revenues
Trading and principal investments	65
Asset management and securities services	18
Investment banking	17

Total assets	$403 billion
Shareholders' equity	$21 billion
Employees	19,000

HSBC
UK-based international bank

8 Canada Square
London E14 5HQ
Website: www.hsbc.com

Principal activities	% share of profit before tax
Personal financial services	43
Corporate, investment banking and markets	31
Commercial banking	22
Private banking	4

Total assets	$1,000 billion
Shareholders' funds	$80 billion
Employees	223,000

Lazard Brothers

UK-based investment bank with associates in New York and Paris

50 Stratton Street
London W1J 8LL
Website: www.lazard.com

Employees	2,500

Lehman Brothers

UK-based investment bank

London European Headquarters
25 Bank Street
London E14 5LE
Website: www.lehman.com

Principal activities	% share of net revenues
Capital markets	70
Investment banking	20
Client services	10

Total assets	$312 billion
Shareholders' equity	$13 billion
Employees	16,200

Lloyds TSB
UK clearing bank

25 Gresham Street
London EC2V 7HN
Website: www.lloydstsb.com

Principal activities	% share of pre-tax profits
Wholesale and international banking	50
Insurance and investments	27
UK retail banking and mortgages	23

Total assets	£252 billion
Shareholders' funds (equity)	£9.6 billion
Employees	79,000

Merrill Lynch
US-based investment bank

Merrill Lynch Financial Centre
2 King Edward Street
London EC1A 1HQ
Website: www.ml.com

Principal activities	% share of net revenues
Global markets and investment banking	49
Global private clients	44
Merrill Lynch investment managers	7

Total assets	$494 billion
Shareholders' equity	$27 billion
Employees	48,000

J.P. Morgan Chase
US-based financial conglomerate

J.P. Morgan Private Bank
125 London Wall
London EC2Y 5AJ
Website: www.jpmorganchase.com

Principal activities	% share of operating revenue
Retail and middle-market financial services	41
Investment banking	38
Treasury and security services	12
Investment management and private banking	8

Total assets	$770 billion
Shareholders' equity	$46 billion
Employees	93,000

Morgan Stanley
US-based investment bank

25 Cabot Square
Canary Wharf
London E14 4QA
Website: www.morganstanley.com

Principal activities	% share of net revenues
Securities	53
Credit services	16
Individual investor group	19
Investment management	12

Total assets	$602 billion
Shareholders' equity	$25 billion
Employees	51,000

Prudential

UK-based international insurance company

Laurence Pountney Hill
London EC4R 0HH
Website: www.prudential.co.uk

Principal activities	% share of profits
UK and Europe operations	51
Prudential Asia	44
US operations	27
Other	−22

Shareholders' funds (equity interests)	£3.2 billion
Total assets	£161 billion
Employees	20,000

N.M. Rothschild

UK-based independent investment bank

New Court
St Swithin's Lane
London EC4P 4DU
Website: www.rothschild.com

Total assets: £4.6 billion
Equity shareholders' funds: £315 million
Employees: 2,000

Royal Bank of Scotland
UK-based international bank

42 St Andrew Square
Edinburgh EH2 2YE
Website: www.rbs.co.uk

Principal activities	% share of total income
Retail lending	45
Corporate banking and financial markets	34
Insurance	16
Wealth management	4
Other	1

Total assets	£455 billion
Shareholders' funds	£28 billion
Employees	120,000

Schroders
UK-based independent asset manager

31 Gresham Street,
London EC2V 7QA
Website: www.schroders.com

Principal activities	% share of net revenues
Asset management	97.5
Private equity	1.5
Group net income	1.0

Funds under management	£98.3 billion
Equity shareholders' funds	£1 billion
Employees	2,000

UBS

Swiss-based universal bank

For addresses see website: www.ubs.com

Principal activities	% share of pre-tax profits
Wealth management and business banking	58
Global asset management	4
Investment bank	47
Wealth management USA	−2
Corporate centre	−7

Total assets	Swfr1,386 billion
Shareholders' equity	Swfr35 billion
Employees	66,000

Appendix 3
Key events 1571–2004

1571	Foundation of Royal Exchange by Sir Thomas Gresham, a leading merchant.
1585	Antwerp loses its role as the leading international financial centre when it is sacked by Spanish troops. Amsterdam becomes the pre-eminent centre. Antwerp bankers also flee to London, fostering its rise as a financial centre.
1600	Formation of the East India Company by Royal Charter with a monopoly on trade with Asia.
1652–74	Three wars with Dutch boost London's emergence as the world's leading port.
1672	The English government defaults on its debts because of the financial strain caused by the third Anglo-Dutch War (1672–74).
1688	Opening of Lloyd's coffee house, which becomes the focus of marine underwriting activity.
1689	Commencement of Nine Years' War (1689–97) against France; growing crisis in government finances.
1694	Establishment of the Bank of England as the government's banker to raise funds to finance war against French.
1711	South Sea Company formed.
1719–20	South Sea Bubble financial crisis and scandal.
1763	End of Seven Years War (1756–63) between Britain and Prussia on one side and France, Austria, Spain and Germany on the other is followed by a financial crisis.
1762	Formation of Baring Brothers.
1773	Establishment of subscription Stock Exchange at New Jonathan's, a City coffee house.
1780	Gordon Riots in London lead to attack on Bank of England, which is provided with a nightly military guard until 1973.

1792–1815	Wars against revolutionary and Napoleonic France, leading to large-scale government borrowing to finance military expenditure and a major expansion of the public debt market.
1795	Capture of Amsterdam by French army results in London's emergence as the world's leading international financial centre.
1798	Formation of N.M. Rothschild.
1801	Foundation of the modern Stock Exchange, with restricted membership and rules.
1804	Formation of Schroders.
1804–05	Building of East India docks and London docks begins massive expansion of the port of London.
1816	The UK adopts the gold standard, making the pound convertible into gold and establishing sterling as the world's leading currency.
1823	Formation of the Baltic Exchange, which laid down membership rules for the conduct of shipbroking.
1822–25	First Latin American debt crisis. A boom in lending to Latin American government borrowers is followed by widespread defaults and a financial crisis in the City.
1837	City crisis. Several leading City firms fail as a result of an economic downturn in the United States.
1839	Formation of Hambros.
1844	Bank Charter Act provides for the separation of the Bank of England's note issue and banking functions.
1845–47	Stockmarket bubble in railway shares is followed by a financial crisis.
1855–57	Another speculative bubble in railway shares is followed by another financial crisis.
1866	Financial crisis provoked by the failure of Overend Gurney, the leading firm of bill brokers.
1866	Transatlantic telegraph cable revolutionises international securities market transactions. Global telegraph network developed in the 1870s.
1867	Comptoir d'Escompte de Paris (forerunner of BNP) is the first European bank to open a City office.
1869	Opening of the Suez Canal promotes growth of international trade.

1865–75   Second Latin American debt crisis. A boom in lending to Latin American and other government borrowers is followed by widespread defaults and a financial crisis in the City.

1873   Deutsche Bank opens a City office.

1875   Parliamentary inquiry into foreign loans in the wake of widespread defaults by foreign government borrowers exposes fraudulent conduct of borrowers and unscrupulous practices of City financiers marketing bonds to investors.

1878   Failure of City of Glasgow Bank, the last major British clearing bank failure.

1879   United States adopts the gold standard, which fosters the spread of an international fixed currency system.

1884   Yokohama Specie Bank (forerunner of Bank of Tokyo) opens a City office.

1888   Formation of London Clearing House.
Opening of London Metal Exchange.

1890   Baring Brothers suffers a liquidity crisis and is rescued by the Bank of England, thus confirming the Bank's function as lender of last resort.

1899–1902   Costs of Boer war in South Africa lead to great increase in British government debt.

1905   National City Bank (forerunner of Citigroup) opens a London office.

1908–13   Boom in international bond issuance in the City.

1914   Opening of Panama Canal further facilitates global trade.

1914–18   City crisis on outbreak of first world war is followed by a massive rise in government borrowing.

1919   UK formally leaves the gold standard (convertibility had been suspended since 1914); currency instability in the early 1920s leads to boom in foreign-exchange dealing. London Gold Fixing established at N.M. Rothschild.

1920   Montagu Norman appointed governor of the Bank of England (and becomes longest-serving governor, leaving office in 1944).

1920s   Emergence of New York as an important international financial centre and the dollar as a significant international currency.

1924	Dawes Loan, a massive loan to Germany by an international banking consortium under the auspices of the League of Nations to pay war reparations.
1925	The UK readopts the gold standard.
1929	Clarence Hatry scandal, involving the sale of shares through false prospectuses, which may have undermined investor confidence before the Wall Street crash.
	Wall Street crash; many UK share prices drop by half.
1930	Young Loan, a further massive international loan to Germany.
1931	Financial and political crisis in Germany and central Europe leads to suspension of repayment of loans outstanding to City merchant banks, which are supported by Bank of England.
	First unit trust launched.
1931–38	German payments moratorium perpetuated by series of Standstill agreements between City creditors and German debtors.
1931	Financial and political crisis in the UK. Sterling leaves the gold standard. Formation of coalition national government to confront economic slump.
	Directors of Royal Mail Shipping Company found guilty of issuing a false prospectus (see page 255).
1932	Bottom of trough of the Great Depression and UK share prices.
1935	Attempted corner of the pepper commodity market to drive up prices prompts Bank of England to intervene to curb commodity speculation.
1935	*Financial News* (*Financial Times* after 1946) Ordinary 30 shares index introduced.
1939–45	Second world war; one-third of City buildings flattened by German bombing.
1940	*Financial News* index falls by one-third.
1944	Bretton Woods Agreement on an international fixed currency regime and new international financial institutions (the IMF and the World Bank).
1946	Bank of England nationalised by Labour government. Formation of S.G. Warburg.

1947	Establishment of General Agreement on Tariffs and Trade (GATT), forerunner of the World Trade Organisation (WTO).
1948	Companies Act 1948. A major reform of corporate accounting provides meaningful financial information for investors for first time.
	Establishment of Organisation of Economic Co-operation and Development (OECD) in Paris.
1949	Sterling devalued by 30%, from $4.03 to $2.80.
	Resumption of use of monetary policy; first interest rate change since 1939.
	London foreign-exchange market reopened.
1950s	Rise of Euromarket in offshore dollar deposits in late 1950s and 1960s.
1954	London gold market reopened.
1956	Launch of Premium Bonds (UK government bonds that are entered in a monthly prize draw).
1958–59	City newcomer S.G. Warburg takes on City old guard in British Aluminium takeover battle.
1960s	A highly publicised and controversial series of hostile takeover bids, notably ICI's unsuccessful bid for Courtaulds and GEC's successful acquisitions of AEI and English Electric, attract public attention to the City.
1962	FT Actuaries All Share index introduced, encompassing the largest 800 or so British companies that account for 98% of the London stockmarket; it is used as a benchmark for asset managers.
1963	First Eurobond issued in London, marking the opening of its international capital market and leading to its re-emergence as a leading international financial centre. (The borrower was Autostrade, the Italian motorways authority, and the lead manager was S.G. Warburg.)
1967	Sterling devalued by 14%, from $2.80 to $2.40.
1968	Formation of the City Takeover Panel, with responsibility for the enforcement of the newly formulated City Code on the conduct of takeover bids to forestall regulatory legislation.
1971–73	Collapse of Bretton Woods system of fixed exchange rates.
1972	Sterling floats and initially drops 6.5% against the dollar.

1973	Oil price quadruples. Euromarkets boom in the City, undertaking recycling of petrodollar deposits by oil producers to borrower countries with balance-of-payments deficits because of the rise in oil prices.
1973–74	Stockmarket slump. FT 30 index drops 70%.
1973–75	Secondary banking crisis. Bank of England organises a "lifeboat" to rescue insolvent so-called secondary banks (specialist lenders that funded themselves in the wholesale interbank market) that threaten the stability of the UK banking system.
1975	UK inflation hits 26%, a peace-time record.
1976	Sterling crisis. IMF loan for Labour government to facilitate the adoption of economic policies to reduce budget deficits and inflation.
1977	Labour government sells part of the country's shareholding in British Petroleum.
1979	Conservative government is elected and embarks on a series of free-market reforms. Exchange controls (imposed in 1939) are abolished, allowing free movement of sterling investments and promoting integration of domestic and international aspects of City activities.
1980	Formation of International Petroleum Exchange. Insider trading (share dealing with privileged information) becomes a criminal offence.
1981	Government sells 51% of its holding in British Aerospace, launching 1980s privatisation programme. (The other 49% is sold in 1985.)
1982	Formation of London International Financial Futures and Options Exchange (LIFFE), a derivatives exchange.
1983	Re-election of Conservative government led by Margaret Thatcher.
1983–6	"Big Bang" deregulation of securities industry leads to acquisition of many securities brokerage firms and a large increase in the presence of American, European and Japanese banks in the City. Financial Services Act 1986 reforms UK financial services regulation, introducing a complex hybrid system of self-regulation and statutory regulation. Comes into force in 1988.

1983–87	Takeover bid boom.
1984	Privatisation of British Telecom. First big privatisation raises £4 billion for the government and 2.3m individual investors become BT shareholders.
	Rescue of Johnson Matthey Bank by Bank of England sparks controversy over the effectiveness of the Bank's supervision of the banking system and marks the beginning of the process by which the Bank loses responsibility for the supervision of the banking system in 1997.
	FTSE 100 index introduced.
1985	Tin market collapses.
1986	Privatisation of British Gas.
	Opening of new Lloyd's of London building.
1986–87	Guinness takeover battle is followed by scandal over illegal takeover tactics and prosecution of perpetrators (see Chapter 13).
1987	Re-election of Conservative government led by Margaret Thatcher.
	Worldwide stockmarket crash.
1989	Morgan Grenfell bought by Deutsche Bank in the wake of the Guinness scandal, which discredited the firm's management.
	Establishment of OM London derivatives exchange.
1990	Guinness fraud trial; four defendants found guilty of conspiracy, theft and false accounting.
1991	Canary Wharf opens.
	Robert Maxwell found dead; subsequent revelations of big thefts.
	Collapse of Bank of Credit and Commerce International (BCCI).
1992	Election of Conservative government led by John Major.
	Launch of the Private Finance Initiative (PFI).
	IRA bomb St Mary Axe.
	UK leaves Exchange Rate Mechanism.
1993	IRA bomb Bishopsgate.
1995	Barings bankrupted by losses incurred by "rogue trader" Nick Leeson. It is acquired by ING, a Dutch bank, for £1.
	S.G. Warburg bought by Swiss Bank Corporation (forerunner of UBS).

	London Stock Exchange opens Alternative Investment Market (AIM).
	Kleinwort Benson, a UK merchant bank, bought by Dresdner Bank.
1996	Settlement of claims against Lloyd's arising from massive losses and a series of scandals in the 1980s and early 1990s; £3.2 billion settlement agreed.
	Pensions mis-selling scandal; 44 firms fined.
1997	Election of Labour government led by Tony Blair.
	Mercury Asset Management, a leading City asset management firm, acquired by Merrill Lynch.
	Bank of England given independence to set monetary policy by chancellor. Financial Services Authority established as unitary regulatory body.
1998–2000	Dotcom bubble.
1999	FTSE 100 peaks at a record 6,720 in December.
2000	Robert Fleming, a UK merchant bank, bought by J.P. Morgan Chase.
	Schroders, a UK merchant bank, sells investment banking operations to Salomon Smith Barney (part of Citigroup).
	Financial Services Markets Act passed by Parliament (June).
2000–03	Downturn in equity markets leads to slowdown in City activity; 35,000 City jobs are lost.
2001	LIFFE acquired by Paris-based Euronext.
	Financial Services Markets Act comes into force (December).
2003	Beginning of revival in City activity and upturn in hirings.

Further reading

Ackrill, M. and Hannah, L., *Barclays: The Business of Banking 1690–1996* (Cambridge University Press, Cambridge, 2001).

Augar, P., *The Death of Gentlemanly Capitalism* (Penguin, London, 2000).

Bank, E., *The Rise and Fall of the Merchant Banks* (Kogan Page, London, 1999).

Blakey, G.G., *The Post-War History of the London Stockmarket* (Management Books, London, 1994).

Buckle, M. and Thomson, J., *The UK Financial System: Theory and Practice* (Manchester University Press, Manchester, 1998).

Centre for Economic and Business Research, *The City's Importance to the EU Economy 2004* (Corporation of London, London, 2004).

Chancellor, E., *The Devil Take the Hindmost: A History of Financial Speculation* (Macmillan, London, 1999).

Clarke, W.M., *How the City of London Works* (Sweet & Maxwell, London, 1999).

Clarke, W.M., *The Golden Thread: World Financial Centres and the Gold Connection* (Sweet & Maxwell, London, 2001).

Cobham, D. (ed.), *Markets & Dealers: The Economics of the London Financial Markets* (Longman, London, 1992).

Coggan, P., *The Money Machine: How the City Works* (Penguin, London, 2002).

Corner, D.C. and Burton, H., *Investment and Unit Trusts in Britain and America* (Elek, London, 1968).

Darling, P.S., *City Cinderella: The Life and Times of Mercury Asset Management* (Weidenfeld & Nicolson, London, 1999).

Davis, S.I., *Investment Banking* (Palgrave, London, 2003).

Diacon, S.R. and Carter, R.L., *Success in Insurance* (John Murray, London, 1992).

Fay, S., *The Collapse of Barings: Panic, Ignorance and Greed* (Arrow, London, 1996).

Gleeson, A., *London Enriched: The development of the foreign banking community in the City over five decades* (FBSA, London, 1997).

Gleeson, A., *People and Their Money: 50 Years of Private Investment* (M & G, London, 1981).

Golding, A., *The City: Inside the Great Expectation Machine. Myth and reality in institutional investment and the stock market* (Financial Times, London, 2001).

Hannah, L., *Inventing Retirement: The development of occupational pensions in Britain* (Cambridge University Press, Cambridge, 1986).

Hayes, S.L. and Hubbard, P.M., *Investment Banking: A Tale of Three Cities* (Harvard Business School Press, Boston MA, 1999).

Hennessy, E., *Coffee House to Cyber Market: 200 Years of the London Stock Exchange* (Ebury Press, London, 2001).

Hobson, D., *The National Wealth: Who Gets What in Britain* (Harper Collins, London, 1999).

Hobson, D., *The Pride of Lucifer: the Unauthorised Biography of a Merchant Bank* (Hamish Hamilton, London, 1990).

Hughes, D., *Asset Management in Theory and Practice* (Financial World Publishing, London, 2002).

IFSL, *Banking* (London, 2004).

IFSL, *Derivatives* (London, 2002).

IFSL, *Fund Management* (London, 2003).

IFSL, *Insurance* (London, 2004).

IFSL, *International Financial Markets in the UK* (London, May 2004).

IFSL, *International Private Wealth Management* (London, 2002).

IFSL, *Management Consultancy* (London, 2003).

IFSL, *Securities Dealing* (London, 2003).

Jaffa, S., *Safe as Houses: The Schemers and Scams Behind Some of the World's Greatest Financial Scandals* (Robson Books, London, 1997).

Kynaston, D., *LIFFE: A Market and its Makers* (Granta, Cambridge, 1997).

Kynaston, D., *The City of London: A Club No More 1945–2000* (Chatto & Windus, London, 2001).

Lascelles, D. and Boleat, M., *Who speaks for the City?: Trade associations galore* (Centre for the Study of Financial Innovation, London, 2002).

Lascelles, D., *Sizing Up the City: London's Ranking as a Financial Centre* (Centre for the Study of Financial Innovation, London, 2003).

Littlewood, John, *The Stock Market: 50 Years of Capitalism at Work* (Financial Times, London, 1998).

Lombard Street Research, *Growth Prospects of City Industries* (Corporation of London, London, 2003).

London Business School, *The City Research Project: Final Report* (Corporation of London, London, 1995).

Loughborough University, *Financial Services Clustering and its Significance for London* (Corporation of London, London, 2003).

McRae, H. and Cairncross, F., *Capital City: London as a Financial Centre* (Methuen, London, 1991).

Plender, J. and Wallace, P., *The Square Mile: A Guide to the New City of London* (LWT, London, 1985).

Roberts, R. and Kynaston, D. (eds), *The Bank of England: Money, Power and Influence 1694–1994* (Oxford University Press, Oxford, 1995).

Roberts, R. and Kynaston, D., *City State: A Contemporary History of the City of London and How Money Triumphed* (Profile Books, London, 2002).

Roberts, R. (ed.), *Global Financial Centres: London, New York, Tokyo* (Edward Elgar, London, 1994).

Roberts, R., *Inside International Finance* (Orion, London, 1998).

Roberts, R., *Schroders: Merchants & Bankers* (Macmillan, London, 1992).

Roberts, R., *Take Your Partners: Orion, the Consortium Banks and the Transformation of the Euromarkets* (Palgrave, London, 2001).

Roberts, R., *Wall Street: The Markets, Mechanisms and Players* (The Economist/Profile Books, London, 2002).

Rogers, D., *The Big Four British Banks: Organisation, Strategy and the Future* (Macmillan, London, 1999).

Thompson, V., *Mastering the Euromarkets: A Guide to International Bonds* (Irwin, London, 1996).

Weyer, M.V., *Falling Eagle: the Decline of Barclays Bank* (Weidenfeld & Nicolson, London, 2000).

Index